SILHOUETTE OF AN EAGLE

BY

LARRY F. SLAUSON

ISBN: 1-4033-0812-8 (e-book)
ISBN: 1-4033-0813-6 (Paperback)
ISBN: 1-4033-0814-4 (Hardcover)

This book is printed on acid free paper.

1stBooks - rev. 07/07/04

THE EAGLE FLIES INTO THE SUN AND SILHOUETTES THE
MOON. IN MEANING HIS FLIGHT IS MORE LASTING THAN
HE. FOR UPON HIS WINGS RESTS AN ETERNAL STANDARD

SILHOUETTE OF AN EAGLE

BOOK I

Larry Slauson

Introduction:

In life there are many birds of a different feather. Most in the flight of life accept the norm or nature of things that have been established. However the spirit of eagles it would seem compels them to search for a deeper meaning. Within the sea of life the eagle senses an added dimension of love and nobility. His drive to ascend to a higher plane is forged in conflict and struggle. Although his flight remains a standard of aspiration, it is often misunderstood by a world that demands conformity. Still in spirit and heart the eagles' course of flight remains inevitable as if willed by grace. One such journey through life is depicted upon the wings of an eagle named - Eric!

Larry Slauson

Contents

AS A YOUNG EAGLET IN THE NEST CAN ATTEST A FLAPPING
OF WINGS ALONE CANNOT BRING FLIGHT. STRENGTH AND
CORRELATION OF SYNCHRONIZED MOVEMENT MUST BE
DIRECTED FOR DESIRED ASCENT.

LOVE LIKE THE WINGS OF AN EAGLE IS MUCH MORE THAN A
MATTER OF MOTION. THE SPIRIT OF FLIGHT IS A GIFT
BUT THE SILHOUETTE OF ONENESS CAN ONLY BE OF HEART.
IF ONE DESIRES TO RISE ABOVE THEN ONE MUST ASCEND
UPON THE WINGS OF EAGLES.

CHAPTER I

Flight of an Eagle

On a Sunday morning during the month of September when the winds of war are gathering around the world an eagle is born. His spirit is of generations of American Bald Eagles. Soon his name will come to pass as Eric.

In the days that follow a keenness of vision comes to him. Thus from the nest towering high upon the cliff, above all creatures large and small, he views the preparation for war in the valley below. He becomes intrigued though without understanding. However his consoling mother swiftly responds with her love and protection.

"Eric," she speaks softly, "you are new to the world. Such solemn matters should not concern you. Your gray feathers are fluffy. Much like your tender wings they will require time to grow. Nourish, be patient and for now abide in my bosom for yet you are mine. Soon enough the world will make its claim. Thereafter you will leave me forever." As the warm nourishment provided by his mother flows into him, a feeling of heaviness weighs upon his eyes. In peaceful sleep he takes leave of the conscious world trusting in her care.

Upon awakening the warm sunlight of the preceding day is nowhere in sight. In its place appear darkened thunder clouds. Soon strong winds begin to blow cold rains upon all below. As he begins to chill in the morning air his mother frequently moves about the nest providing her warmth. She is such a wonderful mother, he contemplates. Her devotion is much deeper than mere instinct. Furthermore her caring brings even greater trust to my being.

Remaining tucked beneath his mother in the nest, he sorely wonders if the rains around him will ever cease. His mind begins to race as he ponders his fate should the sunshine not return. Suddenly he begins to panic. Through the thick feathers of his mother's underside he again pokes his head out to investigate.

Bolts of lightning spread across the heavens which are followed by several loud thunderous booms. His heart quickens as he glances downward upon the world before him. There he can see many fires throughout the forests and meadows. Even odd appearing structures all of which appear strange to his sight.

In the far distance numerous small flashes erupt with deafening echoes rising high into the sky. Eric has never witnessed such unnatural phenomena or arrayed movement before. He further senses a terrible wrong as a tear from his mother's cheek falls upon him. Within her womb he had not experienced such enormous fears nor sensations. How much at this moment he longs to return to that peaceful well-being.

Looking upward and slightly to the side with obvious bewilderment, he observes the fixed glare of his father's eyes upon him. Through his purposeful love he has brought fish to the nest. Although as Eric begins to eat, he acutely senses his fathers look of intense concern. He concludes that food is not foremost upon his mind. Also given his immense size, color of his feathers, and the air of command about him, Eric feels blessed by his father's closeness. He senses protection and has on occasion observed his father to be a cunning and superior hunter among eagles. Thus within his spirit he comes to realize while his mother represents gentleness, his father possesses the quality of strength.

It is not long before Eric is to know the meaning of his fathers fixed glare upon him. "Son!" he exclaims, as he stretches his wings in full extension. "You are too young a bird to understand the ways of this world. However it is time for your education to begin. First, I will tell you to relax as the rains above and your fears will subside in time. Thus the warmth of yesterday's sun will return.

However the downpours of preparation, its echoes, and the resulting fires that you have observed in the lower valley, are caused by man. In duration they will last far beyond many tomorrows. For the winds of war gather below and the clouds associated with them are destructive in nature. Such hostility the world has known before.

In our domain there are no boundaries. Yet in the days to come your spirit will inevitably cause your flight to enter the jet streams of man. It is because of this responsibility and conflict that I must prepare you. The sounds and things that you saw in the distance are the training battlefields. Mankind has sounded a call to arms. Sadly many birds of a different feather will not live to see the peaceful meadows again. Now rest my son for you will need your strength in the days ahead."

However sleep does not come quickly to Eric. Experiencing anxiety he wonders about what his father has told him. Why humans kill and destroy? His mother has on days past explained his birth and about a creator of all things. He has also, been told about love, peacefulness, and of the important meaning of lasting good will. Nevertheless as sleep eventually drifts to his inner spirit his confusion remains most acute. Also unknown to him at the time, the perplexity of contrast between the Great White Eagle's (Creator) purpose and man's warring nature will remain a dilemma to him for years.

Even a young eaglet like Eric can envision the preferred choice of peaceful meadows. Especially one adorned by a multitude of brightly colored flowers. In his scanning from the nest of the many hills and skies without end he has never seen an eagle needlessly harm another. Except for the realm of man there appears to be order in all of nature.

Upon awakening after what seemed to be an endless sleep, Eric feels much joy. As he looks about the surroundings from high on the cliff the sun again fills the sky. A slight breeze blows over the rocks and a heavy dew appears everywhere. Furthermore the warm rays of sunshine bring not only a drying of feathers but a renewing of spirit. He stretches his wings with a strong desire to burst into flight. However the time is not right.

In the distance he can see the trail of flight as his father returns to the nest. His excitement intensifies for he values greatly the hours which they spend together. Following a brief greeting his heart fills with joy as his father tenderly embraces him within the fold of his wings. During the passing moments both eagle and eaglet perch silently. Each drifting into separate individual reflection.

Upon concluding contemplative thought father and offspring venture a short distance to a huge rock. "Eric. I have brought you here purposely that I might talk to you in private. I know that you are troubled. Yet we cannot always control many of the forces of this world. In this respect our destinies are not always of our choosing. Meanwhile let us live a day at a time. Perhaps by blessing we may fortunately escape the ravages of the coming war.

However son, it is time you learn about responsibility. It is expected that you will represent yourself in the manner of our forebearers. Their flights have exemplified the esteemed standard inherent of all eagles. Understand that the Great White Eagle has seen fit to bestow life and purpose to every flock of birds. We eagles are not superior. However we are special by our purposeful endowment.

We alone grace the uppermost heights of the heavens. The splendor of our flights has served as an inspiration throughout time. Also by the will of right we mate for life. We are acclaimed hunters ascending and diving upon prey with swift cunning. Yet we are also sensitive. Therefore we build our nests on high. Although socially competitive by nature, we are also extremely individualistic. In essence we are the guardians of the skies.

In days to come Eric the magnitude of your size will symbolize your stature. Yet remember that real stature is neither measured by length nor breadth but rather by character. The colors of your inspiring feathers will symbolize orderliness. Your many flights will promote pride. For we are proud birds. However remember always to be humble to the ways of your Creator. Furthermore balance each flight to avoid faltering. Lest you, become a victim to one of life's pitfalls.

Your worst enemy in life will be yourself. Conquer your fears and never panic. Still you must cope with man. Most humans are good but some are prone to do evil. More than a few I regret to say have carried banners bearing our image in the name of greed and deceit.

Our eagle forefathers have given to us a worthy heritage. Also your mother and I have endowed you with a wholesome set of values. Retain and give much thought to the guidelines that I have just expressed. Hopefully they will serve as a direction for your life. Now off to your mother as the tests of time will come upon you soon enough."

The weeks and months pass ever so slowly for Eric. His physical development far surpasses his patience. He now strolls quite freely from the nest while constantly flapping his wings with enthusiastic delight. Although only average in body size, the span of his wings proves so immense that he often ponders in self thought his future role.

Thus often in perched seclusion he would beseech the Great White Eagle with an abounding curiosity. It was on one such occasion that he boldly sought a specific response concerning the capacity in which he might serve the Noble Heavenly Eagle. However, before an anticipated reply could be rendered, a sudden gust of wind blew against his extended wings. In an instant he found himself being tossed upon the rock surface rolling head over claws several times before being nearly blown off the cliff. Sorely bruised with a feather or so missing he felt humbled as he recollected his father's advice about the need to balance each flight. Even those of a spirited nature. Wisely he never told his mother about this incident. Still he sensed that somehow she knew.

As the snow of winter blows across the landscape the war escalates abroad. His father though home for brief periods is away much of the time. It is during these many weeks that Eric and his mother's caring relationship forms into the meaningful experience of mother and son. In addition his spirit for life and flight develop ever so strongly during this early phase of maturing. Often he imagines his heart bursting from over excitement.

Typical of his young age and given his intrigue about life he incessantly asks questions. "Mother, now that I am attending the Eagle School of Learning, I cannot but wonder about the peculiar behavior of the female eaglets. Their perspective on life is so contrary to my own. When I approach them and ask basic questions I never get simple answers. Also I fail to understand why in my presence they frequently walk so oddly. They also make strange movements with their eyes. One even chased me! Frankly I had cause to wonder if she had gone mad."

"Son. Kindly slow down. There is no need for you to hasten knowledge to a single season. You have a lifetime to learn about the ways of the world. Still I shall tell you these things. The silliness and related behavior that you have associated to female eaglets is all quite normal. It represents an important part of the maturing process. Think of it as a harmonious blending or coming together of the physical and mental sides of life that in puberty are somewhat at odds in development. Now that your ole mom has enlightened you about the flirtation of birds, your father may wish to speak with you concerning the nature of bees." "Oh mom."

The changing seasons reflect a gradual strengthening of Eric's wings allowing him to lift slightly off the ground. Although impatient for flight, he becomes equally perplexed in spirit to know his intended direction for the future. Thus the frequent talks about life between him and his mother continue. "Do you think mother that I will succeed in life." "Yes, my son. However you should not worry so much about the tomorrows. At your age, life should not be so solemn."

"Nevertheless mother how can you know with certainty that I will not fail. My goals and the future are so obscure to me." "Son, Patience is a virtue. Besides you are so demanding, even of my free time, that if these many talks don't wear us out first, you cannot avoid succeeding." "Oh mother. Can you not accept the seriousness of my dilemma?" She does not respond to his desired resolve. Thus with love and tears of laughter their conversation of the day ends.

Eric's seemingly unsaturable appetite stimulates further his continuing rapid growth. Still the conflict of his spirit preys proportionately upon his happiness. With reverent regard he increasingly turns his attention to the Great White Eagle. Yet nowhere does the angel of his heart appear purposeful of conveying the nature and direction of his believed destiny. He feels troubled and frustration seems to shadow him.

Although Eric is advancing through the Eagle School of Learning something is disturbingly wrong. Other eaglets appear content. Also their thoughts are often contrary to his own. How much he envies them and their supposedly taking things in stride. To him growing up seems so awkward and difficult.

Notwithstanding, his impatience only encourages his eagerness to mature into the eagle that he wishes to become.

His youthful spirit remains assertive and independent. Thus he does not always conform to the established strict standard of behavior. There are occasions when he is grounded to the confines of the nest. Also other times when father eagle sees fit to discipline him with the biting edge of his wing. Still his deep inner sensitivity causes him to continue to question almost everything. Often in contemplation he would ponder how it is possible to pursue goals of a direction that it seems the Great White Eagle keeps secret from him.

Eric also remains disturbed by an incident that occurred early in his schooling. Jackie another male eaglet and he had become close friends. Without exception they walked to school together every day. However one bright sunny morning following a vacation period Jackie was not waiting. Upon approaching the nest Jackie's mother greeted him instead. "Where is my friend Jackie?"

With tears of sorrow in her eyes she replied that Jackie had gone to live with the Creator. Eric didn't understand. Perhaps in part due to his young age. But also in result of his intense feeling of emotional loss. A response to his spiritual nature that could not accept his friend's dying. Because to him it seemed so untimely and out of order with things.

Only old eagles he thought who had lived out their lives in purpose and happiness were supposed to die. In the direness of pain associated with imagined guilt he had asked himself what wrong he had committed to be saddened so deeply. He began to wonder if he might die as well. In feeling of agony he trembled in fear that he might never fly. From this day forth whenever Eric would see an ant on the path he would step aside. Life had taken on a new and precious meaning to him.

In reflection Eric continues to remember Jackie and how alive their spirits were in sharing. Still however young and close their valued relationship was the loss of Jackie does not devastate the daring of Eric's eaglet spirit. Yet the dilemma of premature death was not fully resolved within him. Certainly given his eccentric nature it would remain more difficult for him to sever the ties of those close to him in heart.

Screeching from the cliff across the valley he had echoed his painful thoughts. "Is it the passing for his sake or my own suffering that perplexes me the most." How tragic Jackie's fate of unfulfilled experiences and unachieved goals denied of purpose. "Oh Creator, divulge to me the secrets of life that I might better understand. Lest I not try so hard to change the realm of things which you have willed."

Life is neither all happiness nor all sorrow. As the seasons continue to pass Eric comes to experience a blending of both aspects. He like all high-spirited eaglets is learning that growing up is difficult. Furthermore time has brought change. The war has ended abroad. The landscape beyond the cliff has renewed its splendor. Also the outer structures of Eric's wings have strengthened sufficiently. In his eagerness to grow up he is elated that the season of flight has arrived.

It is a beautiful early morning. The warm currents of air rise rapidly from the valley floor. High upon the cliff he proclaims this the day of his first flight. His heart pounds with exhilaration. It matters little to him that elsewhere thousands of other eaglets are feeling similar sensations.

Full of eagerness with readiness at his back he proudly moves to the edge of the steep escarpment. His wings feel young and strong. It is the beginning of his destiny. He is determined to ride the winds in search of glory. Typical of exorbitant youthful enthusiasm he feels the sensation of immortality. Fear is all but a stranger to him. In asserting proclamation he screeches across the open sky. I shall not merely rise upon the wings of an eagle. For I am an eagle; the most magnificent of all birds. I shall fly in bidding venture into the majestic heights of the heavens. In time my purpose will become known to all as will my mark upon this world.

"Eric. Eric." "Oh mother. Why do you bother me at this important moment? Can you not see that I am about to span the two poles in gracious flight." "What poles are you referring to? I see no poles." "My dear mother. Must I explain that my reference is to the opposite extremes of the northern and southern hemispheres." "Son. Stop that confounded flapping of your wings and sit with me a spell.""But mother." "Yes. Now that you have recognized my loving care and authority, please perch." "It has just occurred to me that my nature is no longer conducive to accepting commands from the weaker gender." "Eric. I am not accustomed to your arrogance nor will I tolerate such behavior. Needless to say, I am not one of your so-called girlfriends. Also I will remind you that as your mother respect is due." "Yes, I know. Besides I do love you very much. However mother, don't you realize that I have grown-up." "Yes, my son. Although it pains me. For very soon you will leave the nest forever. Nevertheless for a few moments humor your ole mother and listen intently to what I have to say.

Considering your excitement this day may seem short to you. However it will live long in your memory. Your first flight is both symbolic of a beginning and an end. It is the beginning of your taking up your place in the world. Yet as you depart from the nest it is nearly the end of our time together. Selfishly I wish that as a youthful eaglet that you could remain at my side throughout life. It is always difficult for a devoted mother to sever the bond of parenthood." "Nonetheless mother, why must you cry? Are you not delighted for me."

"Eric, I am extremely joyful for you. Someday when you are a parent you will better understand the meaning of my tears. For now know that they are tears of love and that you are of a special meaning to me. Also as I have told you before you have a gift of sensitivity that enables you to feel life in a deeper sense than most young eagles. However this trait also makes you somewhat more vulnerable as you are too trusting in nature."

"Are you suggesting mother that I am naive." "No, my son. I just believe should you make the wrong choice of a mate that you could be hurt very deeply. Beware that not all birds in the world are as noble in thought as yourself. In my fear for you, I pray that you will never experience such painful unhappiness. For you it would likely prove more devastating. Also of profound importance the resulting bitterness could ruin the gift that sets you apart. Do your mom a favor. Never let life take away the love that I know to be in your heart." "I promise."

"I do hope that some of your youthful charm will linger. Notwithstanding As you mature in the ways of the world eaglehood will seal your fate. I hope and pray that the changes will be gradual for you. To my utter sorrow the time is rapidly approaching when you will never be able to return home again.

With concern I have chosen this moment to express these things to you. The days of our lives are not guaranteed. None of us can foretell with promise what the tomorrows may bring. As you embark upon your first flight also remember the sound advice of your father. Let his contribution represent the strength of your flight. Not only the first, but in all of your flights throughout life.

Eric, Your mother loves you very much. I so wish that your first flight would become lost in the tomorrows. However in spite of your mother's sentiment the morning is still young. If you feel that the time is right, go with my blessing. Although be careful. Remember well my son that greatness in the realm of nature is most accurately determined by surviving."

"Mother there is much gratitude in my heart. I do love you dearly. Also you should not worry about me. I shall return safely. However tell me why are you crying again?" "Go my son. Leave your mother to her reminiscent thoughts. These are heartfelt tears of the happy times that we have shared."

Upon departing Eric hugs his mother and gives her an affectionate peck on the cheek. How deeply he feels for her pain. Yet there exists an inner calling to the edge of the cliff which he cannot deny.

While gazing across the verdant lower valley, he gives concerned thought to the things that his mother has said to him.

"How fortunate I am to have a mother like her. She so represents the epitome of motherhood. I know that if necessary she would sacrifice her life for me. In a peculiar sort of way a part of me also yearns to remain a youngster at her side."

Turning in concentration Eric realizes that he must rely upon his instincts. For in all flights there is an element of danger. Standing firmly on the edge of the cliff he proudly extends his wings. Almost immediately he comes to feel the strain on his muscles as the wing feathers from tip to tip begin to quiver in the prevailing breeze. Looking upon the enormous wing span that reaches far beyond his body the whole of his being fills with a sense of aroused self-importance.

Slowly with determinate zeal he begins to flap his wings up and down. So pleasant is the sound of the resulting breeze beneath them. Like the soft humming of a faint wind against the side of the cliff. The right moment has arrived. There can be no hesitation or ceasing of the vibrant motion of the wings. It is as though an inner voice is conveying to him an unrelenting command. With all of your might, lift into the sky. The whole of life awaits you.

Like taut springs suddenly released, his legs catapult him from the escarpment into the heavens. "At last I am finally airborne. However there is something extremely wrong. I should be ascending in height, not losing altitude. The pressure against my extended wings, is almost more than I can bear. If only momentarily, I could fold them back to ease the pain. That strange shrill sound complicates my thoughts. Furthermore I am at odds to understand the thin lines of white mist which trail from the outer edges of my wings.

I feel so sleepy and my mind is oblivious to what is happening around me. My eyes water incessantly clouding my vision. It is as though I am locked in a trance or trapped within a dream. Yet consciously I can feel myself being rocked and bounced about as if thrust upon a choppy sea. Even the wind rushes and lashes at me like a turbulent storm."

In reaction to his plight, Eric commences to shake his head from side to side hopeful of improving the flow of blood to his upper extremity. To his relief his conscious thinking gradually becomes more clear. I must have entered a pocket of cool dense air which in effect is hurling me like a projectile towards the ground. This would explain the strange noise and the mist flowing from the tips of my wings. As both are caused by the immense velocity of my downward flight.

Whether instinctively, or by a miracle his wings remain extended. Almost as if they were frozen in position. Even so awareness of an involuntary crash dive prevails. The resulting pain is becoming excruciating. Again numbness darts at his head and he fears that at any second he might blackout. In desperation though avoiding panic, he instantly fans his tail feathers in an upward position of alignment. With correlated movement he also raises his head slightly. Then with all the strength that he can muster, he arches his wings.

Spontaneously the forces of nature that have been working against him now begin zooming him in a semicircular pattern of motion. Still with fearful emotion he surmises: "If I don't crash onto the ground the intense velocity of my flight will cause my demise. Yet to my amazement I am beginning to slow in acceleration. Also my flight has altered in direction. I know this to be true as the sunlight now glares upon my eyes. How profoundly I welcome the sight of white clouds dotting a blue sky."

With near disbelief he begins checking himself for injuries. There are none. Although as he looks upon his wings he gestures a despairing sigh.

Folded over the outer edges of the fore fronts are several strands of native grass.

His ordeal had brought him within inches of death. Although because he did not panic he has survived. Now more than ever he feels a purpose to his destiny. However obscure it remains to him. With determination of will he asserts that he shall fly again on this very day. Nonetheless he must first rest as the toll of his misfortunate endeavor has drained his strength. Banking his wings he begins to descend towards a flat ledge formation approximately halfway up the cliff. Slowing in his approach he is able to make a near perfect landing.

Soon after given his zeal for life and flight, the pain subsides within the muscles of his young wings. While reason does not always prevail especially in youth he subdues his joy over having survived. He also concludes that no worthwhile purpose exists for relating the near fatal experience to his parents. After all he contemplates, they have enough worries in life without my adding to them.

Besides he further ponders "the lesson is mine. Moreover with gratitude I am alive and well. Although I shall not soon dismiss the value of this experience that has taught me so perilously the critical importance of coordination and timing. Nor will I forget that it is wiser to bend with the forces of nature than to oppose them."

For an hour or so Eric rests. Upon awakening he feels refreshed with only a slight feeling of soreness. The sky remains clear. Save for the warm rays of the western sun shining over the valley. How much they enhance the colors of his feathers in all the radiance of his youth. With only momentary hesitation he spreads his wings and again lifts into flight. However unlike before the warm air currents rising into the heavens gently buffet his underside.

As he masters the art of gliding, some of the heated updrafts swiftly lift him several hundred feet. Passing from one upsurge to another only rarely is it necessary for him to flap his wings. In the skillful pattern of his maneuvering they are proving to be a precision instrument of flight.

Never before has he known such elation and control of power. It is good to be alive. Proudly a part of him now wishes that the day of his first flight would last forever. His youthful spirit is truly at play.

In earnest he seeks tremendous delight in perfecting rollovers, banking his wings, flying in circles, and abruptly diving with all of his might. With equal fervor he zooms at low levels over the floor of the valley arching his wings and ascending rapidly to great heights. If not upon the realm of the earth, he is on this day making his mark in the skies.

However the intense heat of the afternoon is sorely taxing his limited youthful strength. He realizes in the days and weeks ahead that maturing will provide additional endurance. Even greater coordination of his wings. Regarding his willingness to learn he vows to keep an open mind. For in contrast of the morning's dreadful experience, he has already learned the hard way that even in the flight of an eagle there exists a margin of error.

The sun now low on the horizon signifies that it is time to bank his wings and head for home. How beautiful he concludes the long casted orange rays which in reflection enhance the many subtle tones of everything below. As he begins to descend towards the nest amidst the escarpment he feels a strong sense of accomplishment. Soon as he makes his approach adjacent the rock cliff there appears a large shadow which reflects even onto his dark shiny eyes. It is without question the Silhouette of an Eagle.

If his first flight indicated an attempt to achieve perfection it was never his intentional desire to alter his feathers. He is what he wants to be and perfection in his way of thinking simply represents a respect for orderliness. Besides even to him it is common knowledge that most eagles fly with endowed skill. Although in searching his spirit, he seems to sense vividly that the flight that will remain foremost in meaning throughout his life will be of heart rather than wings. In this regard he yearns for a queen. Thus his ultimate flight can only in purpose reflect this caring.

Eric has long expressed a desire to make his mark upon the world. However given his eccentric spirit ambition becomes primarily an endeavor for the support of endearment. Thus achievement can never be more than an emptiness absent the meaningful sharing with a rightful mate. In perspective the gift of true nobility is much more than an inherited standard of values. Rather it encompasses the whole embodiment of fulfillment adding a thoroughly rewarding dimension to the flight of life. Therefore in heart he identifies himself with that rare love that embraces the deepest of feeling and devotion.

A LONE EAGLE TOWERS HIGH ABOVE. HIS FLIGHT IS IN
SEARCH OF QUEEN AND LIFE'S DEEPER MEANING. HE IS
NOT LIKE OTHER BIRDS AND BY KNOWING FEATHERS
DIFFERENCE THERE IS A UNISON OF FLIGHT.

CHAPTER II

The Conflict of Adolescent Flight

During the weeks following his return to the nest Eric's parents teach him the art and prowess expected of an eagle in flight. He becomes an experienced bird of prey procuring much food. Yet frequently he would feel acutely sensitive whenever an injured prey in his grasp would manage to escape. Acceptance of a miscalculated dive or an untimely extending of his large claws came with utmost difficulty. The knowledge that an escaped victim, suffering and possibly dying vainly in some hole or den, proved unforgivable. Justifying the need for food was simple enough but waste was another thing.

It is common knowledge that the burden of responsibilities increases with age and maturing. Although for Eric, the self-inflicted harsh demands far exceed the normal expectations imposed by his parents. "What drives me to excel at the price of serenity within my soul, he would ask himself over and over. I desire peace. Yet such eludes my inner well-being. Also in contrariness I cannot deny my thoughtful interest on the subject of war. My claws are like a compelling weapon that draws me to an unknown hostility. Perhaps even my own destruction. How ignorant and impatient I am in youth. Yet I continue to sense that there is much more to this realm called life."

The swiftness of the passing weeks marks the close of another season. One sunny afternoon as Eric perches reflecting upon days gone by, he is pleasantly drawn in attention to a young and attractive eaglet of the female gender. She shines upon his eyes. In an instant his heart begins to quicken. As they communicate he becomes enthralled by the joy and fullness of life that radiates from her. In mutual fondness they soon begin to share many flights together.

Thereafter on a brightly colored autumn day as Eric returns from school his mother calls to him. The sound of her normal gentle voice reflects concern. "Come and perch with me as I have something I wish to discuss with you. It has been brought to my attention that you are making many unnatural solo flights late into the nights. I believe this to be true as I look upon your somewhat darkened eyes from a lack of proper rest. You are a good eagle and I am not questioning your behavior. However, I sense that you are deeply troubled."

"Mother, It is no secret that I hold much fondness of feeling for my female companion." "Yes. She is a fine gender and I believe son that her

19

heart is for you." "Nevertheless mother following our graduation from the Eagle School of Learning, she desires that I accompany her to the Eagle College of Advanced Learning. Because of my applied work with nest design, she has somehow concluded that I would make a great innovator." "I can understand your feeling somewhat pressured son. However your mother doesn't think this to be the cause for your late flights. Why don't you level with your ole mom?"

"Well, she understands our devotional difference to the Great White Eagle. Graciously she does not even ask that I accept her beliefs. However we cannot nest without the conditional consent of her elders to raise our future offspring in her faith. Mother. Why do you stare at me? Please say something. Do you think that we have already nested?" "No, my son. I do know you so. Now I understand what is bothering you."

"Mother, she is a considerate eagle and vows upon their reaching maturity that the eaglets can decide their own future. However, in spite of her commendable gesture, I feel that the early restricted influential instruction will be detrimental in prejudicing a truly free choice later. While I respect her faith with sincere admiration I remain deeply troubled."

"Son, I wish that it was within my heart and mind to bring you the peace that you seek. Unfortunately your ole mom just can't help you in resolving this particular problem. Nevertheless I would advise you to seek additional rest that will help to clear your thoughts. Also remember your father's wisdom regarding time solving fifty percent of your problems. You only have need to concentrate on resolving those remaining dilemmas that endure."

That night Eric does rest. The following morning after eating, they again converse. While his mother never brings total consoling peace to his soul, she does bring forth much understanding. She begins this particular conversation by stating: "Son, you are not like any male eagle whom I have ever known. Perhaps in part this is why I cannot help you more. Yet for the love and deep sensitivity within you, it is not difficult for me to understand the feeling of your inner turmoil.

Eric when you were younger I would observe you in the meadows and fields. You have always been such a lone eagle. On occasion in the midst of other eaglets, I have observed your perseverance long after they had given up on a trying ordeal. For you defeat always seemed like an intolerable fate. However agonizing your flight in life it could never be satisfied short of perfection. Still because of the resulting unhappiness, from your unwillingness to compromise, I hope that age will slightly curtail this demanding characteristic within you. There are times when you are too hard on yourself not to mention your high expectations of others." "Mother.

Might you have someone particular in mind." With a smile she responds: "Yes. Me for one."

"Tell me more about myself." "Eric you have such an inquisitive nature. Alright. I shall relent. However, don't you dare become conceited. Very early in youth you proclaimed that what you wanted most in life was a rightful mate and eaglets of your own. You have never changed in this spirit of desire. Most male eaglets do not aspire to a goal or dream of this nature. Especially one with such devoted aspiration until a much later age. I sincerely hope that I live long enough to gaze upon your choice. For as demanding as you are she will undoubtedly be extremely special." "Mother. Must you poke fun at me." However all that he hears in response is her amusing laughter that echoes the genuine love of a superb parent.

"Son it is not for your mother to know what field of endeavor you will eventually pursue. However I have never known an eagle to be so serious and intrigued about life itself. Still your endless questions and impatience to grow up causes you unnecessary unhappiness. Try to enjoy your youthful seasons for they are truly the best years of your life." "No mother. They are not. For one thing, father is too demanding in his expectations of me." "Son there are times when I would agree. However it is your father's intention to prepare you with the learning essentials of flight which he feels you shall require for a successful future."

Eric pauses momentarily. Then in an emotional outburst he asserts: "What he is doing by his unreasonable demands and incessant criticism is making me miserable." "Son. You are becoming angry. I might add that if there is a negative aspect to your personality it is your temper. Sometime your temperament is going to get you into trouble unless you learn restraint. Remember self-control. If some of your father's tactics are questionable his profound love for you is not. Besides your blatant behavior is unbecoming of your better side. Even if somewhat typical of a teen among eagles.

You have such love in your heart. Often I have witnessed your compassion come forth like a fountain of water bursting from the ground. On numerous occasions I have observed your nurturing a broken wing or freeing creatures torturously trapped. Also I am proud of your having consoled troubled and ailing elders when their hurt touched your sensitivity. Continue to strengthen these noble qualities my son. Never let hate enter your heart.

Choose a mate carefully and allow yourself ample time to learn. Nevertheless I fear by the complexity of some of your questions that you may never have all of them answered. In your maturing seek the assistance of the Great White Eagle. And for your mother try to become more patient. Lastly it would behoove you to be more tolerant in your relationships with other eagles. I sense a growing mistrust within your spirit."

During the months of autumn and winter there were many more talks between Eric and his mother. Then spring came and his graduation from the Eagle School of Learning. As he had not fully found himself in life or concluded his direction for the future the event was not particularly of great meaning to him. Nevertheless the related celebration proved of lasting memory. Affectionately both Eric and his sweetheart of the day believed that their joy would last far beyond. In their heart's, fondness had brought much happiness. Their flights had been many. Also through their frequent sharing they had experienced a fair amount of maturing.

Although unknown at the time, with exactness of meaning other influences had begun to shape Eric's destiny. The Eagle School of Learning was now behind thus requiring a decision of direction for the future. As summer trails, his endeared companion takes flight to the Eagle College of Advanced Learning. In her caring she persistently urges Eric to join her for the fall semester. So many times she spoke of her concern that if they did not remain together that something might happen to end their relationship.

Yet coincidentally a fear of failure begins to grip Eric's spirit. As a young eagle he lacks a genuine sense of real confidence. The latter is something earned by achievement. Also because of his age, his experiences are somewhat limited. Frequently in despair during this period of his life he would often beseech the Great White Eagle. Where is the angel holding the message of my purpose he would earnestly inquire in prayer. "Why Creator, have you given me life only to abandon me?"

A few days later Eric is high in the sky heading for home when the twilight begins to replace the setting sun. Typical of most eagles it is not his natural desire to remain aloft at night. Thus he banks his wings and begins to descend to a perch in a tall pine. As he lands with fixed claws and his wings still partially spread, his eyes immediately scan the surroundings. It is uncertain whether he has invaded unfriendly territory.

All seems well as he nestles in for the night. Suddenly a strange voice utters: "What's your name son?" In dire fright Eric nearly topples from the branch of the tree. Notwithstanding his young eyes instantly focus upon the source of the screech. To his immense surprise there is an old gray eagle. His stature is that of a very large bird. The look about him exemplifies wisdom. Upon gathering his ruffled feathers, Eric nervously expresses his name. "That is a distinguishing name. Quite befitting the masculinity of an eagle," retorts the elder bird. "Also I am sorry for having frightened you."

"May I ask your name?" "Why certainly. I am known as Alexander." "Well, Alexander. It is I that owes you an apology for having invaded your territory." "Nonsense. Besides I welcome your company." "Without sounding rude Alexander might I inquire why you are here instead of the warmth of your family's nest on high?"

"Eric, my nest is now with the winds of the past. Do you not know what your eyes tell you." "What do you mean Alexander? Truthfully I do not understand." "Lad, your youth betrays you. For I am old and my days of flight are over. According to the traditional law of nature I am an outcast. I have come here to wait upon death." "Oh Alexander. It is a ridiculous tradition. One that I shall never accept." "Eric. It is the way. We were put on the earth to serve and our pride prevents us from becoming a burden."

"Alexander can your mate not find satisfaction in caring for you?" "Sadly no. Still do not be sorrowful. In losing her and of late my ability to fly, life no longer holds the same meaning for me. Always be positive in your thoughts Eric. For example, I have many happy memories of sharing with Katie and as a Master Philosopher at the Eagle College of Advanced Learning."

"Sir. I am extremely impressed." "Quite frankly Eric your presence represents one last honor for me to instruct. That is if you are willing?" "Oh yes, Master. Please teach me that I may become as learned as yourself." "There is not time for that my youthful friend. However perhaps, I can stimulate your thinking in the right direction.

First, tell me which birds of flight in your opinion are the greatest?" "Why eagles of course. They grace the highest elevations." "Yet only a moment ago Eric you implied that I do you an honor. Yet I am very old and incapable of flight." "Yes Master. Nevertheless you are learned and therefore wise in the ways of life." "I am flattered by your compliment. Furthermore I can tell that you possess a keenness of mind. Now in challenge of our exchange of thought tell me which you believe to be more important. The eagle or the flight?" "Most assuredly the flight." "Explain yourself."

"All birds including eagles are restricted in flight by the measure and formation of their wings. Although knowledge, even without wings and a fair breeze is boundless in the pursuit of understanding. Thus education transcends ignorance providing a purposeful direction towards noble contribution. In essence this represents our serving."

"It is most evident my young friend that you are an eagle of much respect. I truly wish that we had met under different circumstances. For you represent a student of my heart. Concerning wisdom and your destiny perhaps time will prove to be your most worthy instructor. However in complimenting the value of time permit me to leave this additional thought with you. Never forget in life that the greatest of all flights is charity. Also as you indirectly suggested, it is not who you are but what you are in flight that is important."

As Eric turns away in thought notwithstanding a feeling of sleepiness a cool gentle breeze passes through the trees. However he can still hear

Alexander continuing to speak about love and the need to keep up a guard against all forms of hate. Then momentarily the master's voice becomes broken. As Eric looks back upon him, he is silent. It is all that he can do to raise one of his large wings. Instinctively Eric knows that this represents his gesture of farewell. Alexander is gone. With sorrow in his heart Eric gives thought to how quickly death has come to him.

Considering the brevity of a few brief hours, Eric has not known Alexander long. Yet the bond of a meaningful friendship has been formed. Subsequently the loss of a master and friend is no small matter. With grieving pain Eric screeches across the heights of the trees. Perhaps he concludes, even Alexander's warm concern for him, had been intended to inspire a final lesson. The important value of friendship. He further senses that the enrichment of contribution by the able master will remain with him indefinitely.

In life there can be no set price fixed upon the true value of education or upon real friendship. Thus the merit of Alexander according to Eric is character. With heartfelt regard he becomes determined that not even in death will Alexander's fate be left to the whims of vultures.

Gazing upward Eric selects a stable site within the confines of the tallest pine. Thereupon in the moonlight shining through the scattered clouds, he begins to build a nest suitable for a recognized master. As the twilight ebbs the task is completed. Ever so gently he carries Alexander aloft to rest overlooking the life below to which he had contributed so much.

For a few moments Eric relaxes and gives thought to his friend above including all that had been said between them. Then upon spreading his wings he lifts into flight for the journey home. As he clears the tree tops, Alexander appears to be at peace. His facial expression seems to convey a felt regard for his final student. Also a kept promise of life fulfilled. However trying Eric concludes that his own life must go on. Respectfully he rocks his wings in a gesture of farewell.

Through the still of dusk his flight home is filled with emotion. Although he is consoled by the belief that Alexander's spirit is again gracing the skies. Yet he remains perplexed in his understanding and acceptance of death. Nonetheless he possesses youthfulness and an eagerness for life. Even in nature this is a form of healing. Also on the distant horizon of time and flight his own destiny awaits.

As the days of summer wane, Eric's permanent departure from the nest becomes inevitable. In addition he and father eagle have not gotten along well during this particular season. However this represents a normal or semi-normal developmental phase. As most young eagles in their late adolescence asserting strong individualism do not have a harmonious relationship with one or both parents.

Although it remains that Eric is most unhappy. On one occasion following an angry dispute with his father, he had even left the nest for three days. During the period after, they saw little of one another and spoke even less. This was also a trying period for Eric's mother who felt obliged to act as ago between or arbitrator. A friend of the family related to Eric his disapproval that he be imposed by so many tedious tasks. However he further asserted that complaining would by futile. "Your father is determined to impress upon you the hardships of a cruel world. While I may not agree with your father's harsh methods I respect him. Certainly he loves you. He just does not want you to forget the important need to continue your education at a later date on a formal level."

In spite of differences of opinion Eric's admiration for his father never changes. Furthermore his father's intended message to maintain learning as a high priority becomes deeply branded upon his mind. In part the undesirable laborious assignments beyond the nest curtail ever taking education for granted again. Eventually Eric will reflect a more grateful attitude for his father's love. For even though he remembers his father as possibly being too demanding, he could not recall a single troubled time when he had not come to his aid. He further senses that many of the strict rules of the nest reflecting strong values will prove helpful in enabling him to persevere the storms of life.

By late August, Eric must reach a decision regarding his future. Classes will begin in early September at the Eagle College of Advanced Learning. His adolescent sweetheart awaits his flight to her. However Eric has absolutely no idea about what field of study to embark upon. And though he is aware that advanced courses will open additional doors of opportunity, he ponders his ability to satisfy the admission requirements.

Considering his young age, to include parental pressure, and social expectations, that he feels imposed upon him, causes agonizing pain. His exaggerated fear that he might fail seems a fate worse than death. Only later will he come to learn that his anxiety of feeling is common to most young eagles destined by opportunity to seek a higher plane of flight.

In boldness Eric begins to drown his fear with disillusionment of self-importance, fanciful dreams, and soundly with a resolved determination to excel. "Have I not been told on numerous occasions that most fears are unfounded he asserts. Did my sweetheart not say that she would tutor me regarding areas of study that might prove troublesome. Besides eagles do not fear high places. In perspective doesn't this pursuit merely represent a place of higher learning?"

As Eric concentrates on bolstering his confidence, his father requests a private conversation. For a moment or so Eric feels only his father's silent gaze upon him. Never before has he experienced such hesitation. It is obvious that his father's words are not going to come forth easily. In fact it is his love for Eric that makes his purpose difficult. Certainly his intention is not to cause despair. However hurt at times is inevitable in the growing up process. Moreover parenthood is endowed with much responsibility.

"Son," he begins to speak. "You are a good eagle. Moreover you have never brought embarrassment upon your mother nor myself. Frankly I don't know quite how to say this, but have you given any thought relative to possibly attending the Eagle School of Military Training? I personally believe this to represent a beneficial direction pertinent to your future." "Absolutely not!" Eric replies as he initially rejects all consideration of the subject. However in expressing the emotional aspect of his heart he seems to sense that he cannot suppress indefinitely his practical side.

"Eric, I want only what is best for you. Also without a doubt your girlfriend is a fine bird. Nevertheless I fear that your affection for one another is likely to lead to an untimely nest of your own. Perhaps even eaglets at the cost of your education. This is the last thing that either she or you can afford at this critical time in your lives. I would strongly urge that you give the military opportunity some thought."

In the days following Eric does give his father's encouraging suggestion warranted consideration. He even takes flight to gain the available information pertaining to the military opportunities being offered. Perhaps what is more important he seeks counsel with a friend of his father. An eagle with whom he has previously developed a trusting bond. Thus it represents an association that he believes will provide equal deliberation regarding his fondness for Marianne.

With life pulling him in two different directions Eric continues to contemplate why growing up must be so painfully complicated. Concerning his deep feelings for Marianne the dilemma of choice seems almost unsurmountable. Nor does it appear to matter to him that thousands of young eagles elsewhere are having to make a similar decision. Also of a perplexing nature Eric has come to believe in result of surrounding influences that happiness is measured by the degree of one's success.

Life is a complicated phenomenon. Even difficult decisions are rarely solved easily even in the presence of wisdom. For this reason Eric does not formulate a final determination to his problem for several additional days. However the direction has become somewhat more clear. While some confusion and anxiety remain the alternatives are simple in number to resolve. Subsequently the situation has inevitably been a problem of Eric coming to grips with himself. Sometimes in life the right path of flight is not always desirable. However it should ultimately be followed.

To some extent Eric is aware that his young age and a period of three years apart might prove detrimental to what began as a cherished adolescent romance. Again his memory recalls her words: "I fear that if we are not together that something might happen to our relationship." However also in his thinking is the ever persistent feeling that lacking maturity he is not ready for the Eagle College of Advanced Learning. The weight of the decision also brings to bear a conscious awareness that a mistaken judgment could prove devastating in nature for years to come. In time Eric will come to regret that not all equally important decisions in his life received as meaningful attention.

Eric's mother either by higher command, meaning father eagle, or by her own grace of feeling what is best, does not interfere with Eric's decision to attend the Eagle School of Military Training. Also Marianne expresses more understanding than he had anticipated. They agree to communicate often. However, there will be no sharing of flights, as Eric is destined to a place mankind calls Germany.

For Eric attending the Eagle College of Advanced Learning will be postponed until another day. Perhaps naively he believes that young love will transcend both ocean and time. He certainly is not alone in this wishful thought. Many young male eagles have been told by their sweethearts of promises to wait a lifetime if necessary.

Yet in awareness he senses that just because one graduate's from a secondary school or reaches a certain age, that the accomplishment does not always indicate maturity. There are only so many heartbeats in a lifetime. Also timing is so vitally important in making crucial decisions. A wrong decision considering dire issues can jeopardize a lifelong future. Eric's deciding choice to join the Eagle School of Military Training as opposed to the alternative of attending the Eagle College of Advanced Learning is largely based upon trust. A trust in those whom he respects for having greater experience and understanding of life.

It is early September when Eric makes his last flight over the forest. He wonders about the days ahead and if his decision has been at the cost of Marianne. He ponders if war might come during his three year tour of duty. If he might never come home again? And if he does return, if the forest and meadows will be as before. Not to mention his loved ones.

As a teen Eric is going abroad to do an eagle's job. In his determination to serve well he vows in heart to accomplish all that will be asked of him. The decision wise or unwise has been made. There can be no turning back in commitment. Thus he raises a wing in the customary gesture of good-bye. Momentarily he turns in a final glance looking upon what had meant so much to him in youth. Then with obvious sadness intermingled with the joy of independence, he departs from the nest.

Lifting into flight he begins to reflect upon his young life. His thoughts are mixed with emotion. For the most part his adolescence has not been a particularly happy period. Still there have been memorable moments. Besides this unique phase of life he concludes can never totally represent an easy transcending. If Eric's early years in the nest had proven burdensome it was due primarily to his profound sensitivity. Including the pressure to succeed beyond his self-concluded abilities of the day. Also his search for the deeper answers about life.

During his trek towards Germany, Eric passes through verdant valleys and over snowcapped mountains before reaching the wide expanse of the Atlantic ocean. Reality assails his heart. He screeches in response to his inner pain. In contrast his mind is wrought with grand illusions of venture intermingled with heroism. Yet increasingly he realizes that the world that he has loved is being left further and further behind.

The salty breezes of the sea blow gently beneath his wings. For the despair of turbulence is solely within himself. "Why do I remain so troubled about life and my veiled destiny? Why did my mother, while shedding tears, express that military duty will prove difficult for me. Why have so many of my youthful flights been in the storms of life? In my compelling flight to succeed my spirit knows untold misery."

On the horizon of his newly acquired independence, Eric ponders if he might find the happiness and peace that have eluded him in the past. Perhaps the significance rests not so much in the moment of thought but rather in the flight of the day. For in the wake of the flapping of his wings, trails his adolescence.

If Eric's spirit lacks the tranquility of peace the fluttering of his feathers reveals the exorbitant excitement of youth. In this vigorness for life he yearns for adventure. With purpose unresolved he is headed in flight towards an unknown future. While security is more often associated with the known it is the inspiring hope of the unknown that encourages flight. He is proud to be an American Bald Eagle and his dreams loom high. In his eagerness to find himself within a strange world he is boldly prepared to fly the skies in dauntless pursuit of success. Even if need be in the storm of sacrifice and struggle.

THE EAGLE BY MASTERY AND CUNNING IS A BIRD OF PREY.
BUT BY GRACE AND HEART HIS FLIGHT FINDS PURPOSE
THROUGH LOVE. THOUGH A LONER BY NATURE BLESSED IS
HIS NEST. AND GIVEN BEAUTY IN EXPRESSION HE MATES
FOR LIFE.

CHAPTER III

Military Duty and Unresolved Conflict

Upon arriving at the Eagle School of Military Training Eric settles in for the night. As the days of autumn pass he soon learns that individualism is discouraged in the military. Most activity is a group response in accordance to a cadence. Thus for the first time in his life he is learning the significant meaning of a Gathering of Eagles.

It is a strange sort of circumstance. For in a normal sense, eagles do not form armies from their ranks. Nor do they go to war as throughout nature a need has never arisen per se. Still military preparation continues in response to a potential threat from their enemies. As territorial disputes constantly threaten the peace.

Eric learns that nobility and the height of the eagle domain restricts the number of their enemies. The vultures represent the greatest threat. It is not their plight in life that makes them dangerous he is told. Rather it is their lust for power and greed. Next are the hawks who thirst for combat and kill for sport. The third enemy is of a different nature. Considering their characteristics they are capable of being both hawk and vulture. Although acknowledging their compassion, they can be like doves as well. Such individuals are called man. Most men are good but do not be deceived as it is they who cause world wars. And their encroachment upon the eagle domain is an unjust infraction upon nature.

For several weeks Eric receives intensive training. He becomes dedicated to learning the prowess of military expertise. Nevertheless the conflict within his spirit grows as his skills are being developed for destructive purposes. Thus he is beginning to understand why his mother had expressed that the military would prove difficult for him.

As a bird of prey he demonstrates a natural talent for the execution of tactical attacks. However he is torn in heart by a contrasting desire to build rather than to destroy. Within himself he feels the futility of war. Yet in part his daring instincts cannot disavow a certain unexplainable drawing to battle. Perhaps it is the sense of power over life and death that he holds within his wings and claws. However during the mock war games, he occasionally witnesses the dying of proud birds. He quivers at the sight of death having learned that whether the cause is intentional or by accident, it holds the same lifeless permanence.

In any military campaign there are at least two formidable forces. There is of course the declared enemy. Equally dangerous are the hostile forces of nature. Along the vast stretches of the German frontier there are only barren mountains and valleys. In the nest Eric had known the comforts of home. Yet here there is no convenient food, at a claw's reach. And though the temperature might drop to near zero it does not mean that a warm nest can be entered.

The prolonged periods of strenuous training exercises exposing Eric to harsh conditions are establishing character.

However the meaningful values are not wholly appreciated by him at the time. Still he senses that he is changing in a maturing way. The days without food, causes an acute feeling of sympathy for those victims in life who have experienced more prolonged starvation.

In lesson he is further learning that frostbite is not confined to the northern front nor heat exhaustion to the equator. In the chill of rain the comforts of the home nest are but memories that warm only the heart. The bitter sharp winds and freezing snow of winter all but stifle his efforts to adapt to the hostile surroundings. Still he endeavors to maintain self-control in spite of the threatening conditions. From his studies he has already learned that whole armies in the past have perished in the grasp of an enemy as a result of panic. Perhaps most importantly Eric is learning to screech less and to listen more.

If loneliness shadows Eric's flights in a foreign land, promotion and the responsibilities of leadership also befall him. Whenever new recruitment birds arrive at the Eagle School of Military Training, he initially greets them as they come under his charge. His ultimate message to them is always, emphatically expressed: "In the wilderness— listen well, learn quickly, and observe the older eagles. For they have survived here longer than yourselves."

During the month of January, Eric's superiors order him to undertake a flight near Bavaria. In spite of a developing winter storm he is to observe reported infiltrating hawk movements within the region. As he approaches the designated area being unaccustomed to the terrain and high mountains it becomes necessary for him to gain extra altitude. He ascends higher and higher in an attempt to establish his bearings and to scan the locale. However his efforts are all but futile. The onset of darkness has hindered the flight almost from the beginning. To make matters worse the besetting cold is compounded by a blizzard storm that begins to threaten further his ability to observe.

Dark gray clouds blanket the sky as incessant gusts of wind violently flutter the feathers of his wings. Soon snow begins to fall and at first given his body heat only his wings dampen with droplets. However within minutes' crystals of ice begin to form upon both his back and wings. Thereafter it becomes a struggle for him to remain aloft. The mission has reached a critical point of impossibility. Eric has done his best but the elements now dictate the flight to be one of survival.

Although lost with time becoming crucial to his remaining aloft, Eric reminds himself to remain calm. After all, he ponders every problem in life has alternatives and a logical solution. However they may not always be of a desirable choice.

Assessing his predicament Eric is acutely aware of the necessity to attempt a safe landing. He must also seek shelter from the storm to avoid freezing to death. However his plight will not be resolved easily. This particular wilderness is extremely barren save for the nests of the war hawks. Also if captured by them, at the very least, he will be confined for three years. Several other eagles have crossed over their borders and befallen such a fate. As the temperature and visibility drop to near zero the worsening conditions dictate the need to take immediate action. Eric thus banks his stiffening wings in a downward circling descent. Frostbite trails swiftly upon the path of his perilous trek.

Never before has he encountered such ravaging winds and blinding snow. Lower and lower he descends while constantly searching for a place of protection from the dangerous elements. However there are none. Unfortunately the maze of white flakes continues to obscure the hope of finding one.

As he glides near the ground the mountains loom high above but offer little resistance from the biting cruel winds. Turning in direction to a flat open area, he struggles to angle his wings in a position to slow his descent. He can only hope that no jagged rocks protrude just below the surface of the snow. However because of the stiffness of his wings upon impact, he crashes with a thud and plunges deep into a drifted snow bank.

Soon the falling white flakes begin to envelop him. From the weariness of his torturous flight he desires only to sleep. Although cold and alone, he wishes for companionship to battle against involuntary rest. Quite wisely he is aware that to succumb to unconsciousness is to invite freezing from which there will be no awakening. It is also imperative that he remain awake to keep an opening for air. Notwithstanding he has survived the landing and ironically the snow provides some warmth by blocking out the wind. Yet in spite of everything, Eric now wonders if the worse does not lie ahead.

Hours pass before the heavy snow begins to relent. With great difficulty he break's free from his white powdered encampment. Extremely stiff and numb from the bitter cold he can barely walk.

Steam rises from his body similar to a river in early morning. He shakes violently. To his dismay he lacks the energy necessary for flight. Stiffness and deep bruises cause pain even to the quills of his tail feathers.

In the distance he notices a small red light. With joyful hope he wonders if the direction might lead to his rescue. However as he begins to walk toward the glowing amber in parallel diversion it appears to move away from him. Then the light dims and ceases to shine into the night. As he stands in bewilderment he is mindful that distance can be deceiving in a cold, darkened, and snowy wilderness. He contemplates further the possibility of his losing all reasoning due to the freezing elements.

Suddenly another light appears. He questions if it might be a luring trick in the darkness by the war hawks. "I must be careful. I do not wish to die or be captured. A compound for an eagle is a slow death." Although as he cautiously stalks towards this second red glow it also dims and disappears.

At different locations within the vicinity additional lights appear only to fade like the others similar to falling meteors. By this late hour Eric tires sorely from walking towards each glow. What is this strange phenomena he asks himself? "This trick in the night that lures me to such fatigue and my eventual demise."

Still as his instinct for survival commands he walks on persevering and defying his apparent fate. Never before has he experienced such cold, thirst, and hunger. In despair he turns in thought to the past when he had been a young eaglet in the nest of his parents. So much had been taken for granted. There had always been food and warmth providing protection from the elements. Never again he declares in the silent still air will I lack appreciation for such things. However paramount to his agonizing plight fear of capture overwhelmingly dominates his thinking.

As his steps slow and become less sure in exactness Eric approaches desperation. Surely he nervously ponders the Great White Eagle does not will for me to die so young. "Oh Creator," he exclaims: "It must be that you have a purpose for me in life. Please save me lest I perish and cannot fulfill my destiny."

In protest of what is happening to him, he desires to screech. Even to make a bargain with the Great White Eagle purposeful of sparing his life. However, he cannot utter a sound, as fear suddenly engulfs him like a giant shadow. There is a mysterious repetitious trailing echo to his steps that exceeds the sound of crunching snow beneath his feet. As he steps, it too moves in motion. When he stops in his tracks it too ceases in movement.

With fixed claws, Eric bolts to defend himself. Only to gaze upon a jackrabbit a short distance away. His heart pounds as he sighs in relief. In feeling of astonishment he believes it strange that the rabbit has been following him. Given a different set of circumstances the rabbit might have proved a tasty meal. Eric wonders if the animal as himself has merely lost its way. If so he shrugs what an ill-fated rabbit to seek direction in my steps. In any event a few moments later the large jackrabbit disappears into the night.

Upon regaining his composure Eric resumes walking towards a light that shines more brightly than any of the preceding. Yet the hours before twilight pass slowly in what seems to him to be an endless trek. It is both strange and fascinating how the lights in the dark come and go. Almost like the shining eyes of nature's creatures. However this light he concludes has maintained its brilliance like a magnificent star on a clear night.

Having his eyes trained upon the white glow in the distance he fails to notice a gully located to his immediate front. Abruptly he falls head over claws at the will of gravity. Upon coming to rest at the lower extremity of the large ditch he can only contemplate the quandary of his hurt pride.

When again he opens his eyes he lurches backwards believing that he is about to be consumed. Upon shaking his head to clear his thinking reality establishes that his confrontation is actually with a gigantic wooden sign of man. Initially he does not understand the huge configuration. Nonetheless the flashes that he had observed as an eaglet in the nest again suddenly loom to the forefront of his thoughts.

Eric soon realizes that inadvertently he has entered the encroachment zone of man. The symbolic designs on the sign reveal the shapes of the large guns which he had seen in arrayed rows in the meadow of the valley beyond the nest of his parents. While he does not comprehend the words Artillery Impact Area, he nevertheless associates the strange light to man. He is now more adamantly aware that his trek across the wilderness has brought him into harm's way.

Under normal conditions he would not fear encountering a single war hawk. However a flock of hawks could pose a dire threat. As for man, it remains for the most part a live and let live situation. Still he recalls that man is not to be trusted.

Their encroachment, upon the eagle's domain, continues to make them a potential enemy.

He is poised in a neutral zone between man and the reported invading hawks. In nature territory is everything. An uninvited guest often finds it necessary to defend his life. In the midst of two unfriendly foes, Eric now risks life and wing by having to consider crossing an artillery impact area as well. There are many dud shells lying about. Any one of them should he accidentally step on it could explode obliterating him from the face of the earth.

If safety exists beyond the impact area in the direction of the light, he concludes the risk of crossing too great. Furthermore he no longer possesses the strength to go around the vast area of strewn shells and casings. The alternative of freezing to death is not a comforting thought either. Still it seems the better of the two choices. In a state of total exhaustion, sleep weighs heavily upon him.

With staggering motion he retreats a fair distance. On his left side he notices an isolated young tree upon a small knoll. Hesitating only momentarily he decides to perch at the base of the leafless perennial. At least it will provide a reference point should any friendlies happen by. Believing the situation to be hopeless he also decides that he will tuck his head under one of his wings and let fate take its course.

Upon nearing the base of the small hill he becomes startled by a sharp screeching command to show his colors. To the best of his ability he shakes off the snow and ice that clings to his many feathers. He is a morbid sight considering his ordeal. Furthermore he shivers violently in the early morning air. Perhaps part of his quivering is due to not knowing whether the voice is friend or foe.

The length of internment and subsequent harsh conditions of hawk captivity suddenly flash within Eric's mind. A pause of silence follows and he fears the worse. Abruptly the screech of the sentry again resounds exclaiming his name. "Eric. Is that really you?" With elation in his heart Eric sighs the biggest relief of his young life and responds affirmatively.

His evasive action throughout the night had proved to be most effective. Unfortunately his ability to avoid detection had also prolonged his ordeal in the wilderness. An unsuccessful search for him had been conducted by his feathered comrades. Whether by instinct, or coincidence rescue had come by his own volition. Yet in humbleness even he attests to the near fatal timing.

Considering the severity of his ordeal Eric is a very fortunate eagle. On this particular military exercise four other young eagles have lost their lives in a separate incident. Several others suffer from frostbite. And a few in consequence will lose a claw or two.

Eric had escaped the ravage of enemy hawks only to find himself in the grasp of another foe. Nature or the elements can under certain conditions prove as formidable an enemy as any upon the earth. For him there will be other battles in the struggle for survival. However because of his near disaster in the frozen wilderness, an even greater appreciation evolves for the value of all life. Respectful of being spared he expresses intense gratitude to the Great White Eagle.

In each life there are ordeals to be endured. However with the passing of each storm the returning warmth of the sun brings a newness of spirit. Change is ever constant and life goes on. As the warming upon Eric's return from the barren frontier penetrates even his deepest feathers, he realizes that his youthful experiences are teaching him vulnerability. How threatening he surmises life can be. He concludes the need to put himself on guard. "If I am to succeed he proclaims in self-expression, I must learn to conquer the elements that cause failure."

His youthful desire for a family remains a noble dream. Yet what had seemed so right and permanent with his adolescent sweetheart is now but a billowing smoke. The Princess has taken flight due to impatience or for love because another was there and Eric was not, or for reasons now lost in time.

So idealistic is our youth and the resulting projections of perfection. The reality of life beckons not only the affectionate sharing but wills the related responsibilities as well. Because of their young age Eric concludes that they had not known the latter. Certainly it is this factor that gives meaning to all lasting relationships. Thus while the ocean may separate it cannot deny true mature love.

Happiness is a realistic goal in life. However our responsibility to the future is of greater consequence. In keeping with this awareness we must at times follow sound advice not necessarily in harmony with our hearts. Sometimes though it may be painful it is essential to abandon immediate gratification for more worthy long term goals. Through wise decisions the best that any eagle can do is to put the odds of a successful endeavor in his favor. It is senseless to ponder later with regret the other unrealized direction not taken in life. Ultimately it remains a figment of the imagination with glittering fanciful overtones of wishful thinking.

All of these things Eric contemplates regarding his hurt subsequent to the loss of Marianne. In proper perspective he also concludes an appreciation for the fond memories of a youthful flight with her. A female eaglet whom he continues to believe possesses outstanding attributes. Again the turbulent winds have blown hard against his feathers. Yet with a silent good-bye he weathers the storm. When the sunshine returns to his shattered world with a renewed spirit, he will sense that his queen and destiny await in a season beyond.

A young eagle eager to spread his wings, often does not acknowledge that maturing is a life long process. Thus typical of most youth, patience and love are fleeting. Even Eric can no longer deny the unalterable fact that yesteryear is gone. That in a very particular sense, he can never go home again. Vain efforts to recapture the past in an attempt to regain some of the early eaglet gleam only adds permanent awareness that the experience of growing up has been at a price.

The understanding that he can never go home again serves only to cause him additional mental discomfort. For the most part he remains troubled and unhappy. In frustration he concludes his untold hours of earnest meditation as wasted circular thought.

"Why he would ask himself repeatedly can I not be like other young eagles? Enjoy their simple pleasures without ethical regard.

Why do I remain so serious in my outlook and life so perplexing to me? Eric could not adapt to an I don't care attitude." "Why he would ask further, can I not accept life more simply? Why do I feel so compelled philosophically to know its interrelated secrets?"

How cruel he concludes the turmoil of his youth. In self-expression he realizes that his perfectionist leaning only adds to the elusiveness of the inner peace which he so desperately desires. Still he cannot accept the adage of eat, drink, and be merry. He wants more out of life and strives to make sacrifices towards the enhancement of life's more virtuous fulfillment. Within his mind he pictures life in tranquility and beauty. Yet the rains of conflict remain. Thus he finds no lasting shelter from his inner storm.

It was inevitable that several other birds would reflect hostility towards Eric. Especially regarding his non-conforming perspective on life. If being different is of some foreseeable value he does not immediately experience any benefit. In a sense he feels himself alone in a crowd. He is shunned and treated like an outsider. Which is not to say that others didn't share his esteemed aspirations. However few are willing to pay the price of commitment.

Although rejected by many of his peers, Eric's esteemed character does command much respect for his ideals. Also in his longing for queen his search continues with the noble attributes of a young eagle. For he has long envisioned that the flight of nobleness given its inspiring value is greater than the eagle.

In retrospect Eric had left the nest of his parents. He had found a world not in accordance with many of the values and honorable traits that he had been taught. Like other venturing young eagles, he struggled to find himself in a sphere of double standards. Yet in keeping with a positive attitude he had kept an open mind to compromise. For Eric this proves to be somewhat of a difficult endeavor. For in his manner of thinking love represents a fulfillment not a bargain of denial. Also within his yearning to share is his heartfelt desire for a rightful queen. Furthermore those things that are right are naturally sound which in worthiness of flight represents the true essence of life.

If in youth Eric aspires to a higher plane in life he does not always achieve his goal. Like all young eagles he comes to experience the scars of imperfect flights. Not to mention the shortcomings of dreams and more than a few regrets. Yet the course of his lifelong flight never wavers in trueness to his heart.

The seasons pass and the time draws near for him to return from abroad. Although he has not resolved all of his inner conflicts regarding life, he has matured much as a result of his experiences. His commitment to the Eagle School of Military Training won recognition including an honorable graduation and many satisfying memories.

While on duty in Germany, he had also spanned the territory's man calls France, Belgium, Austria, Switzerland, Denmark, and Sweden. A flight to Italy was aborted due to a severe storm over the Alps. Although disappointed, Eric did not panic. He was becoming accustomed to the storms of life.

As the leaves begin to turn golden and crimson color the brisk winds of autumn bring a fresh outlook and a return flight home as well. Eric had flown the skies and had made a small but successful mark upon the world. Still in modesty he does not conclude himself as a leader among eagles. However at the Eagle School of Military Training some of his superiors did. Nevertheless he believes that only time and his destiny will reveal the truth about the merits of his leadership. However the added boost to his level of confidence is of a great complimentary value.

In seeking the noblest clouds of ascent Eric increasingly comes to sense a growing feeling of destiny within the enormous span of his wings. Excited in spirit he screeches across the sky. "Oh Great White Eagle. It is in my heart to know my fate. Tell me the secrets of life that only time in passing tends to reveal. I beseech thee to know if my future beholds fulfillment. And if I shall escape the misfortunate failings of others.

By my yearning to grace the skies, I seek only queen and success. In this endless search I endeavor not for the wealth of the world. Rather, only for the fruit of my ambition. Cast thy breeze beneath my wings that through wisdom I might rise above the turbulence of my inner conflict and experience the serenity of flight." Yet neither the Great White Eagle nor the Messenger Angel whom Eric beckons for during the nights of his youth renders a response.

THE FLIGHT OF THE EAGLE CAN BE ETERNAL ONLY WITH
QUEEN. FOR WITH HER ALONE RESTS HIS FULFILLMENT. HE
DOES NOT RUSH TOWARD STORM BUT ALIGNS HIS WINGS.
FOR IN SPIRIT HE KNOWS THAT LOVE MUST BE TENDERED
OR BECOME FLEETING.

CHAPTER IV

A Season of Maturing and Learning

Upon arriving home Eric experiences much jubilation as he has not seen his parents for nearly three years. However some of his joy is short-lived. For the most part the forest and the meadows appear as he had remembered them. Yet he has changed. He is no longer an adolescent. The maturity that has come upon him by the winds of time has altered the meaning of the past. On a note of sadness he accepts the realization that in a unique sense he can never truly come home again.

Indirectly and quite coincidentally Eric also learns that his adolescent sweetheart Marianne is now with two eaglets and expecting a third. He feels for her happiness. Yet with concern he can only wonder if her early nesting has not been at the sacrifice of her formal education. Although with profound personal satisfaction, he is proud that her nesting relationship had not been denied its sacred chastity. For in queen he aspires the same.

Considering these private thoughts and others Eric begins to adjust again to the ways of a peaceful pursuit. His training as a bird of war is also now a part of the past. Still the future awaits him including a flight to an alternative Eagle College of Advanced Learning. Both time and maturity have put the odds of success within the fold of his wings. He is determined to soar to the best of his ability.

During his brief stay at home he undertakes several solo flights. High above the forest he ascends and glides through the air carefree of events below. This particular period represents an interlude of relaxation and recollection of seasons gone by. However most importantly it is a time of transition. The beginning of a much deeper meditation surrounding philosophical thought. Especially regarding his untrusting acceptance of a hostile world. Following one of his daily flights shortly after dawn an event occurs which forever changes his life.

It is a warm morning in early September when Eric pauses by a clear running brook to quench his thirst. At a certain point he notices that the bedrock acts as a barrier forming a pool of still water. As he leans to drink, he hesitates momentarily to gaze upon his vivid image shining on the surface. Inadvertent of his own motion some ripples suddenly appear on the water abruptly distorting his reflection.

In solemn meditation over whether he or the projection represents reality his eyes grow heavy. Sleep slowly comes upon him. As he drifts deeper and deeper into a slumberous state a part of him resists. However consciousness wanes like the trailing mist of a cloud. His last instinctive thought is indicative that eagles do not invite danger by resting upon the ground.

As he sleeps, a power or spirit beyond his own seems to control his entire being. Against a clear blue sky, he begins to see swift moving clouds. The silence is of a stillness that he has never known. Time appears nonexistent. In an unfamiliar dimension he has become lost in a vision.

Softly though with pronounced clarity he commences to hear his name. "Eric. Eric. For by your spirit you have sought the truest meaning of all life. Furthermore because of the noble calling of your heart, you shall share in the expression of all flight. However concerning the knowledge being imparted to you there is an absolute condition. In meaning you will never fly as before. Not even in the likeness of most other eagles. Nor can your self-will remain as before. Although on occasion you might falter your wings henceforth will be in purpose of serving the Great White Eagle. It is He who has sent me."

"I am so very honored. Yet how am I to determine the precise nature of my serving?" "Be patient Eric. But for now permit me to divulge the wisdom that shall be your guide. Nonetheless do not expect too much at once for it will be up to you to learn understanding." "Please explain." "What I mean to convey Eric is that learning is a lifelong process. Though I impart wisdom to your ears the value rests with your ability to eventually comprehend fully my message.

For example no flight is of value without a positive purpose and a worthwhile priority. The day will come Eric when according to your maturing you shall believe in something greater than yourself. When that time arrives in benefit you will experience the freedom that you seek. Therefore through your understanding your flight will also be more of heart than of wings.

Listen carefully. There is an ancient myth that explains your destiny. However it is much more than a traditional story. In reality it transcends time and bestows your obligation to all life. In the creation of all birds, there came to pass not a single random feather. Orderliness interacts and complements all creatures and all things. Yet by eternal purpose only the eagle is destined as the guardian of the heavens to inspire all who seek the grace of noble flight.

According to the ancient myth: An eagle upon reaching old age will molt. The belief is that he will become overwhelmed and feel compelled to fly towards the sun. As he reaches a certain altitude his feathers will singe. Ultimately he will fall into the sea. However he will emerge renewed of youth."

"Oh sacred one. I am profoundly grateful and my heart is full of glorious elation that you have chosen me to serve the will of the Great White Eagle. Still my spirit is saddened as I do not wish to be forever denied heaven for any reason." "Eric. I alone did not choose you. Although do not despair for myths as I have expressed, are not wholly a matter of fact. It is just that more often than not they are paralleled by a sense of realism. Furthermore it is doubtful that when your time comes that you will be denied access to heaven. In clarification the myth reference to renewed youth implies the knowledge that eagles are endowed with longevity. Thus however misconstrued the vigorous youthful period of eagles extends far beyond the measured years of other birds. Also among eagles molting is an inconspicuous evolving.

Eric, you are inclined to venture. Cease to think in terms of restricted or conditioned learning. Let there be no barriers in your flights of thoughtful pursuit. Go beyond the mode of present day thinking. Search the tomorrows and explore beyond the established horizons. As your spirit seeks total freedom, demand increasingly more of your mind and body.

My feathered friend the parallel of the myth in relationship to your destiny is that on a predetermined day you will be called to a near vertical flight. You will know exactly the precise moment by the compelling spirit of truth and love within you. That you may further know the right time it will follow a chilly rainy night. Your chosen flight will also begin from your perch upon the branch of a forest tree.

It is not for me to say if your flight will terminate at the threshold of heaven. However, I can relate to you, that your destination will be of glory rather than a journey into the sun. Nor Eric will you fall and perish into the sea. For that is neither your purpose nor fate. I cannot tell you more as prophecy is not a realm left to my discretion. Nevertheless be strong in your faith for though many tribulations will cross your flights in the years ahead, you will not be alone.

I must now leave you. Perhaps someday we will meet again. Know that you are loved by He who has sent me. If in the future you should contemplate another image, let it reflect Him. Also Eric, in your learning and understanding, always look upward for the rainbow of your dreams. Farewell my friend. Remember that luck is a matter of faith."

Upon awakening Eric immediately takes to flight. Inadvertently he has broken a cardinal rule of survival by remaining on the ground too long. On this particular occasion he has been fortunate. Or perhaps as he gives thought to his vision duly protected in harm's way. He feels refreshed. Although of greater importance, he senses an enlightened purpose. Thus it is now within him to learn understanding of the wisdom that has come to him through a voice from the past.

Eric's flight to the Eagle College of Advanced Learning begins appropriately. He feels the usual doubts and reservations often associated to a new venture. However foremost he forms a positive attitude. No eagle could be more committed to achieving an educational goal. Yet there exists a lack of full confidence. Thus he vows to himself that if failure is the final eventuality that there will be no regrets. Relevant to not having applied himself to the best of his ability.

During the next four years Eric studies diligently. On rare occasion he undertakes flights above the forests with fanciful female companions. However his dedication remains pursuant to gaining an education. Throughout this phase of his life there are numerous struggles and sacrifices. Yet he has come to realize that anything worthwhile does not come easily. During one especially cold season the severity has caused lean times. He finds himself obliged to solely consume a corn substance for twenty-one days. To his immense pleasure it is vastly satisfying when the flakes of winter give way to the more abundant variety of spring.

Considering the nature of Eric's flight in life it seems only reasonable that his interest would turn to history and evolve towards philosophy. Thus in time his spirit truly becomes curiously devoted to philosophical study. Within this embodiment of knowledge he senses the fulfillment of his educational pursuit.

Eventually Eric excels beyond his self-imposed goals. Honors and honorable mention are bestowed upon him. In view of his achievement and because of his spirit of excitement the other eagles accept him. Also to his gratification his peers frequently seek his advice. During the third year at the Eagle College of Advanced Learning the rector requests him to assume the teaching responsibilities of the Master Eagle of the Philosophy Department. The latter has taken ill and will be absent for several weeks. Conditional on being granted total professorship authority Eric boldly agrees. Compliance is rendered and during the weeks that follow he lives up to the confidence placed upon his young wings.

Some of Eric's superiors both at the Eagle School of Military Training and at the Eagle College of Advanced Learning have recognized qualities in him that he has not equated to himself. In time he will recognize similar attributes in many of his own students. Subsequently encouraging them according to their own developmental flight. For by a caring manner he has also come to conclude that his own destiny rests within the field of instruction.

On graduation morning the sun shines ever so brightly. Eric concludes it to be his day in the sun. In a silent assertive gesture of proudness he exclaims: "The achievement has been realized. Now the potential for real and lasting success is more than a vain dream." It does not matter to him that the accomplishment will not be concluded as magnificent by many others. However he regrets, that proven eagle teachers, are not represented higher on the scale of professional measurement. Still he asserts that life is a noble flight. Also the direction begun is not always indicative of journey's end.

For the next four years, Eric teaches at the Eagle School of Learning. He senses that his contribution is of merit and feels an inner satisfaction. The rapport between him and his students has represented a profound joy along with the learning aspect. Yet two notable concerns begin to prove detrimental to his spirit as an educator of history. Foremost is the lowering of the eagle educational standard. Furthermore in view of his philosophical training he gradually feels a loss of self-challenge.

Thus the season has arrived for Eric to pursue attendance at the Eagle University of Higher Learning. Again his chosen field of specialty becomes philosophy. As in all meaningful endeavors in life, he encounters the usual storms. Still with renewed determination including his prior educational learning, he rises in altitude to meet the challenge of opportunity.

During the passing months at the University, Eric becomes an instructor. Which coincidentally parallels his enrollment as a student. Accordingly and approximate to the beginning of the spring semester, he is assigned the charge of a rather large class of Introduction to Philosophy students. Soon after, a unique and warmly remembered rapport develops between himself and this well meaning, but eccentric untraditional youthful group.

This special interacting educational relationship is no small achievement considering that time has brought social change. Eric's military attributes are no longer as popular as in days gone by. Perhaps it is his meaningful humor and genuine caring which they sense that makes the difference. In any event, many of these fine young eagles soon after, are sent to a war in Asia. They take with them the values and understanding of life that he has taught them. Sorrowfully for some it represents their last flight.

As graduation approaches, The Eagle University offers Eric a departmental professorship. Although most grateful, he declines this most generous offer desiring to settle in the West. He is also aware that acceptance will require pursuing still another higher degree. An endeavor that would curtail much of his teaching. Most emphasis would ultimately shift to research. A direction of opportunity which on a permanent basis is not of great interest to him.

Upon graduation Eric becomes a master by degree. On the occasion reflective thought takes him back in time to his friend Alexander. "Oh Alexander, exclaims Eric in silent contemplation. If only, we could converse again. For all that I have achieved, my spirit remains without peace. I long for my queen. For every flight of learning the ocean of knowledge deepens.

45

Thus the more I learn the more complex life becomes. Also, the more unhappy my heart. A part of me yearns to retreat to the values of the simple life." Realistically life had never been simple for Eric. Furthermore his longing is but an uneasiness of heart. For he senses still that his destiny eludes him.

In spite of his inner troubled discord he resumes a position at the Eagle School of Learning. Because of his interest in teaching and devotion to the young eagles, he remains there for the next three years. Thereafter with much reluctance he decides to leave the teaching profession. He has grown weary of the struggle against developing negative changes as most teachers conclude them. Although steadfast in his persevering to maintain teacher classroom control, the exacting demands have taken a toll upon his personal life. The time has come to bid farewell.

As he departs, a female teacher of long standing, calls out to him. "Eric, I am speaking for all the teachers of this school whom you alone have fought for. Not having our support we owe you an apology. We ask that you understand our dilemma in having to consider the protection or security of our family interests. Many of us have eaglets in the nest and cannot easily take flight elsewhere."

Upon expressing empathy Eric again turns to leave. However again, she calls out to him. "Eric it has been several years since we have seen a teacher of your quality. It will likely be several more before we see another." Following this most moving and gracious compliment Eric departs. However his heart never takes leave of teaching.

During the seasons immediately after, he ventures in search of his spirit's longing. However fulfillment is always elusive. In despair he compromises his dreams and his faith in the vision by the brook. Thus in the midst of loneliness absent the Great White Eagle's blessing of consent, he nests. In time he fathers two little eaglets. Given the love of his heart they remain most precious to him. And though by sheer effort the nest lasts long in the forest, it cannot be sustained indefinitely from the eroding winds.

Eric is learning the hard way that in life some things are meant to be compromised while others are not. It bothers him immensely that the two eaglets will suffer because of his mistake. To his deep and humble satisfaction the eaglets do not hold him accountable. Still it remains that he is responsible for them. Accordingly he nurses them in fatherly love for several seasons. Up to this time obligation's beyond the nest have dominated much of Eric's life. For many reasons he has experienced little happiness. However through these offspring his heart finds much revealed and untold joy. Perhaps because of self-condemnation regarding their plight, he unfairly concludes that his own life is over. Therefore at least inwardly he lives mainly for them.

It had always been Eric's intention to mate but once in life. For this represents the traditional standard of the eagle. Furthermore to him it is in meaning and reward the most valued of pursuit. He is also aware that in relationship to nature that the eagle was not meant to live alone. With feelings of regret he finds it difficult to condone his self-imposed impropriety. In self-pity he wonders why life seems to bring him into harm's way more than others.

Aside from pity his answer soon follows. For at least in theory Eric is demanding more out of life than many others. Thus logically in multiple decision making the potential for error becomes greater. In essence, No decisions! No errors! While concentrating in solemn thought he becomes mindful of a phrase that he had often shared with his students: "In life be all that you can and be all that you can be." With humbleness he further considers his own imperfection.

As all eagle's who take to the skies, Eric will confront additional real storms. Although in his continued search for the answers to life's perplexing problems he ponders the potential harm of those turbulences that are only imagined. He further deduces that the prime importance lies not in the number of storms but rather in our fortitude to weather them.

THE EAGLE IS A NOBLE BIRD BECAUSE HIS FLIGHT
EXEMPLIFIES NOBILITY. IN PROUDNESS HE SEARCHES FOR
HIS DESTINY. YET IN HUMBLENESS HE SURRENDERS HIS
WILL. IN BELIEVING IN SOMETHING GREATER THAN
HIMSELF HE JOURNEY'S IN HEART TO A SPIRITUAL
ONENESS WITH HIS CREATOR

IN THE CAPACITY OF SERVING RESTS HIS PURPOSE AND
AWARENESS OF LIFE'S REAL TREASURE. IT IS ALSO
WITHIN THIS DOMAIN THAT THE MOST VALUED FEATHER OF
LOVE FINDS MEANING—
THE FLIGHT OF CHARITY.

CHAPTER V

A Gathering of Vultures

Spring comes early bringing a renewal of blossoming flowers and verdant grass throughout the meadow. Eric has taken flight for the sole purpose of enjoying the magnificent beauty. Esthetically it beholds a certain peace. On this particular day he is carefree in heart. Almost as if he was reliving the afternoon of his very first flight.

Again he portrays a youthful eagle flying higher and higher in frolic. At approximately thirty-five hundred feet in altitude he banks his wings performing roll after roll before pulling out into a gentle glide.

It is on his fourth pass over the meadow when he glimpses a flash from below. Although smaller, it appears similar to those which he had remembered as an eaglet in the nest. Suddenly he feels a burning pain in his left wing. His heart begins to race. However drowsiness soon proves overwhelming. He struggles desperately to maintain consciousness. In spite of gradually losing control of his coordinated movements instinctively he attempts to ascend in elevation. However this is not to be. In harm's way, blood spews from his wing over and against his body before falling in a downward path that seems his destruction.

"Already the vultures begin to gather and circle below awaiting my demise. Free are the skies though they lick their hideous beaks in eagerness of my fate. Is it their nature to consume everything good or bad without regard? Is their vision so distorted that innocence, beauty, and love, are reduced to a meal? Perhaps it is their selfish desires that equate life to a gutting of all decency. In the wake of my doom such thoughts are futile."

As he weakens in strength his wounded wing begins to flutter and shake violently. Subsequently regardless of grave effort, he can no longer sustain a critical alignment of flight. Within seconds he begins to lose altitude falling into a faltering and nearly uncontrollable dive. The wind rushes by like a hurricane over the land. Even the tips of the pine trees far below appear to be jetting upward.

From the loss of blood and the speed of his descent he begins to chill in the morning air. Fear grips his mind. He senses the nearness of the shadow of death. He begins to wonder if it really matters whether he lives or dies. Or if a choice any longer exists. "I have known only the hurt of misguided love. Also for the most part life has proven unkind. Surely the death of one more eagle will bring little sorrow. After all, the vultures of the world have devastated thousands. Perhaps millions over the centuries. Many have been ravaged only to serve as stuffed trophies in the name of sport.

In life I have battled both hard and long. I have been victorious in overcoming every obstacle. Still I have not known my queen. Moreover happiness has remained just as fleeting. Perhaps in death I shall find the peace that has forsaken me in this dimension. If not for the value of life I would have crashed myself upon the rocks long ago. Why was I given such values that have only become a standard of burden?

My spirit is weary of so many empty flights. Yes. This hunter of sport and trophy who has shot me is my excuse to renounce my responsibilities. He is my escape from a life of disappointment. Apart from my offspring what blame could result should I align my wings in the position true to the dive of death. I would just be another victim of the vultures."

As the winds of a downward flight continue to pound against his every feather, he is gradually aroused by the resounding of his name. "Eric. Eric." Being only half conscious he wonders if the distinctive sound is merely the vibrant whistling of the wind. Although again he hears what sounds like his name being echoed from the clouds overhead.

"This is the Great White Eagle. Your intolerance and defeatism of thought have tried my patience. Also your excessive individualistic will referring to your compromised choice of nesting has annoyed me. Nevertheless it is my will henceforth that you shall serve me. Therefore I shall render unto you the necessary strength to survive your ordeal."

"For gracious sakes. This is going to require a miracle. Why did he not just stop the storm of injustice at its outset?" "Eric. I do not prevent the storms of life. However I help those of my flock through them. It is not important that you understand my intentions. However, I will tell you emphatically, not to tempt me again, or the vultures shall feast upon your carcass. Now bank your fall to that clustered group of young pine trees on your right."

Eric's vision is blurred by the mist that fills his eyes. At such a speed of descent none of his innate coordination's are normal. Even his consciousness is possible only by the numbness that has eased his pain. Nonetheless following the instructions given to him, he musters his strength and begins to direct his fall towards the small trees.

Doubt continues to beset his wings. For even if he survives the impact he will likely be consumed by the vultures. "Oh Eric. You are of such little faith," exclaims the Great White Eagle.

There are no further thoughts or expressions as Eric plunges into the thick growth of tender but pliant branches. In what seems forever at a tremendous velocity he is hurled about through a maze of dense and cracking twigs. Each stem fundamentally acts as a cushioning buffer.

Eventually he comes to rest upon a bed of grass needles and pine cones which have formed upon the ground.

Although stunned, and badly bruised, he is grateful to be alive. Instinctively his spirit for survival encourages his escape. However his wounds prevent such a vain attempt. Besides it is all too obvious that the vultures have descended and surrounded him. Injured and unable to assume flight within their zone of influence he is at their mercy.

Soon after, he is placed in a cage. His feelings of agony and pain are as immeasurable as the drops of blood that continue to flow from his afflicted wing. His eyes fill with contempt as he looks upon a group of vultures standing nearby. So ravenously they lick their chops at the sight of his pooled life's fluid. Still within his heart as he succumbs to sleep, he senses that the Great White Eagle is with him in spirit.

Upon awakening several hours later he is astonished to see that his wounds have been cared for. Yet he quickly concludes the treatment afforded him to be less than a noble deed. For in theory the strewn bones about the compound indicate the abundance of prior vulture victims. He is simply being saved from a postponed fate that will likely befall him at another time of greater scarcity.

For the next several weeks Eric is provided with the essentials to sustain life. Slowly his wounds heal. Nevertheless his predicament remains a nightmare. In misery the reality of his situation seems unacceptable though ironically undeniable. Torn in both heart and mind he wonders if ever he will experience flight again. Even apart from his plight of captivity he cannot be certain if his left wing has suffered permanent damage. Although in the face of death such concern, he concludes is so much superficial nonsense.

One day as he paces aimlessly in his enclosure a lone vulture enters. Although not of impressive features he bears a large frame and walks with the gait of one who has battled long for authority. "I understand," he comments in a deep voice "that your name is Eric." "Yes. However I should not think that to be an important matter to a buzzard." "Perhaps you are wrong.

Not many eagles venture this way. Also from our observation you appear interestingly different. Possibly this reflects your prior domain and education. Furthermore your character indicates a degree of arrogance. If you prefer high spiritedness. Without a doubt you arouse my curiosity eagle. Although we are deemed enemies at the cross road of life, I should like to have many conversations with you. By the way I am known as Brutus."

After disclosing his name, Brutus departs. More than a week will pass before the two of them meet again. He has appeared pleasant and likable. Nevertheless Eric reminds himself that Brutus is a vulture not to be trusted.

51

How contrary this type of thinking is to Eric's heart. Still captivity remains a stark reminder of his misfortune and the need to be distrustful. Also Eric is not so naive to believe that Brutus's expressed interest is actually of any real regard to himself.

Upon his second visit Brutus informs Eric that he has violated the law having entered the vulture air zone. In specific language the charge amounts to an endangerment of the species. He further states, "that there will be a trial held by the master vultures." Although after pausing for a moment, he adds, with a look of manipulation, "that such a misfortunate tribunal experience might be avoided. It is even possible Eric that your freedom can be restored to you."

"Brutus. What unwarrantable price do you seek for my freedom?" "Eric. Your tone of voice indicates an unduly suspicious nature. Have the master vultures and myself not already spared your life. Did we not bind up your wounds and provide for you. Perhaps you should give additional thought to having misjudged us. Actually in simple terms if you will concur to admitting violation of our air space conditional freedom will be granted to you." "Brutus please explain in explicit terms the implied restraint." "Very well eagle. Although I caution you to weigh carefully the alternative choice that is death. In clarity you will be branded by a notching of your wing. We desire that all of nature will come to know you as a violator of vulture law."

"Oh Brutus. Do you think me a fool. It is you and the other vultures of life who make a mockery of justice. There has been no violation of your air zone. Nor is there any truth to your accusation that falsifies endangerment to your species.

Nature dictates the boundaries of the skies. By sacred origin the grace of flight rests upon the wings of eagles. It is through our serving the Great White Eagle who wills all things that we represent the standard of nobility in life. Yet in humbleness unlike yourself and other vultures we do not make claim of the heavens. For we realize that varying purposeful flight has been endowed to all birds of nature. Thus the flight of the eagle is a standard for all of nature to aspire. A mirror if you will of a deeper meaning of life that reflects love and respect. It is within this realm of meaning that my own purpose in life is greater than my freedom. Therefore I can neither agree nor accept your conditional offer."

"Eric, your excessive stubborn pride will be the cause of your condemnation." "Perhaps Brutus. However your misguided displacement of blame will not right your intended wrongful act. Like all birds, I am imperfect. Also I have been humbled many times in life. Still I shall not deny that I am a proud bird for such is my inheritance of flight.

I would suppose Brutus that our conflicting viewpoint is a matter of perspective. For if you truly understood the underlying goodness of life you might be less prone to greed and selfish pursuits. We both share the skies but our devotion to purposeful flight is as different as the sea and the land."

Brutus is angered by Eric's remarks. With heightened emotion he quickly reminds him that a trial awaits the conclusion of their talk. He also begins to pace back and forth as if somehow it bolstered his argumentative position. Suddenly he stops. With a cold and stern glare he blurts: "Do you not think that we vultures are civilized?" This is a trick question Eric acknowledges to himself. If I answer yes he will trap me by asserting civilized enough to render justice.

"Hearken to my words Brutus. Civilization is not a guarantee of justice. If it were so wars would not occur in a civilized world. Also you and I both know that justice in this life reflects varying perspectives of values and conflicting interpretations of such. Furthermore because of iniquitous dispensation of unjust measures many so-called civilized flocks have fallen upon nonexistence since the beginning of time. Notwithstanding, law and order existed in nature long before civilization. Your unethical rationale Brutus is at best only a futile attempt to justify in purpose the persecution of this eagle."

"Reluctantly Eric, I will concede to your argument or point concerning the accounting of civilization. However rhetoric is not something that can be digested in a real sense." "Perhaps not Brutus, but it certainly is food for thought." "I tire of your arrogance eagle. Besides might it have occurred to you that we vultures are the chargers of justice."

"Brutus there is little justice in this world. Notwithstanding most certainly you vultures are the least of the administrators. You are not a separate entity. But rather a single link in a long chain that comprises nature. There are inherent laws that harmoniously bring order to nature. As all other infractions that arise, your bid for power will succumb to her will and not your own. The winds of catastrophe including evolution are not as wayward as your lustful greed.

The noble flight of the eagle is decreed by authority of the Great White Eagle. Thus we are in harmony with nature. The grace of our serving is symbolic of justice. We unlike yourself do not rest in the shadows of treachery.

There was a time in the beginning when you and your flock flew with us in the upper heavens. Other creatures were destined as scavengers to cleanse the land and the sea of carcasses. However as fallen eagles from grace you were banned. Why? Because justice in your eyes was reduced to illicit power, corruption, and greed. Also your appearance came to reflect the injustice and suffering that you have imposed upon others. Now you know exactly what you represent Brutus. Your falling from grace was the result of your own volition. Neither your heart nor those of your vulture followers are any longer full of love. Furthermore I have not violated your air space because your dimension is no longer on high. Thus you will not persecute me in the real sense of justice. For your reality is the lowly realm of vengeance.

In a world of much misunderstanding where knowledge and wisdom are often absent some will be fooled by your claim of being the Administrators of Justice. However you cannot serve two masters. In the end corruption will cause your ruination.

Brutus it is not for me to judge the vultures of this life. I can only enlighten you by screech and deed. Therefore given my own imperfection I cannot change the nature of things intended. These reflections are not for my sake but for yours. Remember that there are those who listen. Yet they do not hear.

Be advised vulture that the carcasses upon which you feed will not save your spirit. It is a mistake to conclude that the external feathers reveal the true nature of a bird. Reality lies within the heart.

In nature there is only one justice. It may be perceived as having many faces. However the image reflects solely the Creator of us all. The distortions of life that appear cruel such as when an egg is stolen from a nest or when a youngster is felled are sorrowful experiences of our limited understanding and attachment. They also reflect our reluctance to accept natures balancing of life as it was intended in the beginning.

It is no secret Brutus that you and your kind promote evil throughout the evolutionary chain. The Great White Eagle denies none his grace. Yet of your own accord you turn from good. You dine upon the spoils of the earth and your appetite is unsaturable. You could change Brutus. However, you will not, for the glory that you seek is your own. Also approval of your ways is sought only from your own wicked flock. Beware vulture for any deviation from the intended way of things is a risk to your own destruction.

I am neither special nor superior of my own right. Thus your charge of violation is vanity. You are a vulture and in your bid to rule the skies you exceed your limitations. I am an eagle though in my flight, I have not desired to alter my feathers. My struggle has been to serve the sacred purpose of another. Sometimes in this endeavor my flight has been awkward. On occasion I have drifted off course. Although I have never wandered far or fallen from grace.

Hear me vulture that you may better serve your own kind. For my words are a gift to an enemy. To this end I serve He who has given purpose to all life. The knowledge that I share with you is His blessing to me. Take heed for though the imparted wisdom may fall upon deafness the meaning is no less important. Nor henceforth can you disavow your responsibility to all life and claim ignorance of your ways.

As for justice Brutus, it may or may not be found in civilization. If it exists at one time it might not at another. However in the presence of compassion you will always find true justice. Much as one finds forgiveness in the expression of love."

"Eric. Your words are not without reason or my respect. Still I fear that we have met too late at the cross road of life. Change comes hard. Also I regret that my personal convictions are not as strong as your own. Especially concerning the Great White Eagle." "With pity, I have already sensed your feelings Brutus. Therefore I can only say that as you dictate my fate you shall also seal your own."

Two weeks later a gathering of the master vultures takes place. Eric's mock trial is held. It is decided that he continue to be caged indefinitely as a protection to the vulture air zone. He is told that the measure represents a gesture of mercy by an advanced civilized flock. Although he questions their authority there is no response. Perhaps he denotes silently there are times in our lives when our destinies take control of us instead of our controlling events.

Ironically during the trial Brutus appeared preoccupied. He seemed unusually solemn in expression. Frequently he held his head down. At one point he was overheard muttering: "This eagle doesn't deserve to be here." With satisfaction Eric hypothesizes that "there is something good in everything I see." Unfortunately Brutus did not come to Eric's defense. Even if the outcome was predetermined. Thus the cast of his fate has been molded. Eric would neither see nor talk with him again.

The seasons pass. Yet in spite of Eric being allowed outside his cage daily he remains a captive. Paradoxically he is not considered a threat. Thus most in time have come to like him. Perhaps in this regard he is a novelty. For certainly there remains a difference that sets him apart.

One day he happens to overhear the voice of a middle aged vulture by the name of Troy. In comment to another of a lesser position he expresses: "If ever an eagle doesn't deserve to be here it is that bird over there." It is gratifying to Eric to know that others also recognize the injustice done to him. Yet what bothers him most is the feeling that the Great White Eagle has seemingly abandoned him.

It is also during his second year of captivity that Eric learns that it had been his former mate who had betrayed him to the vultures. He had suspected such concluding her unfaithfulness and the speed by which the vultures had encircled him. Now he knew with certainty and his heart took pity upon her. Apparently his being shot by a hunter was a coincidental occurrence that only served further an unscrupulous plan previously contrived. And though also betrayed by the vulture acting in his defense at the mock trial, it is the separation from his offspring that weighs most upon his mind.

Considering his noble values and the love of his heart Eric had never taken freedom for granted. Nor given his humble wisdom will he allow bitterness to destroy his enlightened perspective on life. Accordingly with earnest endeavor he maintains a forgiving nature. However by birth he represents a graceful bird devoted to flight. Thus the cage is inevitably a death sentence upon his spirit that daily extracts a toll. His prowess in the sky remains unquestionable. Although on the ground, even he is aware that he is losing the battle of survival. The vultures have decided against branding but have long bound his wings to prevent flight. In consequence though hope has sustained him for several months inwardly life is draining from him.

Sometimes during the storms of life there occurs a compounding downpour of torrential rain that adds to the suffering. Among eagles this also holds true. Like a bolt of lightning it comes to Eric that his mother has passed on. He had long known of her being ill. Still the time is never right to lose a loved one so endeared. He is deeply sorrowed for their relationship had been of profound richness. Time will bring healing. Also a reminder that for all things there is a season.

In spite of his plight and for the sake of his offspring, Eric endures yet another season. However in spirit he can no longer accept the cage except in heightened deterioration. Mind over matter is waning. Before his capture he had existed if not lived in a normal sense. Problems had represented a challenge. Also he had striven to accomplish goals. Now even that stimulation is a denial to him in a degenerate surrounding.

No eagle born into freedom does well in captivity. Perhaps in part this purports of his uniqueness. It may also lend credence to his flight never being aimless. Certainly the pillar upon which Eric's strength of character has rested had been proven many times in the past. Such are the birds of a different feather. Notwithstanding even eagles have limitations.

On the evening of the day his discouragement peaks Eric turns to the Great White Eagle in total surrender and humbleness of this message:

"My life no longer serves me and without
purpose I have no will to live. There is
much which I do not understand for all that
I asked of life was queen, offspring, and
the means to care for them in a befitting
manner. Nor did I seek these things freely
but regarding the fruit of my flights.

By thy grace I have known the blessing of

Eaglets. For the time of joy with them, I am
eternally grateful. Yet in the absence of
destiny I have failed myself and offended
thee. Therefore my serving has been more in
word than heartfelt deed. For this I beg
your forgiveness. Now my life is not my own
to live. In search of meaning I give it and
all my love to you. If by your will there
remains a veiled purpose to my serving I
beseech thee my rescue. Grant ascent from my
enemies for in death my flight cannot
glorify thee."

Eric had never prevailed upon his Creator before with such fervent regard and expression of self-will. He realizes in heart that there is little to his offering of service. Yet not a heartbeat of feeling did he withhold. In the truest sense he is seeking a value of purpose to his restricted life absent of flight. For even in the depth of his most inner spirit, hope in his rescue now appears almost unbelievable. Still he does not doubt that all things are possible with the Great White Eagle. His apparent lack of faith actually represents only a loss of self esteem.

Ironically a few hours later Troy makes a surprise visit. He informs Eric that a special council has been formed to correct the injustice done to him. "Even among vultures," Troy affirms, "there are some who in remorse believe in the Great White Eagle. In our departure from noble flight we became blinded to our true hearts. Since, we have become inspired by your devoted example and shared wisdom. No longer will we silently standby to the evil injustice around us. Our true beauty shall be our spirits. Though we who believe are small in number our love will spread across the skies."

"Troy. Your renewed faith and courage deeply humbles me. However will the other vultures not persecute you for your regard in my behalf." "Eric. It doesn't matter for our commitment goes beyond yourself. Through forgiveness we seek reuniting love and eternal flight with the Great White Eagle." "I can only say Troy, that you and the others of your devoted flock, are truly eagles among vultures."

However due to initiated delays caused by the non-believing vultures the months continue to pass without avail. Eric's hope for freedom again begins to wane. The resulting discouragement causes him much anxiety. Still in spite of his despair he strives to maintain trust in the Great White Eagle. Perhaps in his loneliness he would have been further strengthened by the caring of his loved ones. Nonetheless during this grave period of ebbing confidence all outside influence was prohibited.

A week later while resting in the warm sunlight, he is abruptly awakened by the loud beating of several vulture wings. The surrounding dust rises high into the air. Still it does not stifle the squawking of discontent. He feels perplexed to understand the commotion. Yet it is clear enough that the disturbance is being caused by a flock of enormous size. Within moments the sky quickly fills with the dark gray color of vultures. A slight breeze passes over the encampment. In the wake is a silent calm.

As Eric begins to concern himself over the safety of the vulture believers, Troy approaches. A smile appears upon his face and those who accompany him gesture the due respect of a leader. Upon confronting Eric, Troy joyously embraces him in wing. Jubilantly he exclaims: "You are free!" Eric instantly entreats: "Please, do not express amusement about a fate so solemn as mine." "Unbind him." "Eric, my friend. Truly you are free. Go in the blessing of the Great White Eagle."

"Troy. I cannot leave until you explain the cause of the commotion. Also why so many vultures flew away." "Eric it was in your defense that the battle for justice began. During the scope of deliberation the meaning and intensity arose to a culmination resulting in the dividing of the vulture flock. Those gracefully acknowledging the Great White Eagle are the ones whom you saw rising in the sky. It is our intention to relocate away from the others."

"I detect that you have been elected a leader." "Yes Eric. I have been chosen to lead the believers. In order to establish justice along with other devoted to prevent our ever falling from grace again." "Troy may I express how joyful I am for you. Also in gratitude I shall forever be in your debt." "It is we who thank you Eric. By your inspiring difference it is you who opened our eyes to a better way of life. Indeed we will remember you long after our feathers change. For by our faith we know that someday we will again be eagles.

Eric. "Yes Troy." So often you have expressed the phrase: "Something good in everything I see." Well, you might like to know that at one point we almost lost the battle for your freedom. It did not look promising when suddenly Brutus came forth proclaiming that he had remained silent too long. He fought for your defense as if you were his son. He risked his life in doing so." "Troy. I must speak with him." "Eric. Brutus has departed with the believers. He said to tell you that it is never too late." In further praise he commented: "I thank him for guiding me home and thus for giving back my life."

Eric is momentarily too emotional to speak when Troy blurts: "There remains evil around us. Let us depart from this place. Good-bye Eric. May all of your future flights find happiness and blessing." "Farewell to you my friends. I promise that you will be remembered for your good. It is important that your offspring will think of themselves as eagles with esteemed spirit. Tell them that it is not what enters the mouth that makes one a vulture. Rather the vile that comes forth."

Upon flexing his wings to remove the long acquired stiffness Eric slowly ascends into the heavens. His maturity and the importance of his flight have escalated in elevation to a new dimension of profound meaning. His heart surges with love and gratitude. Then with caring he rocks his wings in a final farewell to his brothers in the sky.

Larry Slauson

TO THE EAGLES HEART THE SOUNDS OF NATURE ARE A
SYMPHONY. ALOFT IN THE WINDS ABOVE HE GLIDES BEYOND
TIME. BY THE SEA HE SENSES THE QUALITY AND LINK TO
ALL LIFE. IN RAPTURE HE YEARNS FOR THE QUALITY THAT
COULD BE.

Chapter VI

Eaglets Ocean and Sea Gulls Calling

For several days immediately following his release Eric adjusts to his newfound freedom. His flights are joyous and extremely meaningful to his heart. He has in spirit moved ever so close to the Great White Eagle. Both gratitude and love shine in his eyes. If there is any sadness it reflects the absence of his mother and the time lost from sharing with his offspring. Time has brought change to many things. Although upon revisiting his father, the same affectionate respect that they had always known in the past prevails.

As Eric's heart has never left teaching he is delighted one morning when a group of gathered eaglets requests him to speak. Upon asking the nature of the subject they hastily reply: "You Master." Eric is flattered by their compliment. However he does not feel his own life worthy of such interest. Still they are persistent. Thus in keeping with purposeful imparting of knowledge he agrees to speak about the meaning of harmony and treasure as each has come upon his wings.

"In the summer of my life," he expresses with an intense voice, "I have come to realize that my ambition is not of the greatness of my destiny. Nor as I perch before you can I truthfully proclaim that I have discovered many of the answers to life's perplexing mysteries. However it is my purpose to bring to your attention what I have learned and believe to be in awareness an important deeper meaning of life. Most birds only flutter their wings in life. Never realizing or committing themselves to its greater values. The true harmony and real treasure of fulfillment lies in the depths of sharing life's intended love.

For many years a battle has ensued within my spirit. A struggle between heartfelt sensitivity and the strength demanded by a somewhat cruel world to survive. In spite of much related agony in my youth most of my conflict has existed only within the realm of my unresolved imagination. Nevertheless some eagles in life often amidst pain possess the gift of a heart which in sensitivity feels a deeper attachment. Unfortunately when we are young such emotions have not been tempered by discipline or the storms of life that give value to experience.

In noble flight, relationships rather than material things are special. Typically by nature we evolve from and are endowed by the love of the Great White Eagle. In the purest sense love is spiritual. Thus my entrusted eaglet friends when you extend sincere caring you are in effect giving expression of the rightful wing of love.

Through awareness, including a strong desire for a better life, our love must inevitably come into harmony with the will of the Great White Eagle. Realization comes from his influential knowledge and wisdom. Thus it becomes a lasting direction of contribution for a loving heart. Remember always that by enhancing the lives of others that we enrich our own.

I am telling you these things because I am convinced that you will never achieve real success without the Great White Eagle in your life. Even within the realm of material gain without him you must weather the storms alone. Therefore build your nests according to actual needs. We exist in the feather but it is feasible for us to evolve to a higher plane through the Spirit that makes all flight possible. It is only within this supreme sphere of dimension that the heartfelt gifts and treasures of this life truly touch upon our wings.

For many birds, life becomes but a sea of procrastination. For them the tomorrows never dawn. Also no one can ascertain with certainty his numbered days upon the earth. Thus the wise eagle meets his responsibilities with diligence. Paradoxically the path of flight to the netherworld is feathered with good intentions.

During your adolescence you are like a tadpole in the water who sees only the world around him. He concludes it to be the best and only existing reality. Yet there is a parallel of developmental relationship to losing one's life to the Great White Eagle and emerging into a vast unexplored dimension. "In analogy the tadpole loses his tail and gills. But within the same process he acquires rear legs and lungs. Thus in his consequential need for food and air a whole new world opens up to him. In a single leap he converges as a newly formed creature."

When your love for the Great White Eagle becomes innocent and unrestricted as most young eaglets, you also will emerge to a sphere of greater freedom. In similarity a whole new world will open before you as well. A dimension of enhanced meaning and purpose whereupon understanding brings forth clarity.

My own flights have been varied. Perhaps somewhat typical of both sunshine and storm that are such natural aspects of life. I have not always been courageous. Yet I have never wavered from obligation or challenge. Remember that there are no great eagles. Only aspiring birds who rise to magnificent challenges. In your development do not despair should you find yourself unable to alter the environment around you. With fortitude you can change your own being. Thus hopefully you will prove to be a positive influence upon others.

Should you hasten to conclude the world hostile bolster your faith and keep a positive attitude. Time heals and all storms have an ending. Under sunlight's gleaming there are many beautiful birds of a different feather and places to see. Also there are many wonderful opportunities to heighten your flight. Enjoy life to its fullest.

Still from time to time pause and reflect upon your life including the world's esthetic surroundings. On occasion ascend in flight over and through the forests to observe the wonder of the brooks and activity of life about. For throughout the creation there is a majestic appeal. Also if you observe closely you will learn that endowed forces are interacting to maintain a balancing of life according to a divine plan. In a related sense balance your own lives to promote an ongoing positive attitude. It will ensure that your problems will retain a true perspective.

To some extent my experiences will remain somewhat different from your own. However a sufficient similarity expressing the meaningfulness of life will prevail. I have faith that you will accomplish much throughout your lifetime. And though we may look downward in flight to keep our bearing let us always strive to look upward in gratitude of blessing.

Although regrettably I have missed opportunities in life my only persistent longing remains for queen. Still I cannot deny oceans calling as a breath of fresh air away from some of the storms which have rocked my wings in the past.

If in the realm of my screeching to you, I have only contributed by nudging a feather, I hope that it has been the right one. In the context of this meaning all that I can do is guide you to the flight of truth. It remains for you to keep yourself on course. Ultimately there are only two choices of directional flight: The way of life and the path of death.

Spread your wings wide. Know that the dimension of flight is narrowed only by your lack of will. Each of you represents the future. In your capacity of responsibility may you grace the skies with humbleness and charity. Farewell!"

Following an early hunt three days later Eric comes to stand by a small stream in the forest. The near silent air abruptly fills with a loud but pronounced hoot. Instinctively Eric bolts and swiftly fixes his eyes upon a rather stout gray owl perched in a nearby tree.

With large glaring yellow eyes the owl again echoes forth another deep toned hoot. "Although I have startled you, be assured eagle that my hooting is instinctive. Certainly contrary to my heart. Actually, I don't give a hoot about anything." "What might be your name," responds Eric. "Considering that your presence has rudely interrupted my daytime rest I shall tell you that most hereabouts call me Bobby. I was so named because of this confounded bobbing motion of my head."

"I can attest to your name being most appropriate. In fact I feel slightly dizzy under the spell of your hypnotic trait. Although no disrespect is intended. However tell me what ails you for I sense a certain feeling of bitterness. First, allow me to express that my name is Eric." "I am honored by your presence eagle. Also your reputation precedes you. However, it seems somewhat strange that we should meet at this cross road of life.

For as nature has dictated you are my enemy in the sky. Furthermore it would appear that we are pitted against one another as well by our contrasting perspectives about life.

Eric, do you think it only a matter of coincidence that man concluded the owl to be the wisest of all birds. Even more clever than the eagle." "Why do you tempt me bird of the trees? Have I offended you in some manner. Never mind you need not respond for I shall answer your question with appropriate dialogue.

Man's associating greater wisdom to the owl is based upon fable not fact. Also wisdom is an ocean of soundly applied knowledge. The tide of which comes and goes. Quite similar to our learning and forgetfulness. Yet the measure of retention is varyingly sustained like the waves that roll upon the shores with exacting purpose. Thus some owls are wiser than others. Just as some eagles are wiser than other eagles. Still it remains in varying degrees that wisdom is equally fleeting to both species."

"By word and reputation Eric it is obvious that you are well rounded in the ways of life. Respectfully I am not offended by you personally. Although your screeching about love, persevering amidst the struggle of life's storms, and seeking noble goals, I conclude as so much vanity. Naively you believe that all birds of a feather upon acknowledging your so-called aspiring values will adoringly flock around them in self-supporting desire.

A starving bird is not swayed by ambition or love. His gratification lies in the goal of finding food. Frankly I take from the barn at will. Also though you may conclude me an outlaw, I eat as well as yourself. But without the struggle. Notwithstanding who shall judge my deed when stealing within the realm of nature is commonplace. Does the kingfisher not steal fish from the ocean and freshly hatched turtles from the beach. Also is it not true that eagles frequently snatch the kingfisher's catch.

Eric. In your disillusionment you make claim to grace and beauty. There is no esthetic appeal to a prey being ripped apart. Notwithstanding in your expressed endeavoring to rise above is there any elegance to be found. It is simply an instinctive effort purposeful of surviving. Also contrary to common belief, the hardy or strong, often perish along with the weak and the crippled. Especially when hunted by roving packs of lions and wild dogs. A pair of hawks in the sky are no less unrelenting.

The only peace in nature is death. Besides if you look realistically at the world around you it is quite apparent that destinies change little. Life is nothing more than a sphere of unending conflicts. Learning only adds sophistication of understanding to the plight of misery that we are all subject to beginning with birth.

It is a satisfying pleasure that I serve myself. For I find neither beauty in my appearance nor life. Or for that matter, benefit in addressing the Great White Eagle. Even if I was to acknowledge his existence my heart can claim no experience of his personal love.

I am offended that in the spirit of your teaching that you inspire hope in youth for a better life. The past centuries attest to the false hope of a better tomorrow which remains a fanciful dream. Is it not true eagle that in spite of all your noble values, proper perspectives, struggles, and education that you remain as miserable as myself. At least considering my own apathetic hooting I am not called upon to make difficult choice's, sacrifices, or decisions.

It is with sadness that you grace the skies to no avail. There is no lasting happiness: Only suffering, betrayal by so-called friends and unfulfilled dreams. Perhaps the only real difference between us in the flight of life is my own excelling wisdom to see life for what it truly is."

"Bobby. It is a matter of respect that I have acknowledged your interpretation of life. I trust in courtesy that you will render unto myself the same accord." "Why certainly Eric. An occasional yielding of the path goes with the territory."

"Well, my friend. It is my observation based upon numerous flights that many birds of a feather disavow life as proposed by the Great White Eagle. However others and I attempt to grace the skies in journey according to his willed intent. This is not to say that we relinquish freely given choices suggesting that our wings are bound in dismal servitude. Rather through our faith we pursue his greater love and wisdom. For we desire to know a better and more lasting way of life.

Through learning much wisdom is revealed. Although in expressing humbleness, I am not wise in my own right. Unfortunately too many birds evaluate life solely upon their own limited experiences. No matter how broad that interpretation only the Great White Eagle who created all things serves as the spiritual basis of all knowledge and understanding.

In effect a bird can fly in any direction of his own choosing. The sky is open for all who seek flight. Yet it remains that ultimate good which promotes our greatest happiness rests primarily through the love and wisdom of our Sacred Creator. Thus our most rewarding ascent in life is determined by how well we follow his path of flight.

Your cause Bobby of seeking pleasure and avoiding struggle is not conducive to your own claim of wisdom. For the very misery that you assail in life you bring to others by your lack of caring. Also by your failure to aspire. Nor is your rationale of my taking from the grasp of the kingfishers of merit. Nature has provided those birds with a greater abundance of food conclusive of shellfish, turtles, and the like. All of which are essential to the eagle diet. Unlike the eagle the kingfishers have unique elongated beaks to facilitate opening the shells and extracting the delicacies within. However in conveying this information it is neither my purpose to justify nor to defend nature. Bobby as you well know the act of stealing in nature is not of the concept of right or wrong. Furthermore it is with all things that live that a struggle to survive manifests itself. Even the starving bird who you stated is not swayed by ambition or love must gather his feathers for a hunt or perish in his laziness. Notwithstanding should he taste only of those things that satisfies his stomach thus ignoring the hunger of heart and mind, he will still fall prey.

Given my thirst I ask more from life than many other birds. Therefore my wants are greater and my excited spirit can only yearn for ascent. Instinct is not a way of living but rather a reflex mode of protection to sustain life amidst harm. Yet in your criticism of the noble life you offer only gloom as a substitute. You would have youth value laziness as an existence void of life's stimulating challenges. Love and life should be compatible not viewed in ugliness and despair. Nor is the esteemed sacred ascent of flight capable of being gutted by mere innuendoes inferring that all tomorrows will lack challenging fulfillment and rainbows.

In your negative hooting there is ample noise but little substance. You claim to posses great wisdom about life and to know what is best for youth. Yet in darkness veiled with selfishness you isolate yourself from life. Also you do not seek flight in care of the young that through them a better tomorrow might be realized. For in self-pity you aspire to neither love nor responsibility. Remember Bobby that change must first come from the heart.

Because of your covert style of living and behavior associated with mice even some of your relatives have grown horns. However it is not my purpose to judge you or them. Or to make claim that in view of my own flight that I am in any way superior.

However it does remain Bobby, that for the most part, you will receive from life just about what you contribute to it.

Perhaps you are correct in concluding that there is little beauty regarding the circumstances of a prey being ripped apart. Yet in most instances of this nature, death comes quickly. In addition a just purpose is served when a life becomes lost to sustain another. Nonetheless little in life is as ugly as a negative attitude.

You and all life are a gift of the Great White Eagle's love. Even your keenness of vision that reaches far into the night represents his graceful attention to your special needs. When you cease to look down on life, and begin to glance upward through your own caring, you also will realize the fulfillment of dreams.

In humbleness it is not wrong that you serve yourself. Essential needs are basic to survival. However broaden your scope of perspective beyond yourself and the obvious horizons. Envision the needs of others. While you are young, set your wings in pursuit of knowledge. For even an owl as wise as yourself to grow must flourish amidst new ideas. Be practical in your approach to life and apply sound reasoning. Never hasten your hooting. It's not only a reflection of poor manners but prudence may escape your pursued flight.

I cannot foretell if peace will follow upon all of your flights. For the gentle breezes of life are often elusive. Notwithstanding knowledge is the embodiment of success. Through increased understanding I believe that a renewing sense of esteem will come unto you. Also in your loneliness turn to the Great White Eagle. Everyone needs a friend and he will not betray you."

"It is through your thoughtful caring Eric that your spirit reveals the nobleness that has touched my heart. Being a curious owl much knowledge has come to me through the years. However my wisdom has been without purposeful flight. Frankly in my perching I have been on the sideline of life. In want of opportunity I have mistakenly expected the world to come knocking upon my door.

Certainly I least of all have no excuse bearing since birth the gift of wings. I promise in the days ahead as my eyes light the darkness that my spirit shall brighten the lives of others. For in gratitude I now realize that my own happiness and peace will come from their joy."

Expressing a respectful farewell gesture Bobby hoots in his usual deep tone. Yet there is a ring of difference to the sound that carries through the trees. It seems to echo a resounding elation of a caring heart.

With immense satisfaction Eric senses Bobby's sincerity to turn his life around. Often the problem causing bitterness can be resolved by forming a more positive attitude. However it takes longer to achieve worthwhile goals. Also one must remain on guard as old negative thoughts like undesirable habits have a way of making return flights unto the wings of all.

In nature there are many orphans. Unfortunately most of them perish. Few are the parents willing to accept the young of another. However though rare some seem so compelled by their inner love that they cannot turn away from the panic cries of the little ones.

Late one afternoon following a long gliding pattern Eric comes to perch upon a crooked branch of a tall oak tree. As he glances towards the ground his eyes become fixed on the remains of a misfortunate female owl. Apparently she had become careless while searching for food. Death in contrast to life is common in the wild. Often it occurs at an exorbitant rate. Nevertheless the numerous strewn feather's lying about reflecting a struggle acts upon Eric's inability to accept violence and premature passing.

During the proceeding moment Eric's attention is abruptly drawn to the peculiar hooting of two barely weaned young owls. It is not their emerging from a hole in the trunk of the tree that perplexes him. Or the scrambling of the young brother and sister down the limb towards him. However when they snuggle under each of his wings he screeches in protest. The least of his intentions is to become an adoptive mother.

He becomes mindful to lift into flight. For however much he represents an uncommon eagle endowment of motherhood to a couple of youngster owls is totally absent. Although because of his sensitivity to the value of life, he cannot bring himself to abandon them. Soon the warmth beneath his folded wings penetrates the contented baby owls and they succumb to sleep.

As the two youngsters continue to rest, Eric takes flight to procure fresh meat for them. Upon returning while in the process of tearing the catch into small pieces, he gazes about the forest.

Not relishing his task, he can only wonder what eyes of nature might be upon him. As the little ones awaken, they quickly devour the food secured for them. Yet not nearly as swiftly as an adoring eagle swallows his pride.

For the time being the two orphans are secure in the care of their self-adopted parent. However for Eric the dilemma heightens during the passing hours. For apart from a willingness standpoint, owls simply are not raised by an eagle.

As the twilight forms, Eric concludes the two alternatives open to him: Either he must kill the young owls to prevent their suffering by starvation or find them a permanent home. Considering his nature the latter represents a more positive solution. Still he is most aware that ideas in life are often more fruitful in the mind than the subsequent action of implementing them. Simply stating something as being practical does not always make it so.

However with a determination to succeed Eric gently secures the youngsters in his claws and lifts into flight. Under a bright full moon, he banks his wings and turns into a gentle breeze. Passing over the tree tops the young owls hoot in delightful excitement. However Eric does not share in their exhilaration. He prefers that they remain silent. Should an observing hawk venture a meal, he will be helpless in defending himself without releasing them to fall to their death.

In the distance he observes an oblong shaped meadow. At the far end stands a small but quaint abandoned barn that reveals the weathering of numerous storms. Yet esthetic appreciation is not foremost upon Eric's mind as he makes his approach to the left. As he lands the two little owls scurry amidst the straw and other debris that has formed upon the wooden planks.

Suddenly a resounding hoot echoes forth from one of the high rafters within the structure. The youngsters are slightly startled. However Eric remains calm in the resounding familiarity of his friend Bobby. "It doesn't look to me for a self-pronounced thief that you actually stole much from this dilapidated barn. Although I mean no offense." "None taken eagle. For I shall admit having possibly exaggerated a bit.

It would appear Eric that your wisdom has taken a new dimension of noble contribution. No doubt your exploit is a first in nature. I am quite impressed by your resourceful adoptive caring." "Perhaps Bobby. However the perpetual winking of your eyes expresses your feeling of amusement as well." "True my friend. However not without due respect. For I am an owl in your debt."

Eric's intention is for Bobby to provide a home for the two young owls. However the wise owl hoots, and at first objects to the idea. Still he eventually concurs that their only chance at life is with him. Also it is Bobby's manner to perpetrate individual gruff and to grumble like a diplomat of nature. Nevertheless his heart is warm and caring.

Upon approaching the young orphans, Bobby takes them into the fold of his wings. He intently turns his head downward though occasionally he glances in Eric's direction. His action appears purposeful of not wishing the eagle to know of his genuine joy. Not because he believes that Eric will not respect and appreciate his inner feelings. But almost in gesture that an owl should not show his happiness outwardly.

The youngsters take to Bobby both instinctively and somewhat emotionally. However they become slightly perplexed by still another change of parent. For they had been abandoned by their real father as well. Nevertheless the love being shed upon them by one of their own kind proves irresistible to their wanting hearts. In spite of Bobby's attempts to conceal his feelings muttered hooting comes forth in disarrayed expression.

As the sun dawns across the meadow the early rays filter through the cracks in the side of the barn. Refreshed after resting with a feeling of satisfaction Eric turns and lifts into flight. He expresses a low sounding farewell. Although as love forms a family of owls, his gesture and final departure go unnoticed.

Ascending into the blue of sky his spirit feels the elation of a superbly successful flight. With boldness he screeches loudly that all of nature might know the power of love. In his heart he senses the joyful reward for having befriended an owl named Bobby. Furthermore, though the proud eagle will never admit it, he had developed an attachment to two young orphaned owls in the forest.

Eric had not merely found a home for two misfortunate young owls. But of profound importance a devoted parent. One by whom security and learning will flourish. For it will be through Bobby's love including his wisdom that normal growth will come to the youngsters. A development that will inspire a furthering contribution to the realm of graceful flight.

The flow of good resulting from an expression of love often radiates in more than one direction. Eric had witnessed the change in Bobby's outlook on life caused by an exchange of knowledge and the renewing of a positive attitude. The youngsters inadvertently contributed to Bobby a needful purpose to his flight. Thus it is in any nest where fulfillment finds abode that there exists an abundance of happiness.

As Eric levels in flight he observes an isolated gray cloud above the far horizon. It serves as an ample reminder that not all days or flights behold rainbows. In parallel within the forests of life there are many whose neglected cries go unattended until peril beckons their silence. Perhaps some are intended to fall victim concluding the ways of nature. However many are not.

In the whole of intelligent life there is a need for love. A time for all things. Yet there is also a need for wisdom. For it is through wisdom that love is nurtured. It is within this context that our emotions must be tempered by sound judgment. By analogy too many rainbows would spoil us. Also too many owls would overrun the forests. Sometimes well intended compassion can result in heartbreak and cruelty.

A week later Eric again lifts into flight to follow his heart's desire to be by the sea. It has long remained a calling or yearning search for peace away from the unhappiness of the past. The ordeals and hard work of yesteryear have taken their toll. Now in fatigue he seeks the quiet of rest and the renewing of spirit.

As he comes to stand upon the sandy shore of the Pacific Ocean he becomes awed by the majesty before him. Never before has he seen such beauty. Large jagged rocks protrude above the waterline as vast monuments reflecting a time when long in the past nature had flexed her hand. Beyond, the vast blue of the sea stretches endlessly. The enormity of magnificence is limited only by the confines of his vision.

Yet in spite of his vision being ultimately limited to a distant fading horizon, his excitement and appreciation proves boundless. His spirit surges with a rare feeling of happiness. With overwhelming enthusiasm he longs to embrace and share with his queen. However she is uncommitted in flight. Thus she remains aloof from him like a floating midnight dream. Meanwhile the white-capped waves beyond the shore rise high into the air before crashing down and dissipating into foam. In wondrous scope they seem to swallow the waters behind them.

Even the blue of the clear western sky appears esthetically more darkened in tone. Save for areas of blanketed white clouds that dot the heavens accenting further the beauty of the surroundings. It is like a perfect garden, he concludes in silent thought. Except for the landscape that is marred by man's dilapidated buildings and litter. There seems to be no end to their destructive encroachment against nature. Still on this day I do not wish to dwell on a dilemma so disheartening. In desire Eric is determined that nothing will interfere with his feeling of delight.

Nevertheless contrary to his euphoric joyfulness a bewildering thought occurs to him. He begins to wonder if this particular region represents the home of his search. If here, he will find lasting happiness. For sometime he has felt older than his years. Yet in sensation reason which had dominated his life now loosens in a revitalization of youth. Although within his heart exists an awareness that even he cannot take prolonged flight from the inherited responsibilities of life. Wherever they might lie. However the winds of achievement that had driven him in the past no longer seem to matter near as much.

Perhaps for all that he feels and thinks the time is right for him to demand from life instead of it extracting so much from him. If his solemn attitude, obligations, and work-inspired outlook, on life as an eaglet had denied him a fair share of leisure, he now endeavors to reclaim the seasons lost. With much exhilaration of spirit he will ascend the skies in worry free youthful play. Should responsibilities trail upon his wings he is resolved to fly evasive maneuvers. I shall only relent during this flight he promises himself should my queen beckon.

In his search for happiness Eric has long experienced struggle and heartbreak. Now by the power within his wings giving rise to a strengthened spirit, he is set to embark upon a dream. Perhaps some birds would think his faithful goal of queen a fantasy. However, because of his belief in the Great White Eagle it does not matter. For the ultimate value complimenting the beauty of all things lies in the eyes of the beholder. Also what Eric envisions and sees before him represents a beautiful and living reality.

The position of the sun indicates that it is about midmorning when the sea begins to subside to a restful calm. While glancing upward towards the Northwest, he observes what appears to be seven sea gulls zooming across the sky in a typical military eagle formation. It is a strange sight enhanced dramatically by the loud squawking chatter of other sea gulls that have gathered along the shoreline.

They appear to be protesting the aerial flight pattern of what some humorously refer to as the Magnificent Seven. However what happens next causes Eric solemn concern. The seven sea gulls aloft begin banking their wings and diving down upon him. Being a large bird of prey, Eric can only conclude the seagulls suicidal to commence an attack upon an eagle.

Nevertheless he does not wish to be caught upon the ground. If a question of territory exists, he knows that he can best defend himself in the sky.

Lifting into the air in an evasive manner he strives to gain as much altitude as possible before encountering the threatening flock. However as he ascends, the lead sea gull abruptly breaks away from the formation. Upon reaching a distance of several yards from the others he positions himself in a stationary vertical pose. Only the flapping of his wings indicates movement.

How very courageous Eric acknowledges the action of this particular sea gull. A swift banking dive on his part concluding an attack would instantly send the smaller bird spiraling to his death. However the intention of this seagull daredevil of the sky is peaceful. His unique pose in midair represents among all flocks a universally accepted friendly invitation. Still Eric has never directly experienced a gesture of this type before. Furthermore, because birds of a different kind seldom intermingle, he descends to the ground with caution.

The seven sea gulls' land and along with Eric, they meet on a rocky knoll. Respectful gestures of wing greetings are exchanged. Thereupon the lead seagull in a very deep voice asks: "What is your name eagle?" "It is Eric." "We are honored by your presence. My name is Oliver. Also in ranking order of age this is Trepid, Charlie, Buttons, Jimmy, Aaron, and Josh. We have been banished from the Society of Seafaring Birds for as long as we aspire to fly like eagles." "Excuse me, Oliver. Although I am greatly flattered and can appreciate your inspiring motivation, what does this circumstance have to do with me?"

"Eric as you well know an eagle is basically a land bird. It is seldom that one of your kind even traverses our territory. Hence our aerial formation was a way of capturing your attention.

It was also our desire to measure your skill in flight. We are most impressed. Also as you know our invitation was not to initiate battle. Because of our devotion and commitment to fly as eagles, we have lost our homes and loved ones. More specifically it is our intention to beseech you to be our instructor. However my friend, we are like poor fishermen of the sea. Unfortunately we can only pay for your contribution with our gratitude.

"Oliver only the Great White Eagle has humbled me more. I wish that compensation were the only consideration. Your gratitude would be of a simple resolve. However there is the issue of maintaining a friendly relationship between our two domains. Must I reiterate that birds of a different feather do not fly together."

"Eric. It is obvious that you are a learned eagle. Therefore I ask are we not having a positive and friendly discussion." "Yes, my friend. I relate to you other sea gulls as well. Nevertheless it is one thing to screech and squawk. However to mix in flight is quite another." "Eric, are you suggesting that you believe us to be unworthy?" "Certainly not. It is not for me to say who is undeserving in this life. Besides I would teach all who are eager for knowledge."

"Master, if your heart is true then instruct us. For we can tell by your words that you are learned in the ways of life." "Master. Master. Are you all right?" "Yes, my friends. I apologize for having drifted in thought. Your words prompted reflection of a similar expression years ago. Like yourselves, I echoed the same to a friend and master named Alexander." "Does your endeared friend still live?" "Only in my heart and within the spirit of flight.

Oliver, Josh, and you other sea gulls, listen carefully to my message. When Alexander lived, he taught me that it is not important who you are. But rather what you are in flight. Over the years, I have learned how meaningful these words are to the whole of life. Every feather of your wings has a definite and distinct purpose. If this were not true the number would be more or less. In proper perspective your number is not the same as upon my wings. Even the structure of our wings is different which indicates a variance of purpose. Also when a feather is lost, another soon grows in its place.

In life purpose is everything. Charity is the most graceful of all flights. Accordingly all birds can share in the truest meaning of flight. It is without saying that your ambition is noble and a compliment to your character. Truly I do not wish to dampen your spirits. However, if in purpose you were meant to be as eagles, you would have been endowed with eagle wings.

Continue in your aspiration of flight. However not as an eagle flies. Rather as a worthy seagull that ascends in heart and purpose. Perfection rests in the nobleness of flight. As I share this knowledge with you, let your greatest ascension be of compassion. Not just wings,in your devoted sharing with brothers and sisters. Each of you has already made a beginning flight by your kindness to me. With gratitude, I value both your aspiring thoughts and friendship. Remember always that though we serve different purposes as birds of a feather we are all brothers in the sky.

Yet within every flock there are those who aspire little in life. Pity and encourage them to flights of higher esteem. To the birds who believe in heart all dimensions of life are attainable. Which is to say that no horizons are beyond the spirit that desires strongly to transcend. Notwithstanding one cannot lose sight of reality without plunging into the sea."

"Master. I do not understand your reference to reality and the contrasting fate of plunging into the sea?" "Trepid. There are many aspects and realms to life. I am an eagle and you are a sea bird. Realistically we cannot alter this fact of our existence. However we can within the realm of our own physical and mental capabilities be all that our creator intended us to be. Most of us think and live within a sphere of single dimension. Broaden your mind. Explore beyond the narrow confines of the material world.

Seek your freedom through new ideas. Let the meaning of life become boundless. When you lose the importance of yourself in the well-being of others you will have achieved the understanding of my intended message. Trepid. When a bird seriously begins to think of himself with self-grandeur, believing himself to be superior to others, he has lost sight with reality. In his despair he will plunge into the sea of death drowning on his own contemptible vanity.

I have expressed that birds of a different feather do not often intermingle in flight. Thus as I have indicated the wings of each species were created in different form to serve varying purposes. This and other unique characteristics rather than color of feathers or the speed of flight for the mere joy of it is what determines separation of flocks. In retrospect never let ignorance be the measure of any flight.

Soon I hope that you will reunite yourselves with your loved ones. We all need sound relationships. No bird can solo indefinitely and survive. Although if the price of being different is banishment as a final measure it may prove necessary to form your own flock. Your commitment to life is supreme. Still I caution you to consider all birds in contemplating your decision. Also be wise in all of your thoughts.

Josh and Aaron have I given cause for your frowning?" "Master. We do not question your wisdom. However words are like empty flights that often fall short of fulfillment." "I see. Aaron, do you agree with Josh?" "Master. I mean no disrespect. However you are an eagle. You represent the symbol of a noble standard. Yet we are merely gatherers of food. Many birds even refer to us indignantly as the chatter boxes of flight. Thus considering our lowly station in life your words Eric are of a foreign meaning to us."

"My friends, your feelings are better understood than you might think. However no discourtesy is intended when I urge you to cease feeling sorry for yourselves. Would many sparrows not say that they wished themselves sea gulls. In their aspiration would they not envy the sea gull for being the greatest of all fishing birds. Would they not admire the powerful size and wings of the sea gull. Even the eagle is partially limited to fishing the lakes and streams. Yet the sea gull hunts widely over the vast oceans.

Also would the sparrow not envy the ability of the sea gull to make long flights out to sea and to sleep while in journey. Even the eagle cannot accomplish this feat. Furthermore the eagle spends much of his time gathering food.

Finally is it not also true that the sea gull represents the important symbol of many coastal areas throughout the world. That for centuries, seamen have relied upon him to locate schools of fish. Remember that criticism is like the wind which blows in all directions. It is not the howling that is important. Rather, you're choosing the right direction of flight throughout life.

Charlie, Buttons, and Jimmy, may I inquire about your thoughts?" "Master. We believe in the things that you have said. If we have doubt, it lies solely in our ability to accept our limitations." "My friends have you not hearkened unto my words. Negative thinking is demeaning to character. Alexander accepted death because of its inevitability. Thus his plight in old age changed the meaning of life for him. However acceptance is similar to a river that is perpetually in a state of change. In this sense reality is not something stagnate. For it is well known that many of yesterdays' aspirations and dreams are todays realizations of ever flowing fulfillment.

Accept in life those things such as your feathers that you cannot change. However do not become complacent in accepting things that can be improved upon in positive ways. Your contentment lies in knowing the difference. Also be proud. Demand from life all that a charitable heart and your wings can achieve. As you ascend accept the limitations of your wings. Yet thirst for knowledge with ample awareness. Lastly develop a sound attitude to promote a boundless spirit.

My words to you are but guidelines of understanding. The meaning of enrichment can only be realized by your own driving spirits. As I have told many others in the past who have sought my instruction, luck has very little to do with a successful flight through life. It is a matter of faith. Also believe in yourself and know that achievement will bring additional confidence. However as you soar to new heights, remember with humbleness that the wind beneath your wings is a blessing not of your origin.

My young friends, I am overjoyed in heart by your enthusiasm for life. I will always remember you with fondness of feeling as the magnificent seven. Perhaps considering your zealous spirits words alone will never fully satisfy. In life there are exceptions to almost everything. As you may already know these are sometimes referred to as the quirks of nature. Well, I came here to play amongst the clouds. I guess that for a day or what remains of it, one more quirk of nature will not hurt. Therefore you shall have your day in the sun upon the wings of an eagle."

As Eric leaps from the rocky knoll over the shoreline water he gestures for the magnificent seven to follow. An overwhelming look of joy appears upon their faces as they lift their almost pure white bodies into the prevailing breeze. Alone and far out to sea, Eric puts them through the paces of several eagle flight patterns. They are quick to learn. They zoom and dive upon one another and perform rollovers with great delight. If in consideration of his broader wing span Eric hedges in speed or slightly

75

alters a maneuver the seagulls are unaware. They are in the splendor of an eagle's flight. Still he does not deceive them as he shares what no eagle has ever dared. For it is within his heart a desire to make this day a memorable one for them.

Upon diving out of the sun, Eric notices a rather large oblong rock protruding slightly above the surface of the ocean. He thinks it strange for such a natural formation to be so far from the shore. However he remains tired from his tedious journey West. Furthermore the seagull daredevils have drained much of his remaining energy by several sharp turning maneuvers that their wings are more suitable to perform.

Thus in need of rest Eric acknowledges the stronger youthful agility of the Magnificent Seven. Thereupon he banks his wings and begins to descend towards the island of darkened rock. Although his descent is rapid, he finds little difficulty in landing upon the huge surface as he pulls up from a steady dive. Soon after, the seven sea gulls approach and begin to hover a few feet above. Diligently they keep a close eye on him with the same concern that most offspring receive from a loving parent. This vigilance pleases Eric as he is beginning to feel slightly dizzy from the ocean water spewing over the immense rock.

With each passing moment he feels more nauseous. In sensation it is as though the rock was floating. Yet in reassuring thought he concludes such a notion as ridiculous and absurd. However immediately upon forming this conclusion, a sudden loud noise echoes forth from the larger frontal extremity of the oblong object. In an instance a steady stream of water in the form of a geyser abruptly rises high into the air. Cautiously the sea gulls continue to hover overhead.

It is no rock which Eric has come to perch upon. Rather a large Gray Whale. In the resulting excitement he almost falls into the ocean. Simultaneously his screeching causes an adverse alarm to the frightened mammal which in a state of panic begins to submerge. Still Eric manages a safe ascent. Although as he climbs in elevation, he cannot escape the immense laughter of his sea gull friends. To his chagrin Oliver and Buttons are so engrossed in humor that they can barely remain aloft.

At three thousand feet of altitude, which Oliver and Buttons have difficulty achieving because of their intense amusement, apologies are rendered. "Master!" Oliver exclaims, in a more solemn tone. "We are most aware that your intention through carefree play was to show us that we are endowed to perform what we do best. We are all grateful for your thoughtful consideration. Yet in honest regard a part of our spirits will continue to envy the majestic flight of the eagle. However because of your caring, we now behold greater pride in our own purposeful eternal calling. From this day forth we shall endeavor to learn. Thus in priority we will gather well the food that best nourishes our minds.

In the days to come, Eric should a sea gull ever venture into the heights and purpose of your domain, it will be one of us. Certainly our gratitude extends far beyond our hearts and wings. In complimenting respect you have demonstrated that even amongst eagles there exists a feather's difference that sets some apart in noble grandness. In the spirit of learning and flight you have taught us how to span a bridge of charity. In our persevering we shall endeavor to cross it with love. Farewell Eric." "Thank you and farewell to each of you."

The following weeks represent some of the most pleasurable Eric has ever experienced. Even the newness of the surroundings brings to him a feeling of youthful serenity. His spirit surges in the meaning and fondness of flight. Even the beauty of the vast Pacific Ocean represents a calm away from the despair of the past.

THE FLIGHT OF THE EAGLE IS LOVE. BUT THE MEASURE IS
SPIRIT AND NOT FEATHER. AND THE TRAIL OF JOURNEY IS
A MIST OF WISDOM AND HUMBLENESS. SWEET IS THE WARM
CALM THAT GIVES ASCENT TO HEART AND WINGS. THUS
HARMONY BECOMES THE COMPLIMENT THAT GIVES RISE TO
THE UNISON AND SILHOUETTE OF ONENESS.

CHAPTER VII

Season of the Visioned Flight

On the eve of autumn, Eric is in flight when a slight chill falls upon the air. The atmosphere had been calm. A breeze soon commences to blow which begins to accelerate in velocity. The feathers of his wings flutter violently. The surging wind increasingly causes control of his flight to become more difficult.

In the distance he observes a gathering formation of darkening clouds. Soon the loud sound of clapping thunder echoes across the late afternoon sky. Intermittently flashes of lightning shoot forth as the turbulence of the storm continues to intensify. Below the tree tops sway furiously in rhythmic motion signifying his impending need to descend and seek refuge in the forest.

As the first raindrops begin to fall, he banks his wings in a steep descent. How quickly the storms of nature and life can erupt. In spite of his having experienced much peace of late there is both longing and conflict within his spirit. In brief reflection he is reminded of his dire agony during those early years which now seem so long ago.

On the first morning of autumn a light rain continues to fall as it had throughout much of the preceding night. A heavy dew blankets the trees and clings to the ground. Eric perches upon a strong branch observing a peaceful verdant meadow in the distance.

Although the light of day is dim he can see clearly. Neither the surroundings nor the dark clouds overhead are unfamiliar to him.

The night has been long much like his search for fulfillment. As the cold droplets of rain trickle down his feathers, in the likeness of silver beads, he begins to chill in the early morning air. In feeling of weariness he gazes upon the flight for food that has convened throughout the meadow and forest. However Eric's thoughts are not focused on food. So often through the years he had heard in compliment the expressions of being different from other eagles. Still he feels that the Great White Eagle had not heard his screeching above the tree tops. However his spirit continues to yearn and ache for the love of his heart.

"I have flown over many of the regions of this earth, he mutters aloud. Yet not lasting happiness have I found. I have known affectionate companionship and the joy of loving children. However the love of queen remains unfulfilled. Knowledge and experience have enlightened me to the valued wealth of this world. Nevertheless only the One who has graced me with wings can bless my flight with unparalleled treasure."

As the rain begins to lighten to a drizzle in observation Eric cannot refrain from wondering why he cannot think and be more like other birds. With some envy he admires their apparent contentment. Their daily lives seem almost programmed as he looks on at their darting flights. They build their nests with such precision and earnest delight. Yet he also senses that something is missing along with a feeling that life should behold more.

Perhaps the Great White Eagle regarding birds of a kind desired a certain mode of conforming. Nevertheless it remains that the material consideration of the forest is not of Eric's heart. Realistically his self-imposed questions are rhetorical in nature. For given the season, he has become a mature and learned eagle. It is simply his solemn manner of venting fatigue respectful of a world that continues to demand his own conformity.

From his perch Eric begins to sense a profound freshness in the air. Even a pleasant stillness spreads throughout the wondrous valley. He becomes moved in spirit. With an aroused vitality he screeches: "I am what I have always been— A lone eagle." He no longer feels confined to the surrounding cliffs', forests, and regions, inhabited by man. In sensation of feeling he further senses an accordance of heart with the Great White Eagle.

From the heavens rays of sunlight begin to emerge through the dissipating thunderclouds. The resulting beauty and tranquility are of immense meaning to him. In days past he had often flown over this particular forest in appreciation of its esthetic appeal. However on this occasion his thoughts become diverted to an inward stimulation of strength and a compelling desire to ascend into the heavens.

His heart quickens in the belief of his life ending with paradise at journey's end. Although the feeling is strange, he feels guided as well as protected by the Great White Eagle's love. A feeling of right and well-being find haven in his trust. Including a resolve of all the conflict which he had ever known.

In the warming radiance of the sun he no longer feels the chill of night. Nor the shivering caused by the dampness of morning. Thus within the peaceful calm he extends his wings and lifts into flight. Passing over the tree tops what he regarded with such importance concerning his life's struggle now shadows. Only the true perspective intended by the Great White Eagle remains impounded upon his heart. Accordingly his last thought is about his recent plans to fly over the ocean waters to breathe further the fresh air away from the past.

During many of his flights over the years, Eric had turned his head upward screeching daringly for the fruit of his achievements. However heaven chose not to hear in acknowledgment that worldly wealth could never make the material of nest into a home of love. The will of the Great White Eagle as Eric had learned reigns supreme in purpose and season. Even the aspiring of a destiny he had come to realize is secondary to what heaven knows is best for all birds.

Pushing his wings downward he steadily ascends higher and higher. The mist of the upper clouds smarts against his eyes. Yet in a determination of will beyond himself, he perseveres in the journey which in calling beckons his spirit. Although some sorrow and regret trails his flight it remains inconsequential. For he is about to enter a timeless realm where forgiveness is eternal.

Upon reaching the upper atmosphere the wind beneath his wings reflects a soft velvet blue which shines onto his eyes. However the air overhead is more white and is thinning rapidly. Instinctively he begins to adjust the alignment of his wings. To his utter astonishment a gleaming white glow gradually transcends every feather's edge. In humbleness of flight he bows his head in awe.

"Oh Great White Eagle. It is with joy that I have come upon the threshold of your dimension. However humbly I beg you to reveal how much further I must go." "Eric! Although you may lift your wings, you shall not gain a measure more of altitude. You have in your trek been homeward bound. However it is not your season to be with me.

Do you recall the vision that I revealed to you by the still water, regarding the mythical fate of eagles?" "Yes." "Well, the right time has arrived for me to divulge to you both your purpose and destiny. I need only to say that by blessing your search is over and that fulfillment awaits you. Serve me well eagle. For I have not always been pleased by your lack of faith." "Farewell my Creator."

The golden rays of the setting sun radiate throughout the reddening sky. Only a fresh gentle breeze breaks the calm. As Eric searches for a place to land, while making his descent, there appears below a mountain that towers above all else. Colorful waterfalls and clear streams meander through the lower verdant valley before draining into an abutting sea. A splendid high cliff adorns the coast while inland tall forest trees stand as far as any eagle can see. With an anxious heart, Eric considers this to be truly an eagle's home.

Thus with untold gratitude he positions his wings to descend in the direction of the concluded paradise below. In sensation of awe he does not question the reason for his blessing. Yet however profound, it remains of yearning thought that neither eagle nor man was meant to live alone.

The whole of Eric's spirit beams with affectionate longing as he abruptly levels in flight. In the far distance to his elated surprise he observes the flapping motion of eagle wings. He soon senses that another heart has been touched by the same grace as his own. It can only be his queen. For in the promise of fulfillment there appears no other in all the sky.

As the distance narrows between them, Eric does not wonder about her nature. For she is an eagle coming to her rightful mate. Her flight represents love and grace gives meaning to her life. Upon approaching his side a gleaming white glow transcends her feathers' edge. And when the tips of their wings touch they sense that they will never part.

Flying abreast they bank their wings and begin to descend towards their blessed domain. The unison movement of their flight soon shadows upon the valley below. However as they near the escarpment there appears only the Silhouette of an Eagle. For in the splendor of flight the touching of their wings has caused a oneness of heart.

With wondrous abounding pleasure Eric turns to his queen. "Our nest will not be of leaves nor twigs. But rather pure love blessed by the Great White Eagle and strengthened by our sharing. We shall build this nest high upon the cliff. Although trust instead of rock, will be our foundation. Except in our serving of noble purpose, we shall not abandon our home or take flight from our hearts. For an elevated love is sensitive to the needs of a devoted mate. In tribute not even our fondness will be measured by time but rather by the joy and happiness of our spirits. Still when a feather does fall, as the winter of life draws near, we shall ignore it. For our memories will be many and dear. Truly the loveliness of queen will never fade for hers is the beauty of flight."

Through affectionate caring for his queen, Eric resounds to all who aspire to become as noble eagles. For it is only the bold spirit of the eagle that can span beyond the valleys and mountain peaks of life in search of lasting happiness. It is through his honorable daring that he perseveres in his determination to conquer the storms of denial. Thus in magnificence of stature he possesses the graceful vision more than any other bird of a feather to see so far beyond. To understand in depth the true treasure of life.

What Eric perceived to be a flight of journey's end was really a beginning. Much like a night's ebbing and the coming of a new dawn. For those eager to spread their wings and in spirit to become as eagles, there is a lesson to be learned. Also a treasure to behold.

Yet in the realization of your own flight, it should be remembered that love is a treasure to be cherished. The blossom of which is sharing. For it remains as in the beginning the most sacred, responsible, and rewarding happiness of life, as we know it. In dimension it exceeds even queen for each petal of the flower of love beckons a different form of expression. It has been wisely prophesied that: "For where your treasure is, there your heart will be also."

EAGLE IN THE SUN

BOOK II

Larry Slauson

Introduction:

Life is a responsibility of love. Often the journey or flight is not of our choosing. In the real world there are both good and evil forces. Yet even in a refuge there are occasions when we cannot avoid the negative perils that befall us. Though we fly from the storms the rain falls upon our wings. However there are seasonable rainbows and the sun's radiance to guide our way. Such is the flight of an eagle named Eric.

Larry Slauson

Contents

IN DEPTH OF SPIRIT AND THE ONENESS OF LOVE, WE WILL
SHARE THE SPLENDOR OF FLIGHT AND SEASON. FOR THE
LOVE OF
OUR SPIRIT HAS EVOLVED ONLY IN PURPOSE OF THIS
JOURNEY.

CHAPTER I

The Season of Love and Friendship

The Great White Eagle (Creator) has blessed Eric and his queen with a home that is an eagles' paradise. As they descend upon the verdant valley beneath the towering mountain peaks, their hearts abound with love. For them fondness holds a special meaning. Also as mature eagles, their season of fulfillment has arrived upon the wings of time.

Although their love is new, their journey to each other has been long in duration. Both have experienced struggle and numerous flights through turbulent storms. However life is full of peril that looms as a shadow upon all flights pursued by eagles. For upon the wings of eagles' rests an eternal standard of nobility. In purpose their flight remains an aspiration for all who seek a higher plane in life. Yet for Eric and his queen the moment of the season holds joy. Abounding in happiness their problems trail like days gone by.

Turning into the wind, their many flights aloft brings them ever closer in heart. With caressing delight their wing tips touch in aerial play. Gracefully they circle downward pulling out, in zooming passes over the valley. Thereupon they rapidly ascend passing from cloud to cloud. In blessing they are meant for each other. Their flight through the sky appears to reflect love's grace of sharing. It is in the early autumn of their lives when they realize a oneness of silhouette. For in the unison flapping of their wings, their hearts become as one. It is also for Eric and his queen, their day in the sun.

Much of Eric's search in life has been for a rightful mate and the related happiness. However he has also sensed in spirit a drive to know life's secrets and meaning in depth. He has yearned for a destiny. A realm of greatness that will provide purpose to his flight. Given his spirit and nature, he concludes his queen to be an intended treasure. As such he does not believe her to be the epitome of perfection. Rather by her pureness of heart, a bond of trust is formed bringing a wholesome feeling to his own being. Within the scope of this meaning is the knowledge that eagles mate for life. Thus Eric's queen remains forever in spirit the wind beneath his wings.

On a clear early morning in April, Eric pauses a short distance from the nest to observe his queen. He momentarily ponders about life's intended fondness. The words that find no tomorrows. The embraces that find no fulfillment. Not desiring his queen to wonder about his heart, he gently takes her into the fold of his wings.

"Our love is boundless. It is not of the
nature of most of the earth. Nor in spirit
do our hearts know the ticking of time.

For we were not born of a day. Rather life
began for us upon our spirits touching.
Although, we shall not share the spring of
life, a tear we will not shed. For in the
season of autumn which reflects the
preparedness of our flight,our sharing will
know its greatest meaning.

Our feathers we will not ruffle. Nor storms
shall we pass through that we cannot endure.
For our divine love has been willed by the
grace of Heaven. In the color of autumn,
all that we cherish will be anew. For in
purpose it will be our season.

Our love will be as a ring of union. For
within the circle of flight, one is always
turning to the other. Also when we speak, it
will not be merely negative screeching. For
the needs of one rest with the other.
The many colors of autumn will reflect the
varied sentiments of our nature. For
though in spirit we are birds of a kind
the nest remains of more than one meaning.
Such I know to be the difference of my
queen and the variance of her flight.
Nor is her heart fleeting as in spirit,
she yearns only for a devoted embrace.

Our love will be as autumn leaves gently
floating to the ground. In tenderness of
thought, what has come to be will continue
forever in heart even beyond our final
flight. Yet though our love will not shed
anew, it will bud and blossom in the flight
of fulfillment.

Our sharing will not know the gravity of
the world. Only the freedom of flight. For
we will not wonder of the meaning of love.
As in our season, we will have come home.
And though I shall cherish the rainbows of
the forest, the beauty that I hold dear will
be you.

Our love when the snow of winter falls will
be warmed by the fondness of memories. In
the spring should wild flowers grow we will
not disturb them. For the blossom will
behold a message that a very special love
came to be."

Apart from Eric's love for his queen there is a fondness in his heart for
the sea. Often his mate would find him perched upon the edge of the shore.
However occasionally she would gaze upward and see him soloing in a sky
blanketed by white clouds. Sometimes she would join him in flight.
However, there were other moments, when she sensed his need to be alone.

On one such particular morning, Eric is perched along the edge of the
sea. His thoughts become captivated by the meaning of the magnificence
before him. Yet there is a certain sadness associated with his awe.

"How gentle and violent the sea can be.
Yet in her natural beauty nothing compares
except perhaps my queen.

Like the softness of a mate's whisper,
she calls men in ships and birds of a
feather to her. Before them, she lays
her bounty. How quickly they take of
her harvest.

The sea is like a mistress. In her hurt
there is a ravage of storm. How she must
ask? Where is my love and he that cares
for me.

How pure and loving this mistress that
gives so freely of herself. So caressing
are her waves. Perhaps, she is not a mistress

at all. For she is like a mother
touching our very spirits.
There is such a pleasing sense to her
aesthetic revealing. Also a warm satisfying fulfillment from her
nourishment. In her pureness she beckons for so little in return.

She cleanses the air. Her tears fall upon
the land. Even the life within her, she does
not forget.

Whether she is called mistress or mother
or of names unfamiliar my fondness for her
remains untainted. She is like a goddess.
However, I can but wonder if her call to
men and birds of a feather will be eternal.

Through her calling in the night, she
has even claimed our dead. They rest in
her care while waiting still another
beckoning.
Now the mistress grows tired. For we have
polluted her soul. She foams along her
shores to proclaim her distrust.
She is the Sea of Life. Without her, we
would perish. Cleanse her body and anoint
her waves with affection. For only by our
love can she continue to give unto all."

It is during this period that Eric begins to reminisce about his past. In his
search and yearning there had been many flights. How valuable he
concludes the warm memories. There had been his attendance at the Eagle
School of Learning. Also the Eagle School of Military Training. Thereafter
he graduated from the Eagle College of Advanced Learning and the Eagle
University of Higher Learning. In fondness he recalls his subsequent years
of teaching. Yet with a sense of sadness, he further recalls his departure
from this field of endeavor.

In the early years, Eric's experiences had been diversified. He had
known affection. However, though there had been some moments of
happiness, the latter had remained fleeting until he met his queen.
Nevertheless friendship and learning had shadowed most of his flights. Also
along the way, he had learned to listen. In particular, he had listened well to
an old gray eagle by the name of Alexander. It was this master teacher, who

had taught Eric that the flight of the eagle is meaningless without noble purpose.

Certainly no flight through life is absent of storm. Eric had experienced his share of troubled waters. However in the realization and love of the Great White Eagle, Eric had persevered the ups and downs associated with life. Throughout his long journey in search of destiny both learning and experience enhanced maturity. Although considering his ambitious nature, patience often eluded him, like stars on a cloudy night.

Eric had learned at the Eagle School of Military Training that Eagles' have few enemies in life. However territorial disputes constantly threaten the peace. The vultures represent the greatest threat. It is not their plight in life that makes them dangerous he is told. Rather it is their lust for power and greed. Next are the hawks who thirst for combat and kill for sport. The third enemy is of a different nature. Considering their characteristics they are capable of being both hawk and vulture. Although acknowledging their compassion, they can be like doves as well. Such individuals are called man.

Through the years, Eric had in flight come into harm's way with each encroaching enemy. In result, a strong sense of distrust had taken a firm grip upon his wings. In search of inner peace, he came to conclude a flight to the Pacific Ocean as a breath of fresh air away from the turmoil of the past. Subsequently, upon the shore of the sea, Eric experienced the most glorious meaning of true friendship.

In relating this story, he would begin by expressing the courage of seven seagulls diving down upon him. How profound and in a sense amusing he thought their action. Nevertheless in respect of their daring, he always referred to them as the Magnificent Seven. Also by the ranking order of their age, he remembers their names: Oliver, Trepid, Charlie, Buttons, Jimmy, Aaron, and Josh.

"Can you imagine that the nonconforming seagulls desired for me to teach them how to fly as eagles? Frankly they paid me such a high tribute that I could not refuse them their day in the sun.

Our flight over the Pacific Ocean is a whale of a story. It was also a rocky mishap. However I have screeched this tale amidst the clouds before. Thus I will not wish your indulgence further. The same is true about the story relating to my captivity by the vultures and Troy. Nevertheless those feathered friends remain ever so dear to my heart."

Turning to his mate, Eric is mindful to express enough talk about the past. "You are my queen. My heart is so full of love for you. Also this is our season. While the best part of this day remains, let us take flight. Kindly humble this lone eagle with your spirited love. Perhaps the oneness of our silhouette will again shadow the valley and please the Great White Eagle."

With unspoken word his queen embraces him in the fold of her wings. She then lifts into the prevailing breeze ascending in flight with Eric at her side.

A week later in the early twilight, Eric perches along the shore. His queen remains at the nest sensing again his need to be alone. In the tranquility of the rising sun, Eric contemplates the life around him. The rolling waves upon the shore are so instrumental in promoting a peaceful resolve. For deep within his spirit, he continues to feel an urging of destiny. He does not wish for his queen to know about his inner turmoil. However, a mate of her particular attributes always knows, if only by intuition.

In the stillness of a sky partially darkened by gray clouds, Eric suddenly hears a muffled cry. There are many sounds in nature. However this particular moaning is not a random utterance, but a calling out in dire pain. With his keen eyes, Eric begins to scan the waters' edge. Several yards beyond he fixes upon a distressed dolphin.

Screeching beyond the sandy shore, Eric spreads his wings and ascends into the heavens. He is a bird of prey. However, there is a difference that sets him apart from most other eagles. In feeling of sensitivity he has developed an acute awareness of the value of life. Also his struggles and the lessons of the Great White Eagle have shaped his destiny.

Landing upon the dolphin's back, Eric conveys that there is no reason to fear. I have come as a friend. However instinctively Eric scans the entire area. As a mature eagle, he knows that in nature danger often lurks when least expected. Ironically this situation is no exception. He glimpses upon four black-tipped sharks in the far distance that have trailed the blood spewed by the dolphin. Fortunately the young dolphin had entered water too shallow for the large sharks to follow.

Nevertheless he has not escaped unscathed. Along his lower back and slightly to the side is a ghastly deep gash. "What is your name?" In a faint reply the strickened dolphin answers—"Marty." "Well, my friend. If I can stop the bleeding you will be fine." By fanning his wings, Eric maneuvers a floating log beneath Marty's head. For it is extremely obvious that should the dolphin lose consciousness and his head lower into the water, that he will drown. "I must leave you for a few moments. However, do not panic or doubt my return." Eric's words are in vain. For in a state of shock Marty succumbs to unconsciousness.

Returning to the shoreline, Eric gathers moss which he pokes into Marty's open wound. After numerous back and forth flights, he further gathers some discarded nylon fishing line. Using his beak to penetrate Marty's tough hide, he nervously tugs and pulls on the line until the wound closes.

For the next several hours the dolphin remains motionless. His breathing is slight. Except for this there are no visible signs of life. Yet of dire importance the bleeding has ceased to a trickle. Upon resting Eric takes flight over the sea to procure fish. Should Marty survive his ordeal, he will be famished. Still it seems to be a vain gesture due to Eric's lingering inability to accept premature death.

Except for the time spent in gathering food, Eric diligently guards over Marty throughout the night. Late the following afternoon to his great delight the still unconscious dolphin begins to stir. His breathing improves and he gradually accepts the bounty of fish. Meanwhile Eric continues to watch over him with a vigilant eye should any smaller sharks venture into the shallow refuge. Inconspicuously Eric's queen guards over both of them from a perch high in a tree along the shore.

Each day brings renewing strength to Marty. Although for Eric, it becomes increasingly more difficult to procure the vast supply of food that the dolphin requires. Of greater importance the mammal has survived. Also his wound caused by the propeller of a boat is healing. Both Eric and his queen continue to guard their new found friend. Certainly it is not a normal occurrence in nature for eagles to assist dolphins in distress. However there are exceptional quirks in all facets of life.

Eventually the time comes for Marty to rejoin his own kind. Like all farewells there is a feeling of sadness. However, there is also a sense of joy. A meaningful exchange of caring and conversation had transformed a tragic situation into a bond of great reward. In the enthusiastic glee of being alive, Marty performs the acrobats typical of the gift endowed to most dolphins. Eric and his queen are moved in heart. Perhaps even the Great White Eagle, as both love and charity find inspiration.

Oddly as the moment of Marty's departure arrives he begs the pardon of Eric's queen. He requests a private conversation. "My friend, I am indebted to you and your queen for my life. I have told her as much. However I did not reveal the knowledge that as you represent a lone eagle, I am a lone dolphin." "But Marty, I did not relate this to you." "Eric! It is not difficult to comprehend that you are a different kind of bird. You are a very noble but somewhat non conforming eagle. I further sense that you are a Master. Perhaps by your inspiring spirit and my continued learning, I too will become a master someday."

"Oh Marty. I do wish you well. Also I applaud your perception of life and myself. It seems strange that we should meet on this shore between two different worlds. Yet each demands our social conformity. How much more we would be at peace if only we accepted the status quo. I wonder if the reality that we seek will always be confined to our spirits?"

"Eric. I can sense your feeling of regret that you have been unable to contribute more to bring change and make this a better world. However, do not despair. Yours is a noble flight. By your difference, you remain in purpose of serving an inspiration. It is what makes you a Master. Love is always a worthy cause. Unfortunately masters of various backgrounds are frequently scorned."

Eric is grateful for Marty's generous compliment. It boosts his confidence during a period when his destiny remains elusive. In spite of being a mature eagle, Eric is still learning which remains a life long process. Certainly the same holds true for Marty. He now has two scars to attest that some experiences in life are more difficult than others. A tuna net almost sealed his fate two years prior. The sun is high in the sky as Eric and his queen bid the young dolphin farewell.

As the weeks pass by, summer draws near. Throughout the landscape the verdant grass grows tall and the blossoms of the wild flowers reflect the beauty of the season. It is a time of renewing. A season when the forest in a befitting manner is alive. Considering their age, for Eric and his queen it is a period of freedom away from the duties of the very young.

They embrace the heavens with the same devotion of enrichment that they grace each other. Many are the hours spent gliding upon the warm air currents rising from their domain. In a teasing manner, Eric occasionally carries a small berry aloft and drops it on his queen. It is of course innocent frolic absent of harm. However, she always gestures a scolding screech, knowing how much he enjoys exciting her spirit. These are the days which they hope will last forever.

Life was not intended to be all sunshine and happiness. According to the Great White Eagle's plan a little rain must fall. Although the journey is often difficult He does guide us through the storms. It is our sorrow that teaches us the value of our moments in the sun. Nevertheless when the clouds of a storm gather the joy of forever is often short-lived.

At the nest, Eric and his queen are enjoying a morning meal when they notice a sea gull in the sky. It seems a strange phenomenon to them as rarely do sea gulls venture so far inland. However the flight of this particular sea gull is of unquestionable mission. As the bird of the sea banks its wings and descends, the distance closes to the eagles' domain. Eric's heart begins to quicken with excitement. Somewhat nervously he wonders if possibly the visitor might be one of the Magnificent Seven. However as the sea gull lands a short distance away in respect of territorial ground, it is apparent that the bird is a female.

As Eric and his queen warmly welcome the young seagull, she abruptly entreats: "Are you Eric?" "Yes, he replies. Also this is my queen. May we inquire about your name?" "Yes, I am Larisa. The sister of Josh." "Well Larisa, Your brother and six of his friends are the brotherhood of my heart. Come! Let us perch upon that high rock overlooking the ocean. You are a very attractive young bird. Furthermore, we are grateful that you have ventured to our abode. Now tell me about the purpose that has brought you here."

"Eric. You are a loved Master. My brother and the others comprising the Magnificent Seven, have related several times the story of your meeting. They have also spoken about your venturous flight over the ocean. They speak of your being different and about your sincere caring. For a day because of you, they flew as eagles. How abounding their gratitude remains." "Larisa. Such a wonderful compliment brings great pleasure. Still the pattern of your flight suggests that you are on a mission. I trust that nothing is wrong? However your voice quivers. Also you speak only of the past."

Momentarily Larisa remains silent. Yet she draws close to Eric. Then in a low screech she utters her heart. "For all that I know about you and in regard of what you did for them, you are like a father to me." Larisa then extends her right wing, partially enclosing it around Eric, in the envelopment of an embrace. However her affectionate attempt to comfort does not cloak the concern wrought in her voice. Furthermore her eyes begin to tear. Her voice becomes choked. Then in a broken whisper she hesitantly divulges the sorrow within her spirit. "I am deeply saddened to express that the Magnificent Seven, have departed from this earth."

As if a bolt of lightning had struck him, the pain darts from one wing tip to another as Eric feels the loss of his beloved friends. "This cannot be," he screeches in agony. His pain echoes through the forest. However within his heart, he knows that Larisa's own grief verifies the truth of her message. Compassionately Eric's queen draws near in feeling of their deep sorrow.

"How did it happen?" "A few weeks after your departure a power struggle ensued within the inner circle of the seagulls. Gradually unrest spread throughout the flock. The strife escalated and eventually a division formed between the elders and the younger birds. After a time, no one seemed to know or understand all the complex issues involved. It became a state of turmoil. However, if any one cause stood out, it was that which circumvented nest rights.

The young seagulls felt the timely need to demand their freedom. It became a cause of the right to flight. They even pledged a constitution declaring their liberty to build nests wherever they might choose. Including the inherited privilege to form their own flocks when deemed warranted.

The elder seagulls have ruled with an ironclad wing for years. Yet the world around them has changed. However they continue to disavow the freedom of the flock to seek new ideas or ways of flight. In desperation to maintain their power of influence, they sought to shift the blame from themselves to a scapegoat. Unfortunately this misguided attention became directed to the Magnificent Seven. The inner circle spread the falsehood that

Josh and the other six seagulls had not conformed with the established rules. The Ruling Elders further decreed if they had not pursued their ambitious desire to fly as eagles, the security of the flock would have prevailed.

Eric. My brother and the other six seagulls spoke to the flock with the proudness of heritage that you had taught them. Although they yearned to be as eagles, they found contentment and pride in being seagulls. As you had conveyed unto them, they in turn told the young to be all that they can be. They further pointed out the attributes of being a seagull. So frequently they would utter your words that you cannot change the nature of your feathers. However they would always emphasize that one's flight can be as boundless as an inner spirit allows. They also echoed your sentiment, that decisions be made with concern for all involved. Every gathering ended by their affirming love. In proclamation they would assert that those present are as brothers and sisters.

However influential in heart the Magnificent Seven became powerless against those in authority. In spite of those who gathered in respect, they were branded as non conforming traitors. They were seized during darkness. Their wings were bound and they were taken before the inner circle of the Ruling Elders. They were not granted a trial. Early the next morning in an attempt to avoid a possible revolt in protest of the judgment, the Magnificent Seven was escorted to the lower floor of a steep escarpment. High above, the elders gathered stones in their beaks and dropped them upon our beloved causing their demise.

When the other seagulls learned about what had happened there was much anger. However those who had supported the Magnificent Seven could do little but weep. Any attempt to oust the elders in authority would bring a swift threat that the same fate would befall them.

Eric. A strange phenomenon occurred when the supporters and friends of the Magnificent Seven went to the site where they were stoned. Everywhere there were mounds of stones that gave evidence of the execution. There were even sea gull feathers strewn about. However Josh and the other condemned were no where to be found. At first we felt that the elders had ordered their bodies removed in fear that they might become martyrs. Yet this was not the case. They were as confused and surprised as ourselves. Equally perplexing were these eagle feathers that laid in the numerical form of 7 just a few yards away." "Do you think that they represent some special meaning?" "I'm not sure."

"Father. Please accept my apology. I should not have addressed you in that manner." "Larisa, you should not be regretful. Jason confided in me the inability of your parents to be with you as all youngsters desire. Nevertheless as you continue to mature, remember that our dreams do not always fade. Love exists throughout nature. Also there are exceptions to almost everything. Consider yourself an extension of our love and respect. Thus you shall be our daughter until you feel another calling." "Do you agree with him?" "Yes. Our sentiment is the same." "I am lost for words. Except to say that I am extremely grateful. However father! What will the other birds say about a seagull in the nest of eagles?" "My daughter. Does it really matter?" "I suppose not. Although I do not wish to be a burden." "Larisa. Only the will of the Great White Eagle matters. Besides has he not guided you to us in heart and in spirit?"

There is much happiness in Larisa's eyes. However some sadness trails like a breeze swept asunder. In her new found joy she has consciously forgotten that the purpose in her coming is more than conveying the fate of the Magnificent Seven.

AN EAGLE DOES NOT SEEK THE PATH OF A STORM.
HOWEVER IF PURSUED, HE WILL NOT TURN FROM BATTLE
FOR RESPONSIBILITY AND DETERMINATION REST UPON HIS
WINGS.
ALSO IF CHALLENGED, EVEN IN THE EYE OF THE STORM,
HE
WILL SEEK VICTORY.

CHAPTER II

A Beacon Amidst the Clouds of Battle

"Larisa. Why are you crying?" "I have just lost my brother. I fear losing you as well." "Do not be foolish. Neither you nor my queen will be rid of me so easily. Besides someone needs to be here to understand these sudden mood changes." Both his mate and Larisa gesture their amusement. However, happiness is often absent or fleeting in most storms of life.

As Larisa begins to speak, her voice trembles almost beyond control. She addresses Eric by name as if a subconscious defense mechanism were denying the relationship between them. Perhaps it represents a form of self-preservation against further extreme suffering. Eric has also attempted to disguise his own hurt over the loss of his friends. He has done so mainly through respectful references to feminine characteristics. However he now realizes with increased empathy the immense tension which Larisa is experiencing.

"Larisa. What causes you so much fear beyond the sorrow felt over the loss of your brother?" "Eric the Inner Circle of the Ruling Seagulls has violated the laws of nature. They have solicited twelve hawks to pursue and cause your demise. The elders have contrived justification of their action by alleging an act of conspiracy. Both you and the Magnificent Seven have been accused of disrupting their power of authority. Fortunately they do not know your exact whereabouts. Also I took precaution to ensure that they could not follow me here." "You did well Larisa. I want you to remain here with my queen. Furthermore do not worry about me. I have many friends."

Eric's queen silently exemplifies the qualities of a very refined eagle. In spite of her own inner fear, she does not show any feelings of emotion. Rather she contains herself in a manner befitting her noble station in life. Also due to her particular attributes she is aware of the need for him to take flight. In response, Eric speaks only about his returning soon. Although his embrace expresses both concern and the love which he feels for her. Also on this occasion he provides a comforting of security to his newly acquired daughter.

As Eric lifts into flight, Larisa asks his queen why he has chosen to leave them? "He knows that we are in no danger. It is he alone that has come into harm's way. Furthermore he is aware that eventually the twelve hawks will find their way to him." "Can we not be of help when that time comes?" "No Larisa. Unfortunately you and I are no match for the cunning of so many hawks. Besides Eric will need his mind free of worry about us when the aerial battle begins."

Eric's destination of flight is to a lighthouse located upon a small island approximately five miles out to sea. The site is uninhabited except for a kind Old Man that serves as the last of a long line of lighthouse keepers. In a changing world automation has replaced the operators of the large lights that have for centuries guided ships away from the peril of danger. Eric has made the long descending flight to the lighthouse many times in the past. If the ocean shore has brought him peace, it is the lighthouse and the surrounding area, which has been a refuge of resolve from life's more perplexing problems.

As he approaches the black and white spiral tower of the lighthouse, the sun is still high in the sky. On this particular day the sea is choppy and the dark blue is broken only by a constant barrage of white-capped waves which come crashing upon the adjacent rocks. However the black roof of the lighthouse and the verdant growth about including the sea reflects the beauty and the serenity that has always touched Eric's heart. In majestic meaning it is a lone eagle's perch in the sun.

The Old Man is working in his garden as Eric had observed on so many former flights. In life there are boundaries which neither bird nor man can deny. However in degree there is a rare passing over where love supersedes differences on a narrow plane of common ground. If Eric in nobleness remains a different kind of eagle the Old Man is equally unique in his love and respect of nature. Although rare in compassion of heart, the Old Man has achieved a partial oneness with the animal kingdom. It is through this sphere of understanding and appreciation that a form of communication with Eric becomes possible. In friendly gesture he waves towards the heavens. Eric screeches and rocks his wings.

Understanding in life is so vital to the expression of love. For some the ability to comprehend seems greater in reflecting a natural radiance. The Old Man by the sea is one of those rare and gifted individuals. For this reason Eric trusts him. However instinctively the genetic factor that has endowed Eric as an eagle, denies ever closing the distance between them completely. In respect the Old Man does not attempt in any way to force Eric into his domestic world.

On a planet where trust is often absent, even the limited relationship between Eric and the Old Man is of a monumental overtone. If in the past Eric's flights to the island had been to seek refuge, events now dictate the need to deal with his grief. Also of paramount importance he must formulate a plan of encounter against the hawks. Even the Old Man considering his gift of perception senses that Eric's flight is of a purpose other than to hunt prey. Because of his goodwill, Eric regularly finds a meal placed before him in the night.

During the first evening on the island, Eric becomes extremely distraught. Not even the soothing sound of the waves washing upon the shore brings relief. The loss of his friends causes such agony. In despair he takes flight to the upper most point of the mast on top of the lighthouse. From this perch he dares to screech his defiance to the heavens for the fate of the Magnificent Seven.

Amidst the brightness of the flickering light that shines far out to sea, a dim silhouette of a bold eagle appears along the shore. It is within the sphere and the shadowing of night that Eric proclaims the injustice of the taking of the good, while the evil doers of the world live on. Overhead the sky is clear. However a sudden flash of lightning arcs across the heavens. In the silence that follows, Eric knows that he has angered the Great White Eagle.

"You are an insolent eagle. As a servant your anger has tried my patience. I might add quite as Moses did in the wilderness when he struck a rock in defiance. Is there no reverence regarding your somewhat questionable faith. As I hearkened unto him and now you, there is some cause to ponder which of us rule's the universe. Who are you to question my sacred will?" In humbleness Eric desires to rectify his displaced anger and to clarify his lowly position of obedience. However he is unable to speak.

"Eric! Hear me well. I warned you about your lack of faith and persistent tempting. As I taught Moses a lesson, I shall also punish you. However, I will not abandon you or deny my love. Still you will find neither friend nor stranger of any feather to assist you in your inevitable battle with the hawks. Also you would be wise not to misjudge your ego as you have me. In spite of numerous blessings including a rightful queen your stance on the top of the lighthouse mast lacks reverence. Furthermore you are not Moses."

In life there are certain thoughts that should be constrained. Certain others should not be dwelt upon in negative reflection. Also there are moments when forgetfulness of sound listening can be an invitation to additional trouble and pain. Eric commits just such an error by pondering aloud. "I might just as well falter from this mast as to encounter twelve hawks. The odds are suicidal."

Again the Great White Eagle beckons unto him. "Eric. I do admire your high-spirited nature. However of course that does remain a compliment unto myself. Still a lack of endeavoring to persevere is evident not to mention a degree of restraint. While I acknowledge your heartfelt reverence, you have tried my forgiving nature too often. Unfortunately that is an error unto yourself.

As a Master of Academic Learning, you have pleased me. However your persistent tempting has annoyed me. Therefore I can but wonder if you are not also a Master of Error. If it were not for my Son's intervening in your behalf, I would not thwart your desire to topple from the mast of the lighthouse. However, I am a loving and forgiving God. Still I am reluctant in this instance. If I gave you flight is it not also feasible for me to know your exact number of feathers? Furthermore if I know these things does it not follow that I also know each of your thoughts? Thus your misgiving will not go unpunished. No matter what the outcome of your battle with the hawks, you will falter in the sky.

Eric. Although I may fault your disobedience I know that your heart remains true. Also I understand your sorrow regarding the loss of your friends. During this time of mourning, I will provide you with comfort. Find strength in my love. In message be patient. A miraculous event will be revealed to you in the days to follow. Meanwhile be obedient and remember that it is my will that you serve.

Frankly, I do not make it a practice to explain my decisions on high. Nevertheless pertaining to what I know is best, I require trust from my servants where understanding may not prevail. Still in spite of your independent and asserting manner, I have found favor in you. Therefore I shall answer your perplexing question about why it seems that the good die young and the evil ones are spared.

You have flown many flights through the storms of life. Some of these turbulences were caused by myself as a test of your faith. Others resulted from your own unruliness and excessive proudness. However regardless of source, you have learned well that life is a complexity of relationships. Often there are no simple explanations or solutions to complex problems. However as a caring Creator, I am quite aware that the spirit of love could not find true expression without freedom. It is equally true that choice is the freedom of flight.

As there is no longer perfection in the world, both good and evil exists. In fact within the spirits of all birds there is a composite of both. Considering all the ramifications involved which hinge upon eternal life, there is no preconceived judgment. Nor does there exist a determination of fate that predisposes good over bad. It is a value judgment based upon nobleness. Thus certain birds are deemed more worthy. Given the greater love, acknowledgment, and contribution of these birds, they are more heartily missed. In essence the face of death has no preference to good or evil."

Following these words, Eric succumbs into a deep sleep. Upon awakening he becomes aware that his voice has been restored. In addition the burden of his heart has been lifted. His spirit feels strengthened. Thus his thoughts turn in purpose to the pending encounter with the twelve hawks. In caring Eric has not been forgotten by the Lighthouse Keeper either. A fresh meal is provided in the usual place.

Throughout much of the following day, Eric ponders his precarious situation. "If the Great White Eagle can turn an evil circumstance into something positive, surely I can be courageous in my own battle. No longer will I think of avenging my friends. I will oppose evil for its own sake. It is right that my spearhead of pursuit be love rather than hate.

It was evil, not the Great White Eagle that caused my grief. He is righteous in punishing me for my disobedience. My anger due to intense hurt was displaced. However there is no excuse. Should I falter in battle, let fate take its course. Surely my demise will be concluded a noble death in the war against evil. Through blessing I have known both queen and eaglets. Now my destiny comes upon my wings. Realistically a lone eagle cannot subdue twelve hawks. Still this will prove to be my finest deed. I shall be cunning in my attack. Yet though I will perish, the inspiration of my flight shall prove victorious."

Eric is no longer a young bird. However his natural instincts as an eagle will definitely be an offsetting factor. In contrast though a distant relative, the hawks are not equal in size. Nevertheless especially in great numbers, they remain a formidable enemy. Although in spite of age, Eric has the advantage of experience which includes the instruction that he received at the Eagle School of Military Training. Furthermore through his acquired wisdom wrought by his many flights, he knows the value of a determined will. To this end he alters his thoughts to a resolve of battle preparedness.

Carefully and with articulate precision he formulates a strategic plan. Initially he decides that it would be an error to wait upon the ground for a confrontation. Thus he decides it best to maintain the element of surprise by taking the fight to the enemy. To achieve this advantage he intends to ascend to a very high altitude and dive from the sun. The blinding rays of sunlight will prevent his being observed by the hawks until he is practically upon them. Also gliding upon the rising warm air currents before the encounter will vastly conserve his energy.

In the stillness of nightfall Eric succumbs to much needed rest. However his mind remains restive. "Something is absent from the strategic plan. What if the hawks observe my flight prematurely and scatter. The sun will be to my advantage. Nonetheless how can I ensure the timely element of surprise at the moment of greatest benefit?" His mind races in search of an answer. In desperation he directs his thinking to the famous battles of man throughout history.

While contemplating the punishment of his disobedience, a clue emerges. "I am being denied the allegiance of other eagles in battle. Still the

Great White Eagle divulged that I will not be abandoned. In recollection, I am reminded of the similarity of the Biblical story portraying the Battle of Gideon. The Creator had instructed Gideon to send vast numbers of his army home leaving only a few soldiers to battle an enemy many times over in number. The decision seemed most unwise. However, by affective maneuvering and the spectacular use of trumpets, Gideon was victorious. What a splendid tactic. Still I remain perplexed to understand the foretelling words of my faltering in the sky."

In spite of his bewilderment Eric concludes the particulars of the upcoming encounter. However in resolve he acknowledges the absence of trumpets. Nevertheless he proclaims in silent meditation my screech will fill the sky. Also if King David could slay a giant named Goliath, with a slingshot and a rock, I shall hurl myself through the sky like a meteor.

Aside from bolstering his determination, Eric realizes that he is being pretentious. The situation appears to be an exercise of futility. After all what can faltering in the sky mean other than a prior downward fall to death. However he cannot afford to let vain feeling's surface. He remains a noble eagle. Should death await on the horizon, perhaps honor and his finest hour do as well. As a bird of prey, he has learned from previous encounters the value of confidence. It is the guardian against fear that can unleash panic in harm's way. In final thought his mind drifts to the past and happier flights shared with his queen.

The light of day is quite dim as Eric awakens in the early twilight. Scattered gray clouds roll swiftly across the heavens. Also a breeze blows gently from the Pacific. He feels refreshed and hunger gnaws at his stomach. Turning towards the lighthouse, he wonders if the Old Man has remembered him. Perhaps on this final occasion. Yes. Nearby is a pan of food. With gratitude Eric glances towards a lower window of the lighthouse. Behind the soil streaked panes, he sees the Old Man. For a moment or two their eyes gaze upon one another. The penetration is more intense than ever before.

Briefly Eric ponders the special meaning of their prolonged stare. He further observes a more pronounced look of sadness upon the weathered face of the only human which he has trusted and befriended. Is it possible that the Old Man senses danger amidst the clouds? It seems doubtful. Perhaps it is only my solemn mood that has conveyed a feeling of something being in disarray? Maybe it is only the jitters of an anticipated encounter. Nevertheless the Old Man is unrelenting in his fixed glare. Only now does he turn away. With some difficulty he is raising his hand and pointing east. It is a warning! In the far distance he has sighted the hawks. How strange when the boundaries of love are removed that the barriers of communication cease to exist.

Abruptly catapulting himself into flight, Eric ascends rapidly. Turning into the wind, he banks his wings towards the clouds to shadow his climb into the sun. At approximately thirty-five hundred feet, he levels off. Valuable energy has been spent in reaching this altitude. However as he spreads his wings in a gliding pattern the warm air rising from below begins to buffet his underside. With cunning skill he begins to scan the skies for any irregular movement.

As the clouds thin, the view broadens unveiling the enormity of the blue Pacific Ocean. The sea lays calm except for an occasional whitecap dotting the surface. In the distance far below the black-roofed lighthouse stands like a miniature model. The surrounding sand graced by clusters of sea oats sparkles in the sunlight. A movement appears a fair distance beyond the shore. This is followed by a bellowing sound and a gusher of water rising high into the air. However, Eric knows by experience that it is merely a whale blowing his ballast. Everything appears so peaceful. However the breeze of battle is poised aloft.

Suddenly Eric's attention is drawn to a flock of birds scavenging near the water's edge. But they are seagulls and pose no threat. However at twenty-five thousand feet of altitude, he observes the pursuing hawks. Folding his wings to enhance the speed of his descent, he commences to dive. The wind whistles past his wings as he aligns them to achieve maximum velocity. A trail of mist soon forms from his feathers' edge. Rapidly the distance to his foe narrows.

The glaring rays of the sun and the speed of his descent ensure the element of surprise. However in a bold maneuver he breaks from the dive. Spontaneously he swoops upward into a broad circling pattern around the advancing hawks. Then with all of his might he screeches in defiance. It is a thunderous blaring as though a hundred trumpets had erupted across the heavens. To the hawks it is a terrifying resound. In panic they scatter in a chaotic state. Still Eric is aware that they will soon regroup. The main battle is still to be fought.

With articulate precision Eric aborts his circling pattern. He then ascends into the haze of a dissipating cloud. At this point of readiness, he banks his wings and begins to dive upon the largest hawk. It is this bird of prey that he believes to be the greatest threat. In a swooping movement Eric descends upon his back before an evasive flight can be pursued. Eric's claws sink deep into the hawk's body. Blood spews into the morning air as the strickened bird falters and falls limply into the Sea.

Eric quickly fixes his eyes upon another of the pursuing hawks. Flying in a vertical circular pattern he aligns himself slightly behind and above the bird. In this attack position he pounces upon the hawk like a bolt of lightning. With a snapped neck, the fated bird collapses and topples into the Sea.

Although the remaining hawks have distanced themselves in confusion, Eric is aware that they will soon attack in force. But to his advantage, two of the hawks limited in the experience of a hunt are committing a critical error. Flying abreast they have prematurely initiated flight to assail the lone eagle. Perhaps in desperation they desire to enhance their social standing within the flock. However it is a misguided venture. Initiating a roll over, Eric swoops across the sky to a position directly above them. With his extended claws, he tears into the left wing of one and the right wing of the other. Together the two hawks plunge into the water below and are quickly consumed by sharks.

Eric has reason to be proud. In his day in the sun, he has downed four of the twelve hawks. However the tide of battle is shifting. Having bolstered their confidence the remaining hawks thirst for revenge. Eric can only ascend in altitude to avoid being dived upon. His foe will now attack across a wide front. Perhaps he might out-maneuver a couple of the attackers but not all of them.

Upon reaching a desired level of altitude, Eric begins to hover in mid air. He feels a strange sensation as he waits for the hawks to attack. However, it does not come for several moments. In the grasp of victory the remaining hawks are eager to torment their prey.

During this lull in the battle, Eric is beckoned by the Great White Eagle. "Why are you merely hovering? Have you lost the will to resist? I would think that you would assume the initiative and become more aggressive." "Oh Creator! Will death not come swiftly enough. If you really want the truth, I would like to take flight from here. Given the enormous span of my wings, I could easily outdistance them." "No! That is neither your way nor my will. Considering that my fate hangs in the balance you might reconsider. Besides I thought that you frowned on suicide." "Eric. Your insolence is beginning to annoy me again."

Upon regaining his composure, Eric is mindful that: "A hero dies but once while a coward dies a thousand deaths." Thus encouraged by the Great White Eagle, he gives a final thought to his queen. He then lowers his head and spreads his wings. Urged in spirit, he again decides to take the battle to the enemy.

As he descends towards the remaining hawks they become confused. However, they remain firm in place. Perhaps they are intrigued by the boldness of his daring. Nevertheless as he closes the distance every hawk along the line lowers his right wing in motionless tribute. Although not deceived, Eric is moved by their gesture of respect. Briefly he acknowledges that something good exists in everything. Yet the nature of the beast is seldom altered. Abruptly the hawks realign their right wings and thirst for his blood.

In a fierce dive with his wings partially folded, Eric continues to close the distance to his foe. Intently the hawks wait to catch him within their grasp. However they are beset by the blood of the fallen that has spewed over Eric's body and wings. The rays of the sun upon him further enhance a ghastly form, masking his true colors. Some of the hawks begin to quiver in panic. However, they remain undaunted in their quest.

Eric concentrates his dive towards the center of the line. As the distance narrows he is hopeful that the hawks will panic and scatter. However as he approaches in flight this fails to happen. In harm's way, he sharply banks his wings. With great impact he strikes the extreme left flanking hawk.

Sorely afflicted the wounded bird tumbles end over end far below into the jaws of a circling shark. A trail of feathers gently floats from the sky in the wake of the fallen intruder.

For Eric the battle is over. Most of his energy has been spent. However his day in the sun has proved to be glorious. On the wing, he has vanquished five of the original twelve hawks. His destiny has been long in coming. Still he is somewhat perplexed. He had always thought that his purpose in life would be of heart rather than as a bird of prey. Maybe if his journey had been different and his time with his queen longer, it would have been so. Nevertheless who can truly ascertain what the Great White Eagle wills for us during a lifetime. For it is His enduring glory that reigns supreme. It is also within the realm of harmony with Him, that our greatest victory in life rests.

Against the backdrop of the sun, Eric resumes to hover in midair. He realizes that the remaining hawks will take no additional risks of vulnerability. They will now attack simultaneously. Defeatism has never been a part of Eric's nature. If somewhat defiant, eagles are also bold. However, in spite of his desire to endeavor, Eric is experiencing extreme weariness. Thus in spite of the readiness of his claws, the end seems near.

The resumption of the hawk pursuit begins slowly. Perhaps in part due to the respect Eric has earned by his cunning. However if nobleness guides the wings of eagles, other less desirable traits spurn the flights embodied by evil.

Nearly exhausted Eric is barely able to defend himself, He is at the mercy of a ruthless foe. Still instinct dictates that every possible attempt be made to survive. Therefore his keen eyes continue to scan the hawks' flight towards him. However it is a vain search for some hesitation or error by his pursuers.

As the hawks press the attack, Eric hovers almost helplessly waiting for the impact. However as the distance closes, something miraculous happens.

The hawks suddenly become befuddled. Seized within a web of untold fear they abruptly cease their pursuit. Their abated flight bewilders Eric. It is a twist of fate. What could possibly cause such a change of event? It is almost unbelievable.

As Eric scans the skies above and behind him, the answer startles his own composure. In near disbelief his heart fills with joy. Across a wide front in spiritual form is the Magnificent Seven. Fanning their wings while in hovering formation is Oliver, Trepid, Charley, Buttons, Jimmy, Aaron, and Josh. With a sigh of relief, Eric screeches his elation across the heavens. I never dreamed that I would ever see my beloved Sea Gull friends again.

Moving abreast of the other sea gulls, Josh squawks fourth a warm greeting of reciprocal reply. "Eric! Kindly forgive our not acknowledging your due as a respected Master. However within the sphere of our new realm of flight, there is but One beholding such esteemed reverence. Also within the glory of our passing all have become graced as brothers and sisters. Yet in your continued nobleness of spirit, you have given our earthly sister Larisa a home. We are of profound gratitude."

Momentarily Eric recollects the joy that had so deeply touched his heart on a day long past. A time when he had taught the Magnificent Seven to fly as eagles. "Eric, we sense your thoughts and our own exalting fades within the grandeur of your charitable heart." Within the splendor of a rare reunion of tribute, the voice of the Great White Eagle carries across the boundless sky. "My sea faring servants! Although I am gratified by the wonder of your fellowship it would behoove you to remember who reigns supreme." "Oh Creator. We shall not forget in our humbleness to render unto you that which is sacred." "Very well."

In the distance the hawks appear to be locked into a grid of still air. Almost as if they were suspended and unable to resume flight. However as large birds of prey they do not feel threatened by the presence of sea gulls. Notwithstanding Eric is certain that they have no intention of retreating. Nervously Eric gazes over his shoulder should a hawk possibly bolt free of the restrictive grid. He does not wish to be attacked from behind. "Eric." "Yes, Trepid." "Fear their evil no more." Somewhat reluctantly Eric trusts in Trepid's assurance. Thus again he devotes his full attention to the Magnificent Seven.

For a while longer Eric basks in the euphoric presence of his feathered friends. However in harm's way, he senses that his blessed reunion with them will soon end in a forever farewell. Sadness gradually begins to fill the void of his heart. "Eric!" "Yes Buttons." "Be of good cheer. Do not despair for our passing has brought us to a dimension of abounding joy and happiness. In transcending we have ascended from the burdens and pain of our former flight. Very soon the blessing of the Great White Eagle will also come upon yourself."

A feeling of relief besets Eric's spirit. However, he is simultaneously intrigued by Button's reference to a pending blessing. Might deliverance also be my fate. "Teacher! Do not be concerned. You are in the protection of the Magnificent Seven. Our mission is of love and indebtedness to you. Also within this domain, we give the lessons."

Again the voice of the Great White Eagle resounds across the heavens. "Enough squawking. The time has come to carry out your mission. Eric! Yes. It is my will that you continue to hover and not resume flight." Knowing the trueness of Eric's heart, the Great White Eagle does not wait upon a response.

A fair breeze begins to flow into the motionless void encircling the hawks. Revitalized their evil intent is resumed. Fear of disgrace further compels the resumption of their treacherous pursuit. The presence of the sea gulls continues to baffle the hawks. However they do not conclude them to be a threat. Nevertheless besides Eric, they are an intended prey.

If triumph shines in the eyes of the wicked hawks the disillusionment will prove ephemeral. For in contrast along a broad line the Magnificent Seven hovers firm in a state of vicissitude. In their serving love, good, and truth represent the embodiment of all who aspire grace. They remain in name: Oliver, Trepid, Charlie, Buttons, Jimmy, Aaron, and Josh.

With claws exposed the hawks swiftly close the distance to Eric. The besieged eagle instinctively is urged to bolt. However, in obedience to the will of the Great White Eagle, he remains in place faithfully flapping his wings. Although near panic, he continues to scan the hawk movements in desperate wanting of a critical error.

Eric's concentration is distracted only by the squawking of Charlie and Jimmy. "Do not fear Eric," resounds Charlie. "However hearken unto my words. You have enriched our being. Also you will live eternally in our hearts. Perhaps when the season is right and you pass into our dimension, we shall all fly as eagles again." "Eric." "Yes, Jimmy." "You have had a splendid day in the sun. Also the noble standard upon your wings is a most worthy aspiration for all who desire to pursue the flight of eagles. Now my friend observe the power and glory of heaven before you."

Eric is moved in heart by the words expressed to him. However, astonishment and near disbelief suddenly overwhelms the whole of his being. Slowly the spiritual form of each of the Seven Sea gulls begins to fade in sequence from left to right, commencing with Oliver. As Josh's form disappears only Eric, the hawks, and the blue of the sky remain.

A cold chill besets Eric. He has never felt so alone, or so abandoned. Yet in panic it is the shadow of death and the near pouncing hawks that alarm him. However in the strength of his faith, he does not bank his wings. However a strange sensation comes over him. As he glances upon his body and wings, the blood of battle vanishes into the air. In the wake only his true colors shine in the sun. I am so undeserving. Even to be anointed in the face of death. After all, I am only a humble servant donned in the feathers of an eagle.

Even more profound on this day in the glory of all eagles, Eric is not alone. In spiritual form the seven sea gulls reappear in the same exactness as before. Greatly startled the hawks cease to advance. Extremely perplexed they again observe the sea faring birds slowly fade from sight. However in their place with the elegance of flight and the speed of lightning, there appears the partial images of seven larger birds. Neither Eric nor the hawks can determine their nature.

In the sequence that follows, a gradual state of transforming becomes evident. Soon a pattern emerges unveiling more distinct features. The clarity of their feathers unfolds delight for Eric and terror to the hawks. The right wing of each bird is folded in a tribute to Eric. Also in unison they screech their loving friendship and farewell. In the glory of the Great White Eagle, the Magnificent Seven, have become the eagles which they longed to be.

It is inconsequential to the hawks whether the seven eagles confronting them have been transformed. What is important is the loss of their superiority. For they are no match against seven eagles. Especially seven whom Eric has taught to fly with cunning skill. In utter desperation the hawks seek evasive flight.

However several yards beyond the most defiant hawk daringly turns to assail Eric from behind. Making his pass at enormous speed, he strikes Eric's right wing. Eric screeches in pain. Although the wing is sorely bruised, the wound is not mortal. Still experience over the year's has taught Eric that he cannot remain aloft much longer.

The Magnificent Seven screech in protest of what they conclude a cowardly act. Eager to flex their newly acquired eagle wings, they turn to Oliver for approval. In response he screeches, What greater glory can be served than our ridding the sky of the remaining evil menace. Yet only six of the transformed eagles bank their wings and begin to pursue the hawks. Josh, the smaller and younger bird remains momentarily behind.

"Eric." "Yes, Josh." "I am beholding to you for giving my sister a home. Thus the honor of attacking the lead hawk who injured you is mine. Farewell." "Farewell my dear entrusted friend."

Banking his wings and excelling in flight, Josh cuts off the retreat of the lead hawk. He then ascends and dives down upon the large-framed hawk sinking his claws deep within his back. Oddly not a single drop of the spewing blood comes to rest upon the gallant eagle. But the mortally afflicted hawk lurches violently before spiralling downward into the sea.

In a caring manner Josh glances back at Eric. He then gestures a final tribute by initiating an eagle roll over. Thereafter, while ascending, his flight becomes guided by the Great White Eagle. As he continues to rise far above the horizon his majestic form gradually fades in the distance.

As the six remaining eagles comprising the Magnificent Seven fly upward in the wake of Josh, they rock their wings in bidding of farewell. Like their brother, they too perform a roll over. The sequence begins with Oliver and ends along a broad line with Aaron. How swiftly they fade from this dimension into the brightness of the heavens.

Continuing to hover as a lone eagle in the sun, Eric is gratified that the Great White Eagle did not abandon him. However he is deeply saddened by the loss of the Magnificent Seven. Their premature and violent death still lingers as a tragedy within his heart. Still he finds comfort in knowing that the flight of his friends represents eternal bliss. For they have ascended beyond the evil of this domain. In their absence a calm spreads across the sky. Even beyond the black roofed lighthouse.

While torn in thought and pain, Eric's bruised right wing begins to quiver. Perhaps I have not escaped the ravage of conflict after all. As the wing begins to shake violently, he folds it closer to his side. However the added strain upon his left wing gradually takes a toll. He begins to falter. He screeches in agony. Although his echoed torment is to no avail. Sinking from the heavens, he begins to plunge towards the sea.

It seems so ironic to escape from the claws of death only to be subjected to a fate of equal consequence. Is there no lasting purpose to my being saved from the clutches of the hideous hawks? His life begins to race past him, almost as swiftly as the wind against his feathers. However in the face of certain doom an inner voice reminds him about the value of life. He becomes mindful that the battle is never over until one submits in defeat.

Nonetheless Eric cannot be pretentious about what seems so obvious. However, situations are not always as dire as they seem. Still in an apparent vain attempt to maintain consciousness, he tucks his head under his left wing. Much like an ostrich that buries its head in the sand. However Eric does not feel as protected from the tragedy of an anticipated impact.

In the likeness of a large ball of feathers, he continues to tumble through the sky. How rapidly the sea seems to race upward to cause his demise. There is no escape or Magnificent Seven to balance the odds. Only the inevitable end zooms near. Yet there exists a driving instinct or inner will to live even in the grasp of peril. In a desperate bid of survival, Eric pokes his head out slightly. Also in spite of near unbearable pain he brings his wings to full extension.

Again he screeches in protest of the fate that has come upon him in harm's way. However the plight of his flight beckons no response. Aligning his tail feathers, he swoops over the surface of the water in a gliding pattern. His dire effort avoids a critical impact and the sharks below. However, his afflicted wing prevents him from remaining aloft. As he descends in flight, the breeze beneath his wings yields to the rushing waves of the Pacific Ocean. For the moment he is safe. However very soon the scavenging sharks will find him.

To remain afloat, Eric fans his wings. My situation is so paradoxical. "In a different dimension, my sea faring friends have become eagles. In sharp contrast, I have become a fated duck. No disrespect intended." "None taken, Eric." The Great White Eagle expresses no additional response.

The stress of Eric's flapping in the water soon alerts the distant sharks. While feasting on the fallen hawks, they had gone into a frenzy. However their insatiable appetites now cause them to abandon the stilled waters for other prey. In pursuit their distinctive dorsal fins protrude slightly above the surface striking fear. Their formidable appearance leaves no doubt about their purpose in the deep.

Eric had always been courageous when the situation warranted. As an eagle, he had resisted and defeated numerous foes aloft in the protection of his domain. Although in the water, he is all but helpless. In a very real sense he is displaced. However in keeping with the order of things it is only the natural instinct of the sharks to rid him from the sea. To this end they continue to close the distance to him.

In frantic Eric observes the voracious sharks dive beneath the surface. At first the perimeter of their stealth cunning is quite large. However, it gradually tightens as they stalk ever closer to him. Numbed by the cold water, Eric buries his head within the fold of his left wing and awaits the inevitable. His appearance as a ball of feathers in the sky becomes similar in the sea. It seems a sad ending for such a noble and gallant eagle.

If sharks represent the deadly scavengers of the oceans, they are not the only inhabitants of the deep. Whether on land, in the skies, or within the fathoms, life remains an interaction of relationships. Thus given the perplexity of the Great White Eagle, life ends and begins anew. It is also congruous throughout this sphere that varying intelligence renders change. Some aspects of life are maternal or instinctive. However others are a flight or journey beyond the ordinary. Such is the meaning of true friendship. What greater love than to risk sacrificing one's self for another.

In the meaning of noble friendship, a dark form appears far below the circling sharks dashing across the ocean floor. With accelerating speed it suddenly turns upward in a near vertical direction. The amount of energy being spent is enormous. Alarmed by the swift ascent, the startled sharks

temporarily veer from their encircling pattern. With sheer aggressiveness there is nothing short of death that will deter this creature from its appointed destiny.

Meanwhile, Eric begins to numb in the cold water. Perhaps more than the chilly temperature he feels the anguish of waiting for the end to come. Often in agony a moment can seem like a lifetime. Still he is grateful that the daughter being left behind will bring comfort to his queen. However concluding this thought his mind races in the belief that the jaws of an approaching shark are about to close upon him. In a final gesture he screeches the despair of his unjust plight.

Although his head remains extended above the surface, he is abruptly seized. In an instance he finds himself being raced across the water. It seems strange to him that he was not instantaneously consumed. In despairing thought he asks, Is there no end to my prolonged torment? Mist spews into his face. With vain anticipation of hope, he ponders if he might drown. Both his pain and the journey of his believed demise seem endless. Certainly he has reason to fear. A few yards behind he gazes upon the dorsal fins of the trailing sharks. In dismay he envisions being ripped apart.

Most sharks readily dispose of their victims. "Why must I be so tantalized? Also why is it my misfortune to be in the grasp of the smallest shark? The larger of the pack would have ended my misery with a single crushing of his powerful jaws. This certainly does not represent a very noble death for an eagle."

As the moments pass, Eric becomes more solemn in thought. Perhaps it is merely accepting the predicament of a cruel reality. He regrets his disobedience and no longer blames the Great White Eagle for his twist of fate. Also unlike many others he has been blessed with a day in the sun.

In a final glance about the surroundings, Eric notices that the depth of the water has become quite shallow. As a result the larger sharks are unable to follow. Oddly in a silent manner he credits the smaller shark for his evasive skill. Apart from this it pleases him that the end has finally come.

Although his vision is partially blurred from the sprays of mist, he focuses upon the sandy shore along the south side of the lighthouse. How reminiscent it lies amidst the esthetic beauty of the landscape. However in total exhaustion Eric soon succumbs to rest. It seems strange that even in the grip of death that one can find peace.

For Eric the tranquility of sleep is briefly disturbed. Although not fully conscious, he feels himself being released and pushed through the inlet. Then momentarily he hearkens to the distressful splashing of the water as if the shark had ventured too close to the shore. Yet beneath the warm rays of the drying sunlight, the slumbering shadows envelop his awareness of the events around him.

During the passing hours the sun ebbs on the horizon and nightfall spreads over the region. It is late in the afternoon on the following day when Eric awakens to loud chattering in the water near the shore. He is both dry and warm not to mention somewhat refreshed. However some soreness persists in his bruised wing. Although of greater significance, he is perplexed about being alive. Also he is uncertain about the surroundings. As he attempts to shake off the drowsiness the nearby chattering becomes more clear in meaning. "Do you think after saving your life I should have need to guard over you until eternity?"

Eric bolts in response. "Rest easy my friend. You are no longer in harm's way." Turning in the direction of the chatter his eyes fix upon the dolphin whom he never thought he would ever see again. It is Marty. For a moment or so Eric is both speechless and motionless. His whole being swells with elation. Then in a burst of excitement, he screeches a resounding joy that carries far out to sea. Marty becomes so engrossed with Eric's happiness that he begins to dance upon the waves.

"Come closer my friend that we might converse." Marty in his young and usual vibrant personality comes darting towards the shore. "I am immensely grateful that you risked your life to save me. I am in your debt." "Eric. Are you not forgetting that you once rescued me from a certain death?" "Still it is of great satisfaction that we have formed such a meaningful bond of friendship."

Eric is confused about how Marty knew of his exact whereabouts when he fell into the sea. After all when he had come to his rescue, Marty was adrift adjacent a far distant shore. Furthermore the lighthouse was several miles away.

Extremely curious he poses this question to Marty. However before Marty can respond, Eric still somewhat shaken by his unfortunate experience, becomes quite startled. To the right beyond the rocky part of the shore shadowed by some pine trees, appear three dorsal fins. For a moment or two their movement follows the contour of the bank. Then they abruptly turn into the direction of Marty. With great distress Eric looks on as Marty casually drifts towards them.

"Is there no end Eric expresses inwardly to the danger beneath the sea."

"The sharks must be underdeveloped to be in such shallow water. However they seem poised to attack. Even their dorsal fins have disappeared from the surface. My goodness! Marty is rising upright and is swimming on his tail fin. I must alert him of the impending danger."

Eric begins flapping his wings rapidly. He further screeches for Marty to approach the shoreline. However almost complacently Marty ignores his message of warning. Somewhat nervously Eric begins pacing the shore.

"That stupid dolphin is going to get himself killed. In spite of my aroused consternation, I can do nothing about it."

A moment after Eric hears the shrieking of chatter and an upsurge of splashing water. It is more than he can bear to look upon. Assuming the worse he is wrought with grief. "How can all this woe happen in a single day?" "Eric! What are you fussing about?" "The loss of a friend." "No one here is in harm's way. Turn around and look for yourself." "I must be going mad. I am beginning to hear voices."

Upon glancing over his shoulder, Eric screeches in panic. In dismay he also lurches and falls backwards onto the sand. He cannot believe his eyes. In the glaring sunlight, he focuses on what appears to be a shark and two smaller dolphins standing on their tail fins next to Marty.

"Try to relax Eric. The shock of your ordeal is playing a game with your mind. However, it is unfortunate that you had to endure such terror. I must understand that your knowledge of my domain is limited. Certainly mine is of your world of flight. Still we must be on guard not to overreact. This is my mate and these are our offspring. Her name is Kim. This is Tad, and this little fellow is Tim." "What a wonderful family. I do cherish our meeting."

Shortly after, Kim and the youngsters depart to engage in some frolic play. During their absence, Eric again asks Marty how he came to know about the lighthouse and the exact place where he had fallen into the sea. "My friend, the posing threat of the hawks had spread throughout the forest and along the shore. We were all aware of course that they were not commonplace to this territory. Kim first learned about them while at the bank of the north shore. However besides a betrayal, I cannot explain how they knew about your being at the lighthouse. In any event by following the pattern of their flight, I was able to come to your rescue.

Someday I would like for you to tell me the story about the sea gulls in the sky that miraculously transformed into eagles." "Yes Marty. I would be happy to do so. But for now I wish only to reemphasize my gratitude. Also I wish to convey to you the immense meaning of your friendship. You are certainly a noble dolphin. Quite different I might add than many related species. Many do not possess such a caring heart."

"Eric. You were spectacular in your flight against the hawks. In my envy, I would also like to fly as an eagle one day." "My friend, I am not to be envied. Besides I am but one of many eagles. However your courage and magnificence of devotion exemplifies the greater meaning of life. You are to be admired."

THE NATURE AND SCOPE OF STORMS IN LIFE VARY DURING
THE COURSE OF FLIGHT. OFTEN THEY CALL FOR SACRIFICE
AND PAIN. SOME DISSIPATE LIKE TRIVIAL MIST. BUT
OTHERS UNLEASH BOTH LIGHTNING AND THUNDER.
WITH RAVAGING WINDS THEY TEND TO DESTROY THE SPIRIT
OF FREEDOM. IN DEFENSE OF NOBLENESS, THE EAGLE WILL
SPREAD HIS WINGS TO MEET THE CHALLENGE.

CHAPTER III

Reckoning With Evil Amidst The Sea Gull Flock

As Eric and Marty converse, they are mindful that in harm's way a conflict can often seem like the longest day. However as the sun dips over the horizon both acknowledge that even the longest day has an end.

In the calm of twilight, Eric hearkens to the familiar call that always touches his heart. Although surprised by her nearness in one of the inlet tree's, he signals for her to join him. Greetings are expressed. A greater abundance of love seems notably present. Certainly the value of life resulting from the battle with the hawks, has been significantly enhanced.

It pleases Eric that Larisa is accepted as one of his own and that she has warmly embraced his dolphin friends. Yet on a day climactic of turmoil in the sun the time for farewell beckons. Still the bond of love and sharing has sealed their friendship. Hence the lighthouse and the surrounding area will serve as a place of rendezvous in seasons to come.

Due to Eric's bruised wing, the eagle family remains at the lighthouse overnight. However before going aloft to the uppermost part of the tall tower, they take flight to where the Old Man normally places food. Again he has not failed the eagle whom he has come to adore. An abundance of fine edibles has been set in the usual spot. Eric is grateful. He further knows by the kindness shown to him that the Keeper has witnessed his day in the sun.

At sunrise, Eric awakens to find most of the soreness has vanished from his wing. He is pleased that his queen and daughter are with him. Also a pleasant breeze blows across the region. In joyfulness of feeling he is eager for the Lighthouse Keeper to share in his pride. However, as he descends in flight to the ground an eerie emptiness comes over him. The hospitable Old Man and his possessions are gone. Even the large clock on the wall is absent. Only the outline of the faded imprint remains.

Gazing through the window at the many lights, buttons, and dials, Eric senses the end of an era. The Old Man by the sea is the last of a vintage that has spanned decades. Progress seems inevitable. Yet for Eric the loss of one's pride and purpose in life reflects a high price.

Sadly he scans the calm waters of the Pacific. Far beyond the shore, he views the wake of a vessel. Screeching his departure to his queen who cannot equal his speed, he ascends in flight. Higher and higher he climbs into the blue sky. At a critical point of altitude, he banks his wings into a jet stream that will carry him aloft to his destination. Fortune has not always smiled upon him. Yet on this day the winds blow favorable beneath his wings. At great speed he is able to close the distance to the vessel. While descending he screeches the loss which he feels within his heart. It is as though he feels this gesture will make everything right. In any event a radiant smile appears upon the face of the Old Man who waves so gratefully.

In a responding manner Eric rocks his wings and performs a roll over. However he does something else far more spectacular that violates his most rudimentary instincts. He comes to perch upon the rail of the stern, within reach of the Old Man. In his eyes, he sees the kindness that has been given so freely. Eric does not even flinch when the weathered hand of his friend begins to caress him. For this is no ordinary man. Rather it is the gentleness of a Lighthouse Keeper who has become one with nature.

The Old Man is aware that the prevailing wind will not carry Eric home. Sadly their time together has come to an end. Genuine caring has transcended their differences. It has also enriched their lives in a meaning beyond words. Thus in the endearment of life, the sharing between them will prove to be of a sustaining value.

Upon returning to the lighthouse, Eric is joyously greeted by his queen and Larisa. High in the tower on the south side protected from the harsh increments, a fabulous home has been built into the wall. Inside the dwelling a message is found written by the Old Man. It reads simply:

"By your difference and elegance of flight
you have touched my heart. I hope that my
gift will warm yours in memory of me. And
if my words are absent understanding, I
know that my love is conveyed."

The home is a unique structure of crafted art. Most befitting an eagle. It is also greatly admired by Eric's queen and daughter. Even the location is ideal. The inlet forest is but a short flight away. Therefore there is no question about occupying the gracious nest.

As the weeks pass, Eric rests and fully regains his strength. During this period they share many delightful flights. It is a season abounding of love and happiness. Also the clouds overhead are peaceful.

On the lower east slope of the island seven small trees have taken root in a row. Abreast of them are three other perennials. In the Old Man's absence it seems strange how they came to grow in such a straight line? However to those who remember with fondness and honor, there is little doubt. In their hearts, The Magnificent Seven, remain in flight. Also in journey are Alexander, Troy, and The Old Man by the Sea.

By late summer the tall verdant grass adorning the area around the lighthouse is browning in the warm sun. The season is giving way to autumn. However the breeze that has altered the landscape is not the only ushering of change. Larisa has experienced puberty and is rapidly reaching full maturity. In spite of her happiness both Eric and his queen recognize that she longs to be with her own kind.

As Eric nestles alone on a balmy afternoon amongst the small trees on the east slope, a vision comes to him. Gray clouds move swiftly across a darkened sky. A raging storm soon unleashes its fury. He further sees a sole white sea gull venturing a path through the turbulence in search of a peaceful calm. However in journey a bolt of lightning strikes the tips of his wings. He can no longer ascend. Foiled in flight, he descends in the midst of others who have preceded him. Yet oddly another bird appears in the storm and the fate is repeated many times over.

Upon wakening Eric ponders at great length the meaning of the vision. In purpose it eventually becomes clear to him. Thus he senses a relationship to his being and a destiny perhaps not fully realized.

Eric concludes that the sole sea gull venturing through the storm represents the composite youth of the Sea Gull Flock. The lightning which struck each bird signifies the evil power of the Ruling Elders. The same authoritative body that had formerly sent the bounty seeking hawks after him. Symbolically the lightning further burns the new and inspiring ideas from the youth who defy conformity. The pursuit of each solo sea gull represents their aspiration for freedom and knowledge of life's greater meaning. In searching for a calm, each lone bird is striving to be all that a sea gull can be. For within heart, they are motivated in awareness that the Great White Eagle aspires all within his spirit.

A few days after, Eric is again called upon by the Great White Eagle. "It is not without understanding of your desire to be with your queen and daughter that I beckon you. In compensation of your service I will double the days of your life that you are away. I am displeased that my little ones are thwarted in their flight for freedom. Long ago I willed that choices prevail in life. The Elder Rulers of the Sea Gull Flock have wantonly negated my sacred authority. Even the old of the flock not in support of their ways have suffered indiscriminately. No longer will I tolerate their wickedness.

Eric. It is my profound wish that you take flight to the coastal area of the lower valley. I want you to remove those wretched rulers from any position of influence. In refusing my love, they will know my wrath. Larisa will accompany you on your mission. However your queen will remain behind."

The next morning Eric and Larisa take flight according to the will of the Great White Eagle. Larisa is unafraid. She trusts in Eric. However she knows little about his devised plan. Notwithstanding neither of them is aware of the havoc that is being devised by the cruel Elders.

As Eric and Larisa approach the coastal area, they zoom in low to avoid being detected. Slowing in their descent they come to land in a cluster of trees. It is here that Eric divulges his plan to relinquish the power of the Elders. However, he is acutely aware that her assistance will be required.

"Larisa. A pretty bird like yourself must have an admirer." "What makes you think so?" "Well, apart from that special sparkle in your eyes, I have often observed you daydreaming. I further sensed that someone's heart was pulling you homeward. Also I knew by the Great White Eagle desiring that you accompany me. Obviously He had read your heart even before myself. Now tell me. Do you have a name to go with this admirer?" "Yes. His name is Nathaniel." "Can he be trusted? Absolutely!"

"During nightfall, I want you to go to Nathaniel. It is important that we learn which sea gulls have disavowed the ruling Elders. Some may be in doubt. Under no circumstances are you to confront them. Seek only those nests that are faithfully loyal to the Great White Eagle. Inform them that their presence at the next execution is absolutely necessary. Also convey that they are to arrive shortly before sunrise. They are to form a circle to contain those who come later. Be sure to clarify that no sea gull is to occupy the knoll at the upper most point of the site. Finally there is to be no exit except through the entrance facing the sea."

"Father, The thought of another execution frightens me." "Try to be courageous." "Who is the condemned?" "I cannot say. However the circle of loyal sea gulls will encompass the cliff preventing the dropping of stones. Tell Nathaniel to appoint trusted leaders to carry out my instructions at the pit. There must be no margin for error. It is time for you to go." With love and the determination to please her father, Larisa lifts into flight.

Eric does not want to cause his daughter undue suffering. However, if he revealed the second phase of his plan, she would not have left his side. It is bitter enough that he must take stock of his own courage. Thus during the next several hours fear shadows the lone eagle. More than ever before the burden of nobility has come to rest upon his wings. However his is aware that the cause is greater than himself.

In the twilight of dawn, he lifts into flight. He has sought council with the Great White Eagle. Now the anticipated moment of reckoning will unfold. There is a still calm over the land. However, an ensuing storm is gathering over the sea.

With ease Eric pinpoints the exact locale of the Inner Circle of Ruling Elders. Their nests are separate from the rest of the flock. In timely fashion he swoops into their encampment. At first they become alarmed believing that he intends to harm them. However to their great surprise, he surrenders to them instead. He expresses wariness from evading the bounty seeking hawks. He further relates that he fears for his loved ones with hope that a peaceful resolve can be negotiated.

In keeping with Eric's plan the Elders remain quite indignant. With atheistic ranting they readily dismiss his noble gestures of cooperative and reasonable resolution. "Eagle. We are the power of authority here and you are guilty of inciting civil insurrection amongst the flock. The penalty is death by stoning. Tomorrow you will know our sense of justice. Perhaps following your demise, we will hang your carcass in the sun as a warning to other so-called noble eagles."

Pursuant with their evil nature, Eric is humiliated and insulted. Insidious mocking is even squawked for his having surrendered. However it saved them the bounty otherwise slated for the mercenary hawks. Nevertheless what happens next represents the epitome of the Elders devised cruelty. While being contained a large jagged "V" is gouged from Eric's left wing. The bleeding is profuse as their beaks have ripped away his flesh. Eventually the blood ceases to drip. Yet the pain sorely lingers. "You would be ill-advised to attempt to escape. For you will not fly far."

Although the day is long and painful, it eventually gives way to nightfall. Eric not knowing of their fate, feels concern for Larisa and Nathaniel. Much depends upon their success. Meanwhile the Ruling Elders decide it would be to their advantage to execute Eric at sunrise. Eric's friendship with the Magnificent Seven had already enhanced his popularity with the flock. The Elders do not want for him to become a martyr. Therefore his execution is to remain a secret without the benefit of a trial or flock witness.

On the morning next, Eric is awakened before sunrise. His left wing is both sore and stiff. During the night he had flapped it hoping that he could possibly resume flight. However the strain proved too painful and he felt it necessary to conserve his remaining strength. He requested food, but was told that it would be wasteful serving a fated eagle.

A short while later the Ruling Elders escort him to the pit below the cliff. However when they arrive, they are extremely surprised to find several members of the flock nesting there. To avoid a protest, they decide to lead Eric to the top of the cliff and execute him there. "This is your lucky day one of them squawks. Instead of stoning, you will be pecked to death." Eric does not respond to the indignant remark.

The walk up the steep path is extremely trying for Eric. Again blood begins to drip from his left wing. His strength is weakening and his steps have become less than steady. The sharp rocks only add to his aggravation. Yet no rest is granted to the condemned eagle. Finally after being prodded numerous times along the dark trail the summit is reached. A few moments after rays of sunlight begin to shine over the horizon.

Eric's predicament is complicated by the absence of a message from Larisa and Nathaniel. It seems strange how the trivial things in life fade in importance when the shadow of death draws so near. Still he is grateful that his queen is not present to look upon his ghastly affliction. However foremost he wonders if his prayer during the night will find blessing with the Great White Eagle. For the request is contingent on the success of his serving.

Upon concluding these thoughts, Eric is led to the center of a circle marked as a point of no return. As he looks about the surroundings, he cannot determine the presence of the sea gull flock. They are nowhere to be seen. Nor is there a sound of any bird in the sky or on the ground save for the evil ones. Yet in spite of the near presence of wickedness, Eric senses the glory of the Great White Eagle. If any sadness is within his spirit, it is the thought that he may never ascend in flight with his queen again.

As the Ruling Sea Gulls and their supporters gather about the perimeter, Eric gazes upon them. He wonders how they came to possess such evil. Their thirst for power and greed is so unquenchable. However the purpose of his quest is not to judge them. Rather he is to deliver them in accordance to the instructions of the Great White Eagle.

As the warm rays of the sun begin to dissipate the early haze, Eric boldly stretches and extends his wings. The Ruling Sea Gulls baffled by his particular show of colors back away in squabbling confusion. However they are reluctant to abandon their wicked intention. Nevertheless their fear and anger are aroused as Eric begins to screech in a loud manner. "You hypocrites that deny freedom and grace. Are you so blind not to know that you cannot serve two masters." In response one of the belligerent Rulers squawks: "Do you think yourself a master?" "No! I am but a humble servant." "Such self concluded flattery. Your status is that of a condemned eagle."

Eric is not swayed by the Ruler's insult. However their iniquitous stance angers him. "There are many apart from yourselves in the sea gull flock that seek the light of love. For them there is hope. Unfortunately you have chosen the path of darkness. Furthermore in your treacherous ways you stoned seven of your most magnificent. Their blood remains upon your wings. Still you will not perish because of them or myself. Rather it is your own evil that will destroy you.

In your lust for power you are demented. You beguile the hearts of the young that inspire nobility of flight. To this end, you demean all decency. Also in all of your endeavoring you betray the Great White Eagle. Truly you are the masters of hate. You represent an abomination to the eternal standard of good."

"Your disregard will not go unpunished eagle." The plump and vicious Elder Ruler named Tyro orders Eric to be held with his left wing extended. Thereupon in a ruthless manner without thought of mercy, he sinks his beak deep within the exposed wound. The flesh is ripped away causing a large amount of blood to drip steadily upon the ground.

Eric screeches in agony. However he does not strike out at his tormentors. Although his murmur is carried upon a gentle breeze that all might hear. "Your treatment of me is no longer of consequence. However your fate has been sealed by the One who has sent me. A part from good that is not of your hearts, you are like thorn birds. Thus the time has come for you to be cast upon the thorns of death."

In a mustering of strength, Eric slightly folds his wings and screeches loudly. Feast your eyes upon the tip of the knoll. Instantly the seven slain sea gulls appear in vivid form. Eric's nightly prayer to the Great White Eagle is being answered. However the Ruling Elders are unimpressed. To them it is only a magical trick. In mockery they begin to chant and make amusement. But when the images begin to fade and are transformed into seven eagles, there develops an overwhelming dread of silence. "Tell them your names," Eric screeches. One by one they resound: "Oliver, Trepid, Charlie, Buttons, Jimmy, Aaron, Josh."

Upon observing the transformation of the Magnificent Seven, the Ruling Elders lurch in dismay. However, in spite of being astonished they reaffirm their composure and dismiss the spectacular occurrence as so much trickery. Until now, Eric had acted with dignity regarding his terrible ordeal. However, he is greatly angered by the accusation that the Great White Eagle is a perpetrator of hoax.

"Josh. Tell the masters of evil about the fate of the hawks." In every detail he relates the doom and finale of the vanquished mercenary birds. Information is also divulged about the sea gull flock that could only have been learned in their former existence. Fear and terror begin to grip the Elder Rulers. However a few of them begin to point out the discrepancy of numbers. There are only eight eagles. Yet we number a hundred strong. Vainly some control is maintained.

In a move to prevent open conflict whereby several of the innocent might be jeopardized, Eric screeches forth the names of Larisa and Nathaniel. Immediately from concealed positions over four-hundred faithful sea gulls ascend in flight. Swiftly they encircle the Ruling Sea Gulls and their supporters. Thus engulfing them in a wall save for the open exit to the sea.

Terrified the evil Elders flee in flight towards the only escape left open to them. Eric, the Magnificent Seven, and the massive flock of loyal sea gulls, quickly pursue. The latter group forms a three-sided stacked formation to ensure that no evil Ruler will escape the fate ahead. How wonderful the commitment when freedom is threatened. However, Eric's attention is drawn to his pain and the need to stay aloft. Blood continues to drip from his wounded wing. Before long he must turn back and descend.

Yet the land fades in the distance. The same is true for the Magnificent Seven. They have completed their task which Eric had asked of the Great White Eagle. In a long upward line they again rock their wings in bidding of farewell.

During the trek out to sea the haze of dawn has since given way to a clear morning. The sky is a velvety blue and white cumulus clouds dart the horizon. However nothing glitters more brightly or beckons greater concern than the red blood spewing downward from Eric's wing. Painfully he recollects a banner bearing these colors which he had looked upon as an eaglet.

To any observer below all that can be seen are two flocks of sea gulls and a towering eagle. Although aloft, Eric's gesture for the faithful flock to return to their nests is unmistakable. As they comply, the squawking of their gratitude fills the heavens. Notwithstanding their eyes shine of freedom. Never again will they forfeit this most meaningful inalienable right.

Larisa wants to come to Eric's side. His afflicted wing has begun to show signs of fluttering. However Eric screeches to Nathaniel not to allow her. He further conveys that the Evil Rulers are no longer a threat and that his own fate now rests with the Great White Eagle. Reluctantly Larisa and Nathaniel depart.

The visibility over the ocean begins to diminish. All birds have taken flight in search of shelter. Except for the villainous Rulers and Eric following in their wake. The vanity of the Elders suggests that their pursuers have turned back in fear of reprisal. They squawk of the suffering that they will vengefully inflict. With hideous intent they gaze back at Eric. Thereupon they bank their wings in haste of his destruction. However their own fate has been cast upon the wind.

Overhead dark thunderous clouds begin to form. Perhaps they are driven by a seasonal violent storm. In the distance a flash of lightning strikes. A volley of thunder abruptly rumbles across the heavens. Barely able to remain aloft Eric aligns his wings towards a small island several miles from shore.

The Elder Rulers rapidly pursue. However, they become riddled by a deluge of pelting hail. Several at a time falter and collapse into the sea.

Some merely dazed descend upon the surface of the water. However they will fair no better. They are about to be devoured by a thousand eels.

How voraciously they consume the vile birds which have entered their domain. Due to the panic flapping of the Elder wings the water churns violently. Yet like the storm which has swept over the region, the light of peace returns and the calm is as before. Eric observes a lone dove high in the heavens. It is chirping merrily further from shore than any dove can normally fly.

Eric slows in flight. His strained wing and weakened condition impedes his ability to reach the island. Increasingly he attempts to glide upon an occasional breeze. Still the remote island remains so far away. It is only a tiny speck upon a vast ocean. It would have remained concealed from him except for the white sand and tall pines. He desperately hopes that the place is inhabited. Without assistance a further loss of blood will result in his demise.

In near faintness Eric is tempted to beseech the help of the Great White Eagle. However he refrains believing himself already blessed beyond the right to ask for more. He has known both queen and destiny. Also his day in the sun has exceeded the flight of his dreams. Perhaps some birds might call it a matter of pride. Nevertheless he already feels himself to be in the fold of his Creator's wings.

Considering his weariness, Eric is gliding more and more upon the rising warm currents of air. For the very young survival is instinctively important. Perhaps there are other reasons as well. With exception the years of their lifetime lie in the future. Untold surprises in life nourish hope. Also their zeal for adventure reflects an exhilaration perhaps stimulated by their first flight. But for Eric youthful dreams and aspirations of a glorious day in the sun are no longer upon the breeze that blows beneath his wings. In agony of pain, he longs for the end to come. However because of the love of his queen, he endeavors to remain aloft.

In the face of grimacing pain this flight seems the longest of his life. Shadowed with drowsiness he recollects how the Pacific Ocean was to represent a breath of fresh air away from the past. In some respects it has been grand. Yet even the most remote flights in life cannot elude the gathering storms.

IN NOBLENESS AND GRACE OF FLIGHT AN EAGLE WILL SEEK
HIS DAY IN THE SUN. ALOFT HE WILL ASPIRE TO THE
HEAVENS. FOR IN AWARENESS HIS HEART KNOWS THE TRUE
WIND BENEATH HIS
WINGS. IN DEVOTION TO LIFE'S INTENDED WAYS HE WILL
LAY DOWN HIS OWN. ALTHOUGH TO HIS DYING BREATH WITH
KEENNESS OF VISION HE WILL SEEK HOPE FROM THE
FOOTPRINTS IN THE SAND.

CHAPTER IV

Remembering An Eagle Above The Cross

For Eric the battles have come and gone. The trumpets have resounded. He has been victorious. However he now seems doomed to an unavoidable fate in the waves below. With his energy spent, he begins to falter.

Spiraling downward the white sand of the island looms forth. Directly beneath he also observes that the waters have become swallow. Mustering the last of his strength he spreads his wings and descends upon the warm shore.

Barely able to stand he rests for a while. However the pain in his wing causes restlessness. As he awakens, a pool of blood lies by his side. To stop the bleeding he gathers some moss. However the wound is too severe. Shivering from the loss of his life's fluid, he nestles in the warm sand. It brings some comfort. Still as he craves to quench his immense thirst, he accepts that death will come to him during the night. Oddly a part of him longs to die while another clings to life.

The island is almost desolate. His hope of surviving dwindles like the sun setting on the horizon. As he painfully peers about the surroundings, he becomes captivated by the beauty. It so reminds him of his queen's loveliness. Yet in distracted thought his eyes become trained upon some footprints in the sand.

Everything seems lost to Eric. However within his spirit he senses a rekindled hope along the path of the footprints near the shore. His attention becomes fixed as he watches the waves roll gently over them. It appears strange to him that the salt water cleanses away not a single granular of sand. Curious about the odd phenomena, he rises to investigate more closely. With each unsteady step he observes his own prints tainted by blood vanish before the sea.

Eric has never experienced such an unusual situation before. In bewilderment he wonders about the man who made the fresh footprints. Might he be a kind and gentle sort of person? Not having fear, Eric becomes mystified. A feeling of trust further prevails within his spirit. As he pauses momentarily, an unexplainable sensation of love seems to emit from the wake of each print.

In tracking the footprints, Eric begins to sense a feeling of friendship. How true each impression becomes revealed in the moist sand. With each additional step, Eric's feelings become more intensified. It is almost as if his heart were converging with the One ahead. Excitement begins to flow throughout his spirit. However the pain of his wounded wing brings clouds of tears upon his eyes. With his vision blurred he is unable to see ahead. Yet he clearly feels the presence of someone very near. It is a miraculous revealing as though the wings of love ahead had given lift to all of his flights.

Nevertheless if love is eternal, Eric remains a mortal bird. In weakness he has taken his last step. There will be no overtaking the One who walks beyond. As his breathing becomes faint he slowly slumps upon the sand. Let the will of the Great White Eagle be done. As Eric takes his final breath there is a look of peace about him. However sadly his appearance conveys the ravaging of many storms.

As he sighs his last breath of air a gentle hand touches upon his head. There is an aperture in the palm that bears the painful affliction of a time long since passed. Eric's heart quickens with empathy and sorrow. But more profoundly in the shadow of death, he becomes gracefully renewed in spirit and body. Even his crippled wing is fully restored. Also the blood spewed upon his feathers vanishes before him.

"Eric. I have healed your affliction. Through your suffering you have learned humbleness. Also the greater meaning of life has come upon your wings. It is because of your love that the Great White Eagle has blessed you with wholeness. Your queen awaits. However first we shall talk.

Eric. Who do you think me to be?" "Your wings are of pure love. The radiance of which shines of the whiteness of light. Also I have been healed beyond what is possible in this world. My heart tells me that you are the Sacred One. The Son of the Great White Eagle. I further believe that you are the wings of the Creator of all birds. Among men, you are known as Jesus.

"In what manner do eagles refer to me?" "As the One who has given noble purpose to our flights. Also, we think of you as the sacred Master of love. Notwithstanding we acknowledge you as the Redeemer or Messiah. You are the wind beneath our wings."

"I am who you say. It is well that you have said these things." "Then I trust that you are not offended by my reference to you as an eagle?" "No, my feathered friend. I know well the voice that scorns. Apart from your occasional disobedience, a lack of reverence has never been a part of your true nature. Eric as you know, there are many different birds of a feather, including mankind. All are intended to ascend in the nobleness of eagles. For you are the bearers of an eternal standard.

The world would be a better place if it accepted Heaven's will. It is upon the wings of eagles that eternal love finds grace. For the exalted flight is an inspiration for all to follow the majestic path of the Creator's caring.

"You seem troubled Eric." "Master! Is it not true that you have thousands of devoted followers who proclaim your love and the Word of the

Great White Eagle. Are they not more worthy than eagles?" For a moment or so Jesus sits silently upon the sand with an intent look in his eyes. Thereupon with a voice reflecting his kindness he responds. "Eric. There is either the presence of love or its absence. In a world that lacks the sharing of its treasure there can never be too much. Also though man was created in the image of the Creator, is my being with you not a testimony of His wings?

Birds of a feather and flight are an endearment to my heart. For they spread my love in the likeness of innocent children. By revealing His word to man, the Creator acknowledged His love and the awareness of needful tending. Also is it not equally true that through His caring for the smallest of birds that He wrote his love upon their hearts as well? Remember that it is the spirit rather than the size of the heart or the wings that enables all birds to become noble eagles."

In these things Eric expresses much understanding. Furthermore he becomes honored by the love of Jesus. Even His mere presence is the greatest gift that he has ever known. Still he wonders beyond the explanation given why Jesus has brought healing to a lone eagle on a remote island.

"Eric. Your thoughts are not unknown to me. The Creator has promised to double the days of your life in compensation of His beckoning. The Great White Eagle does not renege on His promises. Accordingly my presence is a testimony of His glory. Although you are loved, know that the importance is not related to your life on this earth, but to the keeping of His promise. Most often that which is sown freely is what one reaps in life. Thus I have come unto you."

For the next several moments, Jesus sits silently as though He were drifting in thought to another time and place. With a sad expression He looks upon His hands and feet. Eric senses that He is feeling the persecution of His Crucifixion. His eyes fill with tears. However the pain unveiled is more of heart than body. In feeling of empathy, Eric moves closer to His sacred friend to lend comfort. Yet in spite of his love, he does not embrace his heart's desire. For he knows that divinity abides at his side. Instead it is the hand of the Holy One that graces him.

In recollection the thoughts of Jesus intensify. Eric profoundly feels the anguish of Jesus's torment. Greatly overwhelmed by His friends suffering, he bolts and screeches across the sea. However in a breath of forgiveness, peace again returns to Jesus. "I do not know of this pain when I am with the Creator. I feel it only now because of the story I am about to tell you.

A long time ago I was crucified. The world is aware of my sacrifice and suffering upon a cross. But only a few know about the flight that took place above me on that dreadful day. As I hung near death, three buzzards gathered in the sky. They thirsted for the mortal blood that dripped from my wounds. However out of the darkened heavens appeared one of your ancestors. A lone eagle above the cross.

He was not a large bird. Especially in the midst of the three buzzards who had fallen from grace. Nevertheless he was extremely daring. In a noble manner he did not wish to desecrate the sacredness of my crucifixion. Therefore he merely screeched a warning for the evil intruders to depart. However the three buzzards remained unmindful of his urging. With immense courage and willingness to sacrifice himself, he darted towards the sun.

In devotion to me and with great determination the eagle descended upon the buzzards. At first, the bewildered buzzards fled. However, it was not long before they returned to overpower the brave eagle. Although, this was not to be. Yet with vicious intent they commenced to descend upon him. The distance began to close when the defending eagle banked his wings and flew directly into their midst. He swiftly plucked several tail feathers from the buzzards. In spite of their angry squawking, he did not harm them. Yet quite decisively he had made it difficult for them to remain aloft.

Until I arose from the dead, this guardian eagle watched over me both day and night. His flight was of love. He concluded the sky over my resting place to be holy. Thus he allowed no bird or creature to trespass above or below. When I awakened within the sepulcher the first sound I heard was his joyful elation. He had come to nestle in an olive tree near the entrance of my tomb. The removal of the large stone blocking the doorway has remained a mystery to many. However to that faithful eagle it was never in question.

As I walked through the adjoining garden this gallant eagle continued to watch over me. In respect he towered slightly behind in his magnificent gliding. Also in the belief that other fowl might taint the air, he screeched them away. Perhaps unduly so. On occasion he would take of water. Nevertheless he fasted until I ascended to be with the Creator. It was a time when many persecuted me and but a few were devout in worship. Still this humble eagle was willing to lay down his life for me. There is no greater love.

There are those among men who think that nature is inferior. However without her, they would surely perish. Doubt and narrowness of thought so limits the mind. If they do not understand the realm of nature, how can they possibly perceive the ways of heaven? They say that my friends of flight have no spirit. Yet they are blind and ignorant of my heart. I will tell you that the eagle of whom I have spoken continues to glide near my wings. And all of heaven knows him.

Eric. What I have just told you is more than a story. It is a lifting of heart. It is a dimension of love that embraces gratitude. As there are many facets of love, there is more than a single reason why the flights of eagles represent nobleness. The eagle that honored me brings forth blessing upon the wings of all righteous.

In remembrance of the eagle who so loved me and in recognition of yourself, you have found healing." "But Master! I am not worthy of such grace. I have been disobedient." "Eric! Perfection is not of this world. Be more forgiving. Even of yourself. Keep a pure heart and all of your flights will find blessing.

My feathered friend. Soon I must leave you. Do not wonder about the transformed Magnificent Seven. They are quite aware of your being healed. "Jesus. Can I not accompany you?" "No Eric. However, I am pleased that you are so graced in heart. Nevertheless it is not your time. Also, as I have expressed, your queen awaits your return. May you find joy and peace with her in the seasons to come."

In the tranquility of blessing, Eric succumbs to sleep. The following morning he is awakened by the gentle sound of the waves splashing upon the shore. Jesus is gone. So are his footprints in the sand. Although as Eric gazes about, he becomes gratuitously joyful. Beside him upon freshly laid green leaves is a meal of bread and fish.

Eric is grateful for what Jesus has done for him. However in his absence he feels much sadness. Still the love that is synonymous with him in spirit remains behind in Eric's heart. In reverent thought Eric is jubilant that One so kind has brought healing by the touch of his hand. It is regrettable that the world did not feel equally enlightened by His presence.

The sky is clear as Eric lifts into flight. He is homeward bound. Although the footprints in the sand have been washed away, Eric is renewed. Even the wound caused by a trophy hunter years' ago no longer restricts his skillful maneuvering aloft. In his revived youthfulness he screeches and glides through the clouds with a greater happiness than he has ever known. How much his queen remains endeared to his heart.

Although a calm breeze whisper's beneath his wings, Eric is aware that other storms will bring turbulence. But for now there is only sunshine as he ascends higher and higher into the heavens. He is towering above the trivial and troubled aspects of life that tend to put a ceiling on graceful flight.

Eric's queen has kept a vigil. As he nears the lighthouse, she joyously takes flight to him. Again their love finds blossom in flight. They zoom towards each other in frolic play. For hours they glide wing tip to wing tip dancing amidst the thinning clouds. Far below the white-capped waves rush onto the shore. However in the distance the sun gradually dips beyond the horizon. A few moments after as twilight spreads across the region, the light from the lighthouse casts its brightness far out to sea.

Upon returning to their nest, Eric's queen respectfully declines to question his belated flight to her. Nor does Eric volunteer an explanation. He merely screeches that peace has been restored within the sea gull flock. A while after in the early darkness two sea gulls appear in the sky overhead. It is Larisa and Nathaniel.

As they approach the eagle nest, Larisa and Nathaniel cannot believe their eyes. "Oh father! How is it possible that you are still alive? We thought that you succumbed to your wound over the ocean or somewhere in the wilderness. We ascended in flight to bring comfort to your mate." As Larisa embraces him within the fold of her wings, Nathaniel looks on with immense disbelief as well.

"Try to understand that it was the mission that was of special meaning. I was merely instrumental in carrying out the will of the Great White Eagle. Had I returned to the sea gull flock only my self-glorification would have become engendered." "Eric. You are a true hero! Even in the belief of your demise, chanting continues in your memory."

"Nathaniel. In my absence who has been chosen to guide the flock?" "Myself. However you are a Master. Thus much more learned than myself. It would be an honor to be your lieutenant." "Larisa. What do you think?" "Oh. Father, I believe that it would be both right and grand. After all there would not be choices or freedom if it were not for you." "My queen. What is your heart?" "I would like to know the story about your mortal wound. Otherwise my spirit is of a oneness with yours. So long as our flights are together, I will support whatever decision that you feel best."

For a moment or two, Eric pauses. Then with a sureness of voice adverse to persuasion he begins to speak. "You are my loved ones. What you have said touches my heart deeply. Still in accordance to the laws of nature an eagle guiding a flock of sea gulls is a prelude of tragic consequence. The Great White Eagle turned my wings into the wind to defeat evil. However He never intended that nature become altered beyond that endeavor.

Nathaniel. You will be a very able leader. Your spirit is of giving. Also you have learned to listen. Many birds of a feather hear the voices of chatter. However only a few hearken unto wisdom. These sentiments have often been expressed by the One truly endowed to be called Master. His name is Jesus. He represents the hope of this world. Abide by His teaching and the flock will come to know the treasure of peace.

Larisa. I am neither a hero nor a martyr. It is my profound wish that no lasting remembrance be made in my behalf. The appreciation rendered is more than sufficient. While I am humbled by the gesture afforded me, all devotion should be rendered to the Great White Eagle. The accomplished good is a credit to His will. Value your new found freedom. In neglect it can become lost and evil will rule again.

I have been honored by many blessings. In life I searched for the deeper meaning of love. The treasure found came as a result of sharing with my queen. Apart from this some of my flights led to disobedience. In consequence I was punished. However because of the Great White Eagle's caring, I was saved from peril more than once. Certainly I am not special. Still He found favor in me to serve. Through my endeavoring much knowledge or wisdom has come upon my wings. Also in suffering I have come to experience the greatest friendship possible. Notwithstanding, the love of you and Nathaniel remains a quirk of nature. But one I might add of enormous endearment to my heart.

My beloved queen. Concerning my near fatal wound, the Son of the Great White Eagle renewed my life. It was on a remote island. In time I shall tell you the whole story. Although for now let it suffice that my being healed began with sacred footprints in the sand and ended with a story about an eagle above a cross. Yet I am among you today only because of the love of our Creator, who never breaks His promises."

While on the island, Jesus expressed twice, "Your queen awaits you." "He did not say that the flock awaits. I believe in spirit that my intended purpose is to devote myself to her during the autumn of our season. This is also where my heart lies. Yet a part of me longs to go with you in search of other destinies. However in the lateness of my season, I tire of life's storms. Certainly more seasons have passed than lie ahead. Notwithstanding, my day in the sun has become somewhat shadowed.

Through grace I have found lasting happiness. Also by the beauty of the sea a wonderful home has been provided. This is where I will remain. However from the beam of the lighthouse, I will not abandon you during times of need. Still the sea gull flock needs both of you. Respectfully Nathaniel, I already have a lieutenant in the form of my queen. I would only add that given her particular independent nature that she is a sufficient challenge for this most grateful eagle."

Reluctantly Nathaniel and Larisa accept Eric's decision. Also within the surroundings of good cheer they remain temporarily. Thus within the calm of the lighthouse an exchange of love develops forming meaningful memories that will long endure. There are many flights of frolic joy beneath a glimmering sun that shines of a changing season.

Near the ten trees a portion of soil is clawed away upon which a pool of water forms at first rain. It is a symbolic gesture enhancing the meaning that the One who quenches thirst does so for all who seek Him. In addition a fourth tree appears among the three in line to honor the devoted eagle that had ascended above the crucifixion cross.

Neither Eric, his queen, Nathaniel nor Larisa, at the pool of water honoring Jesus, feels that their presence is a gathering of eagles or sea gulls. The union is one of meaningful devotion which is the foundation of all lasting relationships. In the days that follow many in flight journey to this place. Yet not a single one throughout nature concludes differently.

The sea gull flock is vulnerable without sound leadership. Thus the time has come for Nathaniel and Larisa to depart. It is a sad occasion. However responsibility is often demanding. Briefly Eric and Larisa take a private stroll through the garden. They converse of things quite typical of a father and daughter. Eric is losing a princess whom he has come to love as his own. The farewell is no less difficult for Larisa. However for Eric there is satisfaction in knowing that she has chosen her mate well.

Life can be compared to a rose. There is the sweet aesthetic beauty and fragrance. It brings forth both sharing and great pleasure. Yet there is also the bitter. Such are the thorns that prick causing intense hurt and grief. From time to time the thorns represent many misfortunes including the pain of parting. Yet all flights have a beginning and an end. In this mindful thought, Eric embraces Nathaniel and Larisa in a bidding of farewell.

Following promises to return, Nathaniel and Larisa lift into flight. Eric and his queen accompany them a fair distance. Although they soon bank their wings towards the lighthouse. Gradually the two young sea gulls disappear in the distance. The spirit of freedom guides them in journey.

IN THE CALM AND SERENITY OF FLIGHT LOVE FLOURISHES
AND HAPPINESS FILLS THE SKIES. THERE IS A TIME FOR
EVERYTHING AND A SEASON FOR ALL. THE TREES GROW AND
THE RAINBOWS FORM IN ALL THE SPLENDOR OF NATURE.
THE SUN SHINES BRIGHTLY REFLECTING UPON AN EAGLE'S
GLORIOUS DAY IN FLIGHT. YET THE GRAY CLOUDS FORMING
ON THE HORIZON SERVE AS A WARNING OF AN IMPENDING
STORM. SADLY THE JOY OF BLESSING IS OFTEN FLEETING.
FOR THE RAINS WHICH FALL ARE REMINDERS THAT THE
MOMENTS OF LIFE ARE PRECIOUS.

CHAPTER V

Calm And Storms In The Season Of Autumn

The passing weeks bring forth autumn and a crispness to the air. It is a time of splendor. The pastel rays of sunlight seem to add an enrichment of tone to the black and white stripes of the lighthouse. Even beyond to the landscape as far as the waters edge.

Upon the branches of the small trees in the garden the leaves are turning golden and crimson in color. How much they flutter in the breeze and float aimlessly to the ground. In the distance the ocean reflects a deeper blue. Along the surface white-capped waves spew forth a cold mist.

It is a time when Eric and his queen come to know the deepest meaning of their sharing. In their pausing moments they reflect upon the many years of struggle and the turbulent storms. However during this joyful period the encounters aloft and the echoing of sacrifice and struggle become silent. Gone is the pursuit of destiny and all that it encompasses. It is a season of happiness. It is also a treasure of lasting memory during a precious time in the sun.

During early morning flights Eric and his queen would occasionally revisit the remote island. In solemn thought Eric would recollect the glory he found in the footprints. Thereafter he would take great delight strutting along the shore vying for her attention. In frolic play she would ignore him. However soon little berries would begin to fall around her. It always pleased her knowing that in spirit he was acting like an eaglet aloft.

Enjoying his attention she would often refrain from scolding him. However upon descending and approaching her, he always had a look of surprise. "Did you notice my queen that berries have been falling from the sky?" "Indeed I have. Should I believe that you are innocent of such an occurrence?" "Possibly. Certainly some unexplainable things have happened on this island before. However seldom have they occurred on such a fine morning."

Waiting for the right moment, for Eric to be distracted in thought, she would swiftly ascend in flight. Upon banking her wings, she would zoom in low knocking him over onto the damp sand. In passing she would screech with utmost joy. "Have you noticed any eagles dropping from the sky on such a fine day?"

It is never necessary for his queen to have the last word. She remains a very noble eagle in her own right. Yet in heart, she knows Eric better than any other bird. Certainly the restless nights have conveyed to her the storms gathering in his dreams. Thus she desires that he share with her the lighter side of life.

Eric is grateful for his mate's loyal devotion and gifted understanding. Through his caring there is always a wild flower amongst the food brought to the nest. It is his unique way of expressing his love for her and acknowledging that no other is so special. Often she asks, "How the flower happened by?" He always retorts, "I must have clipped it on the wing." Her reply always brings a sparkle to his eyes. "Considering the warmth it brings to my heart, it must have been upon the right wing."

In the absence of storm, the glow of sunlight radiates ever so brightly the happiness of a season. On one such morning, Eric awakens to see the figure of a man sitting idly near the shore. He immediately ascends in flight to investigate the stranger. "Why has he come here? Also I wonder if he is friend or foe?" Spanning his wings and gliding nearer he observes the man slowly extending his hand upward with two fingers making a V sign. Eric's heart fills with joy. It is the Old Man by the sea. He has returned to reminisce about the years when he operated the lighthouse.

Unafraid Eric swiftly descends and goes to the Old Man's side. The former Lighthouse Keeper who faithfully provided food and friendship begins to caress his feathers once again. Somewhat nervously Eric's queen comes near. Still she remains at a distance. She appears to sense his gentleness, but her instinctive fear dominates. The sensitive Old Man who has become one with nature does not coax her.

The reunion of friendship brings a smile. However there is also a forlorn look upon the Old Man's face. He has come home to the only meaningful life that he has known. Perhaps he has returned to his only real friends. Yet a weekend is a very short time when one searches for a meaning in life that has gone by. Although memories are dear they often lack a feeling of purpose. Thus sadly they can be as fleeting as one's youth.

Thoughtfully the Old Man has brought supplies. After sharing his food, he waves Eric and his queen into flight. Ascend into the clouds. For you are as angels in the sky. Besides I have work to do. In delight the two eagles bank their wings towards the mainland forest. It has been a long time since they have taken this journey.

With immense jubilation they screech across the forest valley. The meadow is alive with the familiar sounds that they enjoyed when Larisa first visited them. However in her absence it does not seem the same. It is also different in other ways. While gliding aloft towards the eastern end, they observe vast acres of severed trees that once adorned the area. The felled timber litters the barren hillsides. Adjacent regions also reveal white markings upon the conifers. Trees slated for cutting at a future date. Man's encroachment is devastating the woodlands. Perhaps the river dividing the forest will preserve the western slope.

If scarring plagues the forest untainted beauty remains in the sky and at the lighthouse. Even so Eric's queen senses his solemn dismay. Diverting Eric's attention to herself by fanning her feathers, she is able to persuade him into frolic flight. Her unique and natural display invites the attention of another male eagle in the far distance. However Eric's resounding screech discourages his intent of pursuit. He scolds her as well. However in view of his heartfelt love for her, it is but a nipping of a feather. As they glide along the river a silhouette of oneness appears upon the slow moving water.

Near river's end they bank their wings towards the lighthouse. As they descend, the Old Man greets them with great excitement. Behold he exclaims with a gesture of his hand. The two of them gaze upon their home with great astonishment. It no longer resembles a quaint nest. Innovations have altered the structure. A deck has been added along with fresh new paint. Through alteration it has become a towering castle awaiting noble hearts.

The weathered hands of the Old Man have also crafted trust. Overcoming her instinctive fear Eric's queen befriends the former Lighthouse Keeper. The resulting joy brings tears to his eyes which trail upon the wrinkles of his cheeks. Here is a gentle and loving man as noble in heart as can be found in all of nature. Perhaps Eric ponders, there is truth in the phrase "what one sows in life; they tend to reap."

A moment or so after a stern expression appears upon the Old Man's face. He abruptly rises to his feet and proceeds to the door of the lighthouse. Upon removing a key from beneath a rock known only to himself, he enters. As he begins to speak into the familiar black box on the wall, his face reddens. In a fit of anger he further waves his arms in all directions. Notwithstanding, the loudness of his voice carries far beyond the structure. However, gradually his tone mellows and his composure reveals the true gentleness of his spirit.

Beyond the window both Eric and his queen are puzzled to comprehend the language spoken. However as the weekend passes, and the Old Man remains there evolves an understanding of joy. Apparently, a condition became agreed upon allowing the Old Man to live at the lighthouse for maintaining the grounds. It is in content an agreement absent of monetary gain. However it is a very meaningful gesture in compensation for a life of loyal commitment.

Without further ado the Old Man again hangs the large wooden clock on the wall. There is a revived spirit about him. However the ticking away of time can only tell the hour. It does not convey the sense of worthiness he has found in coming home.

141

As the darkness of night fades to the light of dawn, the Old Man begins to cleanup the grounds. While strolling about he notices the pool of water within the garden of flowers and the two rows of trees. He is greatly puzzled to understand how they came to exist. Pausing for a moment he takes a puff on his pipe and glances in the direction of Eric. However Eric only screeches in a dumbfounded way an unexplainable response. Nevertheless with a sigh, the old man sets to deepening and lining the pool with carved stones. A few days hence he adds a fountain to keep the water pure.

As the weeks pass, the air increasingly chills with each nightfall. However the afternoons warm abundantly beautifying the season of autumn. Eric and his queen venture less afar. However their sharing never wanes. Also aloft in their castle, they are secure from the elements. It is a safe haven that will last through many storms. Although it is their spirit of love and nobility that will endure throughout time.

On a morning blanketed by frost a large group of gray whales appears near the lighthouse. Gigantic funnels of mist spew high above as they clear their ballast. It is a thrill to see these majestic giants of the sea. However, it is equally sad to accept that many of their numbers have met the peril of a harpoon. So often their frantic cries have lingered upon the waves. Perhaps there is a relationship between those who exploit them and the whales that beach themselves upon a lonely shore. It would seem that both have lost their way in life.

Amidst the splendor of the whales frantic bellowing assails the calm closer to the shoreline. It is Marty and Kim. Upon seeing their dolphin friends both Eric and his queen screech excitedly. However it soon becomes apparent that something is terribly wrong. Eric! Exclaims Marty with a dire chatter. Tad and Tim have become trapped in the net of a Tuna boat.

Eric is not sure how he can assist. In the water he is inept. Still he must try. Not wishing to complicate the situation further, he screeches for his queen and Kim to remain at the lighthouse. Thereupon he ascends in flight. With incoherent fearful chatter Marty hastily begins to lead him towards the vessel anchored approximately six miles to the Northwest.

Several moments after the large craft comes into view on the horizon. Slowly the distance closes. Fortunately the net remains in the water and none of the crew are topside. Marty signals to Eric the exact site where Tad and Tim have become trapped. While descending Eric concludes that time is vital. He also gestures to Marty to be alert for any infiltrating sharks.

At set intervals the net has wooden floats that prevent any catch from escaping from the surface of the water. The chance of rescuing the two young dolphins is slim. Nevertheless, Eric comes to perch upon one of the floats. With great intensity he begins to claw and tear at the strands of the net with his beak. However his initial effort is without result. The braided material is too strong. It has been fashioned to hold a vast amount of tonnage. Although as he continues to be steadfast some of the strands begin to rip. Soon the first wooden float drifts away from the binding.

It is a tiring and difficult ordeal. A task that seems endless. Much of the time Eric must hover in the air. Also to his disadvantage some of the floats randomly turn in the water. Often in an awkward manner he must balance one claw on a float with the other beside on the braided line. He is constantly splashed upon by the frantic commotion within the net. Frequently he becomes partially submerged in the cold currents. But in spite of all the disadvantages and unliklihood of success, he is unrelenting. It is as though the victims caught in the net were his own.

However the hours pass and the drain upon his strength begins to take a heavy toll. Time has become critical. Also near exhaustion he cannot sever all the remaining lines securing the floats. In desperation he perseveres to cut through the fourteenth float. His claws are raw and bleeding. The cold water has also caused him to chill. However it is his moisture laden feathers that are of paramount concern. He may not be able to lift into flight.

In desperation Eric screeches to Marty to dive and reach Tad and Tim. Also to make contact with any other dolphins that may be trapped below. They must attempt to surface and crash the net between the first and fourteenth floats. A short time later seven dolphins reach the surface. However ghastly wounds bear the struggle of their plight. Yet in the balance lies their only remaining chance for freedom. Unfortunately Tad and Tim are not among them.

With a low sounding screech Eric signals for Marty to come to his aid. To remain any longer in the cold of the sea will prove fatal. He manages to leap upon Marty's back. However keeping his balance proves extremely difficult. As Marty attempts to maintain a stationary position in the moving currents, Eric shakes away as much moisture from his feathers as possible. Yet he has lost much resilience. Also in weariness he will have but one chance to ascend.

Mustering his remaining strength, he extends his wings and lifts only slightly. Saturated with salt water it is all that he can do to skim the surface. The added strain upon his wing muscles causes agonizing pain. Descending slightly his claws penetrate beneath the surface. To falter further will invite tragedy. For he cannot emerge into flight again. Marty is close to panic when Eric by sheer will begins to rise ever so slowly into the sky.

The motion of flight gradually dries Eric's feathers. Banking his wings, he screeches to Marty to communicate the simultaneous strike against the weakened upper section of the net. In a gliding pattern, Eric becomes dismayed as the initial attempts fail. It seems a futile action.

However in direness Marty begins tugging on the center float. Thereupon a fourth attempt is made at ramming the net. A snapping sound abruptly emerges at the critical points along the weakened section. As the upper portion begins to slip away, a semicircular escape path opens to the surrounding sea. Marty in pulling it towards the ocean bottom to avoid any additional entanglement, inadvertently frees Tad and Tim.

On this particular day the Pacific was able to reclaim a part of her dwindling life. Those fortunate to escape the cruelty of the net will heal. However some perished by drowning in their web of entanglement. Even a few tortoises and periled sharks.

So often the balance of nature is upset by mans' greed. There are those among them who claim that love is of a lesser meaning within the realm of nature. However many canines have fasted upon the graves of their deceased masters' until they too died. The wailing of whales separated at sea by harpooners is a cry of lost love. Throughout nature with some variation the bond of fondness is so strong that mothers have sacrificed themselves to save their young. If the embrace is merely instinctive, there would be no lamenting or existing exceptions.

It seems odd to Eric that he would ponder such thoughts during a moment of danger. Perhaps they are stimulated by the reminder that all life should be highly valued. Certainly the real worth of life is a correlation of wisdom and a loving heart. In conclusion of thought Eric rocks his wings gesturing to Marty the need to return to the lighthouse.

During this rescue attempt Eric had not sought the help of the Great White Eagle. Nevertheless he knew that Providence had provided guidance. They had not been detected while in harms way. Also they had escaped the fate of so many others. In the flight of freedom their wounds will heal quickly.

Still the crew aboard the fishing vessel will receive little sympathy. They have suffered little more than a damaged net. In affixing blame they will undoubtedly conclude that some whale or other sea mammal ran up against it. Even so there will be other days for the crewmen to venture again out to sea. For the harvest of the net is even more vast than the ocean itself. In their wake the caretakers of nature will protest their voyage. Too many of the vessels set sail in greed rather than in purpose of need.

As they approach the lighthouse, Eric screeches joyfully to those who await their safe return. His queen swiftly ascends and Kim, with a jubilant heart, swims out to Marty. Although as Eric's mate closes in flight, she becomes very disconcerted by the ghastly appearance of his wounds. Some of his claws are sorely jagged and his legs reveal a mass of formed blood. In feeling of empathy she screeches across the sky.

"Do not despair my queen. I shall heal quickly in your embrace. Besides have you not expressed on numerous occasions that I am somehow different from other eagles?" "Yes! However, I believe that you are taking liberty of the intended meaning." "Perhaps. But you should look at the positive side of things. Are you not graced by flying with the only red-legged eagle in the world?" Her eyes begin to shine in the nobleness of his intention. However the mist of her tears continues to convey her caring concern.

Far below and near the shore the Old Man joyously dances upon a huge rock. He is grateful that all has turned out well. In the distance he observes the four dolphins closing upon the lighthouse. The ocean so represents the treasure of his heart. How pleasant the sprawling grandeur of its beauty that stirs his spirit. Such enormous joy he feels in seeing the sleek dolphins arching abreast in and out of the tide. They are such graceful swimmers. Also in a fascinating way the sounds of nature are pleasing to one who hearkens with appreciation. To the gentle Old Man even the chattering of the four dolphins represents music to his ears.

Eric knows that his wounds are more severe than he is willing to acknowledge. He ponders his ability to land safely. Not wishing for young Tad and Tim to witness his possible demise, he rocks his wings in gesture of Marty taking his family homeward. However Marty sensing Eric's motive disobeys. If for any reason his friend should falter and drop into the sea, he intends to save him.

Apart from Eric's obvious wounds, he suddenly feels a sharp twitch in his right wing. Although unnoticed by his queen, the wing further dips sharply in alignment. "Do not be alarmed my feathered servant. Also no other can hear my voice." "Oh Great White Eagle. I am extremely honored. However why have you chosen to broaden my suffering?" "Eric. I am pleased by your noble deed on this day. In the distant future I shall reward you. Although because your action was charitable as opposed to the mission that I formerly willed, you cannot be renewed again in this dimension.

Still you should not despair. The twitch in your wing will be short-lived. The added discomfort is to convey a strong message. You are no longer a young eagle. However your eagerness to take flight into the turbulence of storms endures. Your journey has been long and trying. Nevertheless in your remaining seasons there should be only peace. My desire for you is not absent thoughtfulness for your queen and the Old Man by the sea.

I have found favor in your serving and your disobedience of the past has come upon my forgetfulness. As such all has been forgiven. It is unlikely that I shall come unto you again in speech. However I will remain the true and lasting wind beneath your wings.

You have boldly found splendor in the sun. Still you should remember the shadowing in the autumn of your life. Also many flights have taken you

145

through numerous storms. Yet the pelting rains have taken a toll. In the days ahead elude the wayward clouds. Through wisdom accept, "What you can change and know what you cannot." It is more than a factor of age. Also remember that the significance of each season in your life varies with intended purpose.

Before departing might I render a wish unto you?" "Oh, Creator. I am humbled by your kindness. Also I am mindful of your words that neither birds of a feather or man was meant to live alone. Truly I have been blessed with queen and many friends. Yet within my heart, I know the loneliness of the Old Man by the sea. I would like to ask that he find solace through a loving and devoted mate."

"Your request is most noble. Also because you did not ask for yourself, I will bless you as well. Be of good cheer and farewell my feathered one. As the voice of The Great White Eagle grows faint the twitch in Eric's wing fades as well."

A moment after both Eric and his queen bank their wings and begin to descend. Lower and lower they glide towards the sandy shore. However Eric suddenly feels a dragging sensation upon his wings. Although oddly, his queen experiences no such breeze. The cross wind is compelling him in a direction not of his choosing. In concern for her safety he sternly screeches that she abandon him. Perhaps due to the sharpness of his screech or the trust that she has acquired in his judgment, she reluctantly obeys.

Gradually she comes to descend upon the rock with the Old Man. However, she is frantic as Eric makes his approach. The sandy shore looms only yards away. However for Eric it might just as well lie across the ocean. In spite of his resistance the cross wind is carrying him over the water. The pressure is too great. In his weakened condition he submits and at seven feet in flight he falters.

Although stunned by the occurrence, Marty begins to swim to him. Eric's queen and the Old Man converge on the shore. In the water Eric desperately fans his wings to remain afloat. He is only a few feet from the shoreline. However the cross wind change's direction before Marty or the Old Man can reach him. Eric begins to drift towards them. Then strangely the breeze abruptly subsides. To their utter astonishment Eric wades through the shallow water and comes ashore. However the sight of him causes them to lurch in amazement and near disbelief. There is neither a gash nor cut nor sign of a mark upon his legs. Also his claws are as true as the blessing of the Great White Eagle.

It has been a day unlike many others. Again in harm's way, goodness has shone upon the noble eagle. As the sun begins to set on the horizon, feelings of joy and gratitude continue to linger at the lighthouse. It also happens a few days after that a woman who had befriended the Old Man in youth felt compelled to visit. The evolving happiness flows like the waves upon the sandy shore. For both have found eternal blessing.

During the following weeks an enduring peacefulness comes to settle over the region of the lighthouse. Eric and his queen's flights become enhanced with a greater joy than ever before. Happiness trails wherever they ascend and the clouds of storm remain afar. Their oneness of heart is a gratifying epitome of their reflected love in the heavens. A fondness that depicts the wholesome purpose of life.

The season of autumn has been both colorful and serene. However change is constant. Similar to age shadowing life, the northern winds of winter cloak the fall. Typical of the season the waves of the Pacific become increasingly choppy. Even the air chills with an occasional frost along the shores.

A violent wind comes to blow off the sea pounding against the area of the lighthouse. Yet high above the colossal beams of light shine far out to sea. A warning that the rocks and barrier reef remain a greater threat than the howling winds. However none of the elements weather away the smile upon the Old Man's face. Nor do they stay his vicarious journey in providing food for Eric and his queen.

About mid winter following a rare moderate snow the gray clouds dissipate. The rays of sunlight begin to shine brightly upon the gathered white flakes that sparkle of freshness. Eric and his queen, gracefully lift into flight towards the mainland forest. In frolic play they glide over the ocean. Although the ice caps below serve as a warning that an error in flight will result in a certain death in the frigid water.

Gradually the tall snow-laden pines appear in the distance. In beauty and sound the forest on this particular day is a wonderland. Briefly the two eagles rest and gather berries upon the areas of ground that lay barren. The Old Man has been wise not to over provide lest they abandon the hunt and become too dependent.

Eric decides to keep a vigilance from the top of a pine while his queen hunts below. Although in the spirit of play he drops a few small pine cones which strike all around her. Except for one misguided by a branch. It harmlessly hit upon her head. Nevertheless she lurches in fright. Ascending to his side she scolds him in her usual fond manner.

In a show of confused innocence, Eric descends to the ground leaving her on top of the pine. However she is joyfully aware of his frolic misbehavior. With similar intent she begins to flap her extended wings sending a barrage of snow clinging to the branches down upon him. She is mindful not to bring harm to him. However when he shakes off the snow and screeches scornfully, she merely gestures her astonishment.

As the afternoon passes, they adorn the skies. However darkness comes early during the months of winter. Banking their wings, they turn in the direction of the lighthouse. It has not been a day of noble inspiring purpose. Although as life was meant to be a blending, it has been a journey of hearts' delight.

Approximately two-third's the distance to the lighthouse a strong wintry wind begins to blow. Another cold front is closing in upon the region. Eric and his queen are caught off guard. Also the northwest drift is making their flight a battle against a powerful head wind.

Staying aloft is increasingly difficult. Yet they cannot descend for only the crashing waves of the sea lie below.

The return distance to the forest is too far. Their feathers begin to whip in the lashing wind. Even worse their wings are being tossed about almost uncontrollably. It has rapidly become a flight of survival. With acute determination they endeavor to edge forward. Yet there is nothing to measure their headway if any, or their bearing. Also to their dismay dark clouds have blanketed the twilight.

If only, they had not delayed their journey from the forest. However vain thought will not cease the heavy mist that is filling the sky. There is no time to fear and panic will lead to a certain death. All remaining strength is directed to their wings. In a dire effort they attempt to ascend above the storm. However they are unsuccessful. The tossing winds are too violent. She flies abreast of her mate but at a safe distance to avoid being tossed into him by the turbulence.

How swiftly their energy drains in the midst of the battering cold and cruel wind. Still they continue to persevere through the heavy mist. Although their hope of reaching the shore slowly dwindles. However through the darkness of the storm the flickering light of the lighthouse appears far beyond. Nevertheless it provides both hope and a bearing to safety. As the intensity of the light brightens, they know that the distance to it is narrowing.

Frequently Eric glances back to reassure that his queen is still trailing in his wake. Although exhausted she begins to screech at set intervals to keep a steady fix on the light. It often becomes shadowed by the dark rolling clouds. But the tragic consequence of their plight is strain. Neither of them can continue to maintain the flapping rate of their wings necessary for forward movement. Burdened further by the cold mist and ice that has formed upon the tips of their wings, they are perilously doomed.

Nature is not always kind. By means of storm and other natural phenomena she balances her flocks. The instinctive signs are endowed to all. Yet there are those who become careless or venture too far from a protective shelter. Only a few live to benefit from the experience. Still not all storms are violent or long in duration. This is the fortune of Eric and his queen. To their great relief and surprise the cold front begins to weaken. Perhaps it is only a temporary lull. Nevertheless it is a stroke of unexpected luck.

As the storm relents, Eric and his queen finally reach the shore. Their eyes smart sorely from the wind of the storm not to mention from the glare of the lighthouse beam. Still they are able to see the waves crashing violently upon the rocks below. How fortunate they are to have survived such a freak turbulence. Yet the flexing of nature is seldom amiss. A sudden twister wind thrusts them several yards to the right side of the lighthouse. Although able to descend, they are tossed about the ground.

As the twisting wind passes, they come to stand. Facing the ocean they observe the Old Man along the shoreline. It seems odd to them that he has ventured out into the elements. However in an instant their attention becomes drawn to an erupting large ball of flame far out to sea. In the wake of three additional explosions the land beneath them trembles. It is as though the sun has fallen from the sky and is lighting the heavens.

Frightened and bewildered, both Eric and his queen seek the Old Man's consoling. Meanwhile a large section of mangled debris drifts near the waters' edge. It foretells the story of the blazing fire further out to sea. Driven by huge waves a passenger vessel has foundered off course upon the barrier reef.

Except for a lingering breeze the strong winds have passed. However given the explosions and icy water it is unlikely that any passengers have survived. During the passing moments some of the bodies begin to wash ashore. It is a ghastly sight as some come to float limply amongst the debris. The Old Man has notified the authorities. Although there is little that can be accomplished until the waves subside.

In the midst of a light snow the vessel begins to list. The ocean water pours into her hull amidst the steam rising from her hot but stilled boilers. On a dreadful night the hissing noise and the sounds of twisting steel carry through the air. It is the resounding of a dying ship.

It is an extremely terrible tragedy in the wake of a midwinter storm. Tears flowing down the Old Man's cheeks are a testimony of his sorrow for those loved one's left behind. Amidst the calamity Eric looks intently into the eyes of his queen. Both are aware of how narrowly they had escaped the claw of peril that had crossed their flight as well.

In this thought, Eric encourages his queen to seek the warmth of their towering home. He observes her flight knowing that the snow has intensified. Ice has crusted upon their feathers resulting in additional stiffness. In promise he will soon join her. However he first wishes to lend comfort to his friend.

Due to the Old Man's preoccupation with the tragedy at sea, he never realized the near fatal flight of Eric and his queen. Nor have they revealed the incident to him. Although in the bitter of cold, the Old Man kneels down and gently takes Eric into his arms. In caring trust the warmth penetrates both of their hearts.

Although the winds have calmed, the waves continue to roar and pound upon the rocks. Perhaps as a powerful force of destiny sent forth to cleanse the sea, the debris breaks up into small fragments. The under tide swiftly consumes the wreckage until none remains. In the wake those lost at sea also find a resting peace in the fathoms. Meanwhile the vessel bellows a final bludgeoned sound relinquishing her claim to the surface.

Burdened with grave sorrow Eric and the Old Man, retire to their respective homes. The snow continues to fall throughout much of the night. However the beauty of the white flakes has been lost in the tragedy of the storm. While Eric does not fully understand the consequence of the event, he is in restlessness of sleep aware of the violent loss of life.

By midmorning the storm has traveled eastward over the forest and beyond. The enormous waves upon the sea during the night now lie dormant. Barely a trace of the calamity remains. Yet the magnitude of the disaster clings to those on shore like moss upon rocks. Sadly the severity of natural catastrophes lingers far beyond the realm of rainbows shining.

ALTHOUGH SEASONS BEGIN AND END LIKE WAVES RUSHING
TOWARDS A SHORE, IT IS THEIR QUALITY THAT REMAINS
IN HEART AND MEMORY.
THE SAME CAN BE SAID ABOUT THE NOBLE FLIGHT OF THE
EAGLE. ALTHOUGH TO EMBRACE THE SHORE HE MUST OFTEN
SEEK A GUIDING LIGHT WITHIN THE RAVAGING STORM.

THE FINAL FLIGHT OF AN EAGLE IS THROUGH THE ARCH OF
A RAINBOW. ALTHOUGH THE WINTER OF HIS LIFE IS
CONCLUDED AMIDST THE PASSING OF HIS WINGS. YET HIS
SPIRIT WILL KNOW ONLY OF SPRING AND TREASURE. A
TRAIL OF LOVE WILL FOLLOW HIS SEASON THOUGH
CHERISHED MEMORIES WILL REMAIN.

CHAPTER VI

The Spirit and Direction of Noble Flight

With storm's passing the radiance of sunlight gradually returns to the region. Springtime soon follows and the warming brings forth new growth.

In their gliding through the tranquil sky, Eric and his queen often observe the Old Man working in the flower garden. In frolic play the two eagles frequently zoom close to the adjoining trees. Even the mature in life experience a renewing of spirit during the springtime.

Wherever the Old Man ventures, the sweet familiar aroma of his pipe fills the air. In his understanding regarding the purpose of the trees and the esthetic pool, an additional seedling is planted. It is a thoughtful gesture honoring the memory of those who had perished at sea aboard the fatal vessel. His gracious mate in reverence to the Lord plants more flowers and puts a few lilies in the pool.

The beauty of spring also brings forth a migration of many birds of a feather. However because of the remote locale of the lighthouse from land, only the lost seem to venture near. Although as Eric perches alone in the midst of the trees on a bright early morning, he hears screeching. While gazing upward, his eyes fix upon a very young eagle hovering aloft. In respect of territorial rights, the young bird seeks permission to descend. Eric kindly grants his approval.

"Might you be Eric?" "Yes. However, I am surprised that you are acquainted with my name." "Master. Your reputation is widely known. I am called Jason. Frankly I have been sent to you for instruction." "I am most flattered. But whom may I ask feels me so worthy of such an undertaking?" "May I simply divulge that my humbleness and enthusiasm have directed me here. Master! Does it really matter?" "I suppose not. Your want of knowledge is ample reason. Not to mention your respect. However I remain intrigued about the nature of your flight.

When would you like my instruction to begin?" "Immediately!" "Is it not your desire to first drink and rest? Perhaps you would like to become more familiar with the surroundings?" "They are quite beautiful. Later if you do not mind?" "Alright.

You are an eager beaver." "I am not a beaver." "I do apologize. It was not my intention to sound impertinent. Well son. You are not very patient either." "Master! I am the son of other parents. However you are correct about my lack of patience. Perhaps you can also teach me greater forbearance?" "Time will tell. Still I am quite impressed by your confidence and quickness of response. As for your touch of arrogance, I am not offended. As I recall that was a similar trait in my own youth.

What subject do you wish for me to instruct?" "Master! The One who sent me desires that you impart all knowledge possible to me." "If I was to undertake such a noble deed, how do I know that the wisdom imparted will be for the good of nature?" "Master! Your question is rhetorical. You are a learned and noble eagle with righteous intent. If I were of less intention, I would seek a master of evil."

"Your parents have served you well." "Master! My parents are no longer of this world. They perished in a forest fire. However your compliment is not absent of merit. Even in memory they continue to be an inspiration to me. "I offer my sympathy Jason. Also kindly refer to me by my first name. You shall nest here until your instruction ends and you desire to leave."

During the next several weeks Jason comes to feel an attachment to the surroundings. The Old Man in kindness has built a wonderful home for him in the garden near the trees. Also he and Eric have formed a close rapport. He is swift to learn and is grateful for the caring hospitality shown to him. Through love he is learning the meaning of true friendship and the experience of being a family member again. This caring further promotes greater patience and his own ability to be more affectionate. Eric had sensed that bitterness had resulted from the loss of Jason's parents.

In his enthusiasm to learn Jason would often coax Eric to continue long after the morning hours set aside for him. It was not a selfish yearning, but rather an overflowing of ambitious youthful energy. Nevertheless Eric is seldom swayed. He has long learned in life that there is a time and a season for all things. In devotion the afternoons are a private time for sharing with his queen.

Still it remains that seasons do not end abruptly. Similarly neither does the time devoted to Jason. Late one afternoon Jason frantically comes to Eric and his queen exclaiming that the Old Man had taken down his home. "Pray tell lad! What has he done with it?" "For mercy sake he has stored it in the lighthouse."

In a clever manner both Eric and his queen pretend to be astonished. "It is most strange that could happen considering the benevolent character of the Old Man. What we have here my queen is a young eagle ousted from complacency. The day will come Jason when you shall find need to fend for yourself. However until that time we thought it best that you abide with us."

Jason screeches forth his joy. Although in the passing weeks Eric and his queen maintain the private moments that have proved so precious in their season. However in the sharing of family love many flights aloft include Jason. It is beneath the shining rays of sunlight that he learns the skills of his parents dominance in the skies. A gift that instinct alone could never provide.

Jason continues to mature in a variety of ways. Thus it comes as no surprise when he begins to address his foster parents as mother and father. Still it proves of gracious meaning to them and bonds the family ties with enhanced belonging. Also unlike in the past Jason grows fond of the title son. However it is not Eric's or his queen's intention, that Jason should ever forget his real parents.

To endure their memory, at sunrise one morning Eric and his queen draw Jason's attention to the wife of the Old Man. To his great inner joy, he observes her planting two new seedlings in the grove. Each small tree has been pecked with the name of the one being honored and remembered. Jason becomes overwhelmed with emotional gratitude. Love has directed his flight. Also in blessing he has found treasure at the lighthouse.

With the season of spring there is a warming of the ocean water. It is a beautiful and splendid time of year. Beyond the shore the magnificent Gray whales have returned. As they blow their ballast the mist spews high above adding to the familiar sounds and sights of nature's renewing. On occasion Marty and Kim visit the shore. Although having matured both Tad and Tim, have since ventured on their own out to sea. However Marty has befriended Jason. This brings immense satisfaction to Eric who desires that versatility of influence be a part of Jason's education.

One blustery day when the sky is gray with dark clouds, Jason appears puzzled in thought. "Father! Tell me about the storms of life. I sense that many of my flights will be turbulent." "Son. Do you not also feel that in blessing your day in the sun will dawn?" "Only vaguely. Yet I do seem compelled within to seek the deeper meaning of life. There also exists a yearning of destiny within my spirit.

A dream or some elusive vision comes to me in the night. However it is unclear to me in message. Still I am certain that my future beholds both struggle and suffering. Although father, do not become unnecessarily concerned. It may only be my imagination. Yet within the mysterious mist there is a persistent but vague purpose. It is so unexplainable. Still I sense that my happiness will lie in some sort of serving. Also I believe that a relationship exists between my learning and the vision."

"Son. Nature is a formidable force. It can reign both calm and havoc. In your many flights you will come to experience her as a caring mother. On other occasion's death and destruction will lie in her wake. As you have come to know my queen and me, learn about her. Always be strong for though she can be protective, seldom is pity flexed upon the weak. Also be humble unto her. However in your quest to survive be daring. Remember that you are an eagle. Never give up on any noble pursuit.

Your wings are a precision instrument of flight. However, you must coordinate both skill and strength to ensure that the prevailing winds work to your benefit. Still be aware that some turbulent gusts will lash out violently. Never panic lest you lose control and perish. Always remain calm and rely upon your wisdom. By applying sound thinking you can conquer most obstacles in harm's way. Avoid the barriers that might prove to be overwhelming."

"But father. Realistically there are storms which when confronted cannot be avoided." "True! Therefore trust in the Great White Eagle. Also know thyself. Bolster your confidence. Most often alternatives exist. Many eagles mistakenly magnify the storms of life. The threat is seldom as great as our potential to weather them.

It is easier to fly into the sun than into the eye of the storm. Naturally no bird can elude all the turbulences in life. Nevertheless choose wisely those worthy of purposeful flight." "I am not sure of your exact meaning father." "Son certain elements in nature are of a detrimental force. Also some storms are voluntary while others are involuntary. The latter predicament will negate your ability to deny it. The best that you can do is to prepare wisely for the tomorrows. Remember when making sound choices to consider their long term effect upon others.

Be of courage my son. Also never assume anything. Rely upon facts and calculate every aspect of a given situation. My wonderful mother once expressed to me what constitutes a successful flight. It is one of survival! However in considering the value of nobleness this cannot be an excuse to avoid responsibility. The wise eagle learns quickly from observing the mistakes of others. It is the easier way. Also it lessens his chances of becoming a fallen eagle as well.

The sun is now high in the sky. Would you like to end our session for the day?" "No father. Please continue." "Alright. But only for a short while. Always apply common sense. It will guide you through more rainbows than storms. When in flight, turn into the wind rather than against it. Align your wings for maximum lift. Jason opportunities both in flight and in life are rare. Weigh each carefully and seize upon them before they escape your grasp. Also minimize your mistakes. Of equal importance avoid repeating them. Regrets will trail upon your many flights but persevere.

If battle should come upon your wings, descend from the sun. Often the seemingly unimportant advantages in life frequently determine the difference between life and death. In a similar regard the achievement of success over failure often rests with a positive attitude. Try to understand that life is an interaction of multiple forces and occurrences. Storms can cause an overcast aloft and within your mind. Yet they represent only the dark side of life. The return of sun's gleaming will renew your hopes, dreams, and aspirations.

Always be your own eagle. Do your own thinking and make your own decisions. Never be influenced by negative persuasion. Many birds will self-assert themselves by availing squawking advice. Seek only those who genuinely care. Their flight in life should further bear the wisdom of age and noble experience.

Son. Every bird is endowed with certain innate abilities. Yet often in youth they elude our awareness. One must know thyself to realize our dormant potential. Also within these guidelines are our limitations. While they vary individually each developed trait can enhance our purpose in life. Thus while I can guide your learning, only you can fully develop your unique attributes. Also for your enhancement of flight remember the crucial importance of timing. Only peril awaits those who rush into flight or a storm prematurely."

As his lesson comes to a close, Jason perches in solemn thought. His love and respect for Eric are unquestionable. Eric's devotion to him also reveals his tremendous caring. However it is Jason's future well-being that rests upon the aging eagle's wings. Therefore through his guidance he is careful not to push his son too rapidly or severely. Still the young eagle's survival in the wilderness may depend upon the stern obedience of his instruction. Notwithstanding Eric desires in heart that Jason will surpass his own day in the sun.

"Come along son! Your dreams of glory and happiness will only find fulfillment should you survive in harm's way." Ascending aloft into the clear blue sky, Jason is eager to spread his wings in frolic play. However Eric's queen in a daring lesson of her own begins to put him through several grueling maneuvers. "Father. Is this really necessary." "Yes! Knowledge comes from many sources. Life will test your every weakness."

"Father. Where has she disappeared? My eyes have scanned the heavens and she is nowhere." "Jason, remember what you have been taught." However before he could even take evasive flight, Eric's queen diving from the glare of the sun gently pricks his back with her extended claws. Jason screeches forth the pain inflicted upon his vanity. He reels slightly from the impact but is swift to realign his wings.

Upon bolstering his confidence, Jason then initiates a couple of barrel turns. He then ascends and rapidly dives performing a well-executed loop. However on this particular afternoon Eric's mate is not impressed by his frolic vying for attention. She abruptly banks her wings and dives down pouncing even more firmly upon his back. A feather is plucked which floats aimlessly to earth. Jason screeches in protest. Although to no avail. Find solace son in knowing that if I had been a hawk, you would have perished.

As the hours pass, Jason loses a few more feathers. However as the sun dips low on the horizon, he dives in an evasive pattern. Swiftly descending he banks his wings in a half circular turn. Approaching from behind he quickly comes abreast of her. The mere velocity of his flight causes her to lurch and screech in fear. In the growing darkness the eagle family descends to the lighthouse.

In private she tells Eric that he has taught their son well. However reluctantly she does not praise Jason directly. She is concerned that he might become too confident. Still she does relate to him that he is learning. She also retorts: "Do you think that a son should frighten his mother like that?" Jason offers an apology. Nevertheless he senses the proudness of her heart.

Spring gradually turns into summer. Like the trees in the grove, Jason continues to mature under the watchful eyes of his parents. His dream or vision persists. Yet slowly the mist that cloaks his understanding dissipates.

In the splendor of the season the happiness of those abiding at the lighthouse blossoms. All are grateful for the serenity of blessing beneath the sun. However a vigil of alertness remains. For the storms that shadow the heavens are always gathering to unleash their fury. In their rumbling even eagles often falter.

Jason continues diligently to devote himself to the pursuit of knowledge. On occasion he is joined by a curious cardinal, sea gull, eagle, or other feathered friend. However though many pass by in flight and indulge in learning few are as committed in heart.

About midsummer three eagles befriend Jason. Two of them strive to learn everything that is being taught. Gradually adolescent play and the sharing between them establish fond memories. Yet oddly Jason continues to show the distinctive aloofness that so reflects his personality. Perhaps it is an indication somehow related to his future destiny. Nonetheless in all other aspects his behavior reflects an amicable devotion.

A week later Eric and Jason casually perch within the grove of trees. The leaves flutter upon the branches in the early morning breeze. Across the way the Old Man and his wife are tending to the garden. It is an atmosphere of great serenity.

However Jason's eyes reveal a look of solicitude. "Son! What troubles you?" "Master! How does one know if the direction taken in life is the right course? Sorry. I meant to address you as father."

"Son. As I have expressed many times throughout the years, purpose is what gives flight nobility. Often a particular feeling or desire provides a clear direction of pursuit. Although occasionally, the right choice is obscured in confusion. Attempt to formulate all that you have learned. By ascertaining your unique qualities and interests the right course for the future will become increasingly more resolved. Also allow maturing to be a helpful guide.

Happiness is a byproduct of life. It is a worthwhile goal. However remember in formulating your priorities that love and good should be foremost. Search within your heart for the right choice, not outwardly. Also I would caution you not to listen to the whims of others. Seek your intended flight in life through the guidance of the Great White Eagle. Only upon this path will you find harmony of flight.

Jason. By nature you are a lone eagle. As such your spirit will demand more from life. Conforming to the standards established by the complacent will not come easily to you. However those who realistically set high goals to become all that they can be, will endure greater hardship. Also in your search for the deeper meaning of life, you will encounter more storms. Sacrifice and perseverance represent the price of worthy achievement. Furthermore learn to be patient. Some birds have found their true calling quite unexpectedly.

Many birds aspire great things. Others are content to scratch about the forest floor. The latter in lack of commitment will never know the splendor of flight that yields lasting treasure. In their bid to achieve self-denial will slow the momentum of their hearts' spirit. Some in result of envy will fault those of success. In bitterness they may even betray friendships and themselves in a zeal of falsehoods. Sadly their plight becomes a web of misery and struggle. Wealth is reduced to a compromised dream.

Jason. Your flight in the sun will be to no avail within clouds shadowing or snows falling. Nor is the sun a true destiny or direction in life. Glory is always fleeting. Pursue knowledge to enhance a greater understanding including the messages of your heart. Apply your experiences in a beneficial manner. Also keep an open mind as you're particular shining in life may be multiple rather than singular in purpose. Lastly you should remember that often a flight begins in one direction only to end in another."

During the period of Jason's learning the days of summer wane. The golden and crimson colors of autumn lead to winter's sparkle. Soon other seasons pass in their spectacular splendor as well. With the passing of time the trees in the grove have grown quite tall. Change has also brought maturing to Jason. Including a greater understanding about the direction he wishes to pursue in life. As for those abiding within the lighthouse the beacon continues to shine of their love and happiness far out to sea.

As a new spring dawns amidst the verdant landscape the lighter side of life prevails. So joyful are the occasional visits by Marty and Kim. Happiness also blossoms when Nathaniel and Larisa again make their presence. With squawking delight they announce their expectation of offspring. They further express that the sea gull flock continues to be firmly rooted in freedom.

Within the depths of the sea the magnificent whales have returned according to their timely migration. The blowing of their ballast continues to be but one of the pleasant sounds of spring. Amidst the love and friendship that adorns the surroundings, the ocean waves roll gently upon the shore. However in their diminishing upon the sandy shore lies a reminder of the precious few seasons that remain for an aging eagle. For though the quality of life is paramount, the chronological aspect remains a matter of numbered heartbeats.

Following a brief rainstorm a couple of weeks hence, Jason approaches Eric. Both are aware that an anticipated though dreaded time has arrived. "Father. There is a mingling of sadness, love, and joy within my heart. I have already told mother about my intended flight into the mainland forest. No simple screech will express the gratitude that I feel for all that you and she have done for me. I will sorely miss both of you. Respectfully I further intend to express farewell to the Old Man and his mate."

For a moment or two, Eric perches silently. Jason is moved in heart by his caring emotion. "Son. I love you dearly. Also you are a good eagle. I suppose that we both know that your leaving is the way of things." "Father. You have taught me well. I will be fine." In a somewhat surprise gesture Eric embraces Jason within the fold of his wings. Eagles were not intended to be sentimental birds.

"I have always liked the name Jason. It is my hope that you will remember your mother and me. Also on occasion take flight to your loving sister Larisa. In your many flights never forget the value of true friendship." "Father. I have learned from a Master. Also I am indebted for his love. Mother has also shed her affection upon me. Quite I might add in the manner of a noble queen. In the warmness of memory I shall never forget a single moment."

In their bidding of farewell Eric and Jason stroll about the grove of trees. They also pay homage at the pool of water that honors Jesus. For a few additional moments they pause idly gazing upon the surroundings. With an intense look Eric thereupon expresses his intuitiveness of thought. "Jason there is more than an eternal standard upon your wings." "How do you know this father? For I have not spoken of the vision in a long while." "Son, there is no beginning or end in serving the Great White Eagle. Both love and devotion are eternal.

All who believe in the Great White Eagle serve Him in some manner. But through His infinite wisdom a few are chosen along more specific guidelines. They are not special or favored except in purpose of flight to carry out His will. Such was my mission when I was called upon to rid the sea gull flock of evil."

"Father. I am curious. When did you know that the Great White Eagle willed my destiny?" "I expected as much on the first day when you arrived here. You expressed a strong desire to learn. However you never divulged who sent you. I realize that at the time you did not clearly know yourself. Nevertheless the message was revealed by your compelling flight." "Still father, the question remains why I was sent here? Apart from your being a renowned Master." "Perhaps son the love of a master is greater than the knowledge he possesses. The Great White Eagle in His infinite wisdom knew that the season had past for my queen to bear offspring."

"Do you think that mother knows?" "Yes! Your mother is a befitting queen. Through her noble understanding I believe that she has known for sometime. Of the numerous flights that the three of us have shared, not all were of frolic intention. While I taught you the cunning of an eagle, it was she who tested your ability to survive.

In your serving the Great White Eagle remember that only He is perfect. Still it is within your ability to improve. Always keep a positive attitude and conclude something good in everything you see. If the Creator should decide to test your wings never despair. Also love His sacred Son. When you become disheartened, He will renew the breeze of your spirit. Notwithstanding do not value the material of this world. Rather seek the fulfillment and treasure that you desire through Him. Only relationships lead to rainbows.

Jason. Strive to be a noble eagle. Bring honor to the One who graces the wind beneath your wings. I would also urge that you not become too concerned about your destiny. You are young and the sun shines brightly without any shadowing. Education is your edge. Through your learning you are already towering in the gleaming light."

"Father. Please explain in greater detail." "Son. Your learning has opened up a vast new realm to explore. Many birds of a feather merely learn the essentials in life. Others like yourself seek greater in-depth perception. To acknowledge something without understanding its intrinsic value restricts the mind to a single dimension. Life is a composite of many complex horizons."

"It is doubtful father that I shall ever know as much as you." "Son. I am flattered by your compliment. However there is much that has escaped my understanding through the years. In time you will come to know much more. This is true with each consecutive generation.

Observe the leaves on this tree. They are but a singular part that makes up the whole of the perennial. Other elements comprise the balance. In your journey through life let your flights represent the leaves. Balance your seasons and with the values that have been taught, achieve wholeness."

In pondering thought Jason departs to extend his respect to the Old Man and his mate. A while after he spends a few additional moments with his mother. Leaving the nest proves extremely difficult. However his own destiny awaits in the sun. Upon sensing Jason's doleful heart, Eric draws him into the fold of his wings. "Son. The Master of all masters awaits your flight. Farewell!" "Good bye father."

As Jason ascends into flight, both Eric and his queen sadly comfort each other. Gradually the son who has been a treasure unto their hearts rises above the tree tops. In his love and honor of them, he banks his wings and circles twice before fading into the distance.

Eric and his queen remain amongst the trees in the grove. It has always been a place for all who pass by to find haven. But to them the meaning has a deeper enrichment. It avails the story of their lives. As the clouds begin to dissipate the pastel rays of the sun shine across the region. Affectionately the two eagles embrace in reminiscence of their wonderful years together. A light breeze passing through the trees seems to whisper that their love has always been what was intended.

As the sun comes to dip low in the western sky, the Old Man and his mate join them. She has brought food. However it is what the Old Man is carrying that excites their gratitude. In the palm of his hand is yet another seedling. Following the planting of the small tree honoring Jason, the four of them come to look upon the pool of water. It appears crystal clear in the mirror of their caring.

The warmth of sunlight brings forth a renewing of youthful spirit. In delight Eric and his queen ascend into the heavens. Gliding above the orange rays of sunlight stretching across the blue of the sea, the lighter side of life lingers on. The clouds of storm are nowhere to be found. Yet small berries gently fall from the sky all around his queen. However on this particular occasion she does not scold him. With extended wings she ascends to his side and expresses her love.

Although it is the autumn of their lives, Eric and his queen will share many more seasons under the sun. Yet when winter shadows, it will be of little consequence to them. For the spirit of their love will forever remain in flight.

EPILOGUE

The essence of Eric's flight through life rests upon the pillar of love. By his innate difference there exists a unique sensitivity of feeling to life's intended meaning and values. He contributes these attributes being endowed by his Creator, whom he knows as the Great White Eagle.

Humbled by formal learning, life's experiences, and correcting for disobedience by the Creator, he does not believe himself to be of chosen distinction. Rather he identifies with those in life who strive for the treasures of the heart in the grace of noble flight. Through this endeavor he is adamantly aware of the true wind beneath his wings.

In early flight Eric struggled within a world which he believed to be in conflict with his ideals. Reality to him was the love within his heart as opposed to the double standards and discord beyond. However with youthful ambition he perseveres in an attempt to satisfy both worlds. Yet he falters in the effort to please two masters. How much he yearns for purpose in flight. Both waste and cruelty are an empty ocean to his spirit. Nevertheless resolve of his inner turmoil remains fleeting until the Great White Eagle blesses him with queen and a glorious day in the sun.

Eric believes that the pursuit of knowledge will bring peace of mind through greater understanding. He further concludes that he will find greater acceptance of a world that continues to demand his conformity. However contrary to this belief, wisdom only broadens and deepens an ocean of knowledge.

It is within this realm that he seeks the truth about his existence and the acceptance of a world that is consuming his love. In search of purpose both knowledge and faith harmoniously represent the truth. For Eric it remains a chosen direction of survival. Perhaps more specifically it remains the axiom of his relationship with the Great White Eagle.

Through learning Eric desires to rise above the wayward world. He does not feel superior to other birds of a feather. Rather in his desire to ascend as an eagle, he hopes to experience the deeper meaning of noble love. In purpose he yearns to share the heartfelt treasure that it beholds. This he eventually achieves in serving the Great White Eagle and through his unrestricted sharing with his queen.

As an eagle, Eric realizes his minor role in life. He is not determined to change the world or to alter his feathers. Throughout his seasons he merely desires to be all that he can be. Yet he believes in One greater than himself.

In flight Eric feels lost without sanction from either the world at large or the Great White Eagle. The storms within seem severe and unending. Beset by weariness and hopelessness he seeks a refuge from the high expectations of noble pursuit. After so much sacrifice he questions why the Great White Eagle has denied him the fruit of his ambition and dreams. Still he is aspired by his inner spirit. Also he cannot bank his wings from the One he knows represents the rightful way.

Life is full of disappointments and lost opportunities. Quite often feelings of dismay tend to influence perspectives in a negative manner. However difficult Eric has learned patience. In time he finds both maturity and the blessing of a mission purposeful of the Great White Eagle. In the perseverance of storm also comes renewing and a strengthening of faith. Certainly the impatience of youth does not hasten a time and season for all things.

In dire of flight, Eric eventually returns from his self-imposed wilderness. He wisely accepts the storms of life as a blending with the warm rays of happiness. Through the turbulence he finds the purpose of his pursuit and determination further brings an inner resolve. He also realizes that he had never been abandoned in the storms. Through enriched love and a positive attitude the rainbows that follow every storm become enhanced with greater beauty.

Eric weathered many of life's storms. He learned that not all tragedies are followed by the joy of rainbows. Often for the misfortunate left behind in sorrow, the shining lies only within the strength of our comforting. It is also a reminder of our own good fortune. However no matter how tramatic the storms or problems in life, they are but an integral part of the whole. There is as well the love and happiness which Eric's queen referred to as the lighter side of life.

Eric's flight in life ended much differently than it began. In spite of despair, he found hope and a day in the sun that became a season of long enduring. He learned that relationships which are true to heart are of noble value. Yet none of these things would he have found so abundantly had he not pursued the footprints in the sand.

Eric eventually found treasure in flight because the values he pursued in direction were of an eternal standard. Within this context rests the word and caring love of the Creator. There are other words and many claim other masters in their pursuit of fanciful dreams and the chasing of stars. But the flight of Eric has never wavered from the embodiment of truth. To this end only in flight did his wings find purpose.

Should you find in life the storms and escarpments too difficult to ascend, turn to the One who carries the burden of all across the sand. His sacred love knows no boundary. Also, if he remembers an eagle above his cross and renewed another, believe in his true and greater love for you.

AN EAGLE NAMED JASON

BOOK III

Larry Slauson

Introduction:

Growing up in a hostile world can be a very perplexing journey. Many eagles are swept up in storms of peril and do not reach maturity. However others seem spared as if destined through struggle and blessing to serve a more noble purpose. Such is the flight of an eagle named—Jason.

Larry Slauson

Contents

Larry Slauson

IN THE FREEDOM OF LIFE'S CHOICES THE EAGLE DOES NOT
MERELY
FLUTTER HIS WINGS IN THE WIND. RATHER HE CONTROLS
HIS EMOTION
AND IN PURSUIT OF KNOWLEDGE HE PREPARES FOR THE
TOMORROWS.

CHAPTER I

The Wilderness and Beyond

Beneath dark gray clouds Jason aligns his wings as he passes over the body of water into the wilderness. It has been a long flight from the lighthouse. However he eventually comes to perch upon the branch of a tall pine. Anxiety more than fatigue dominates his thoughts. Certainly this is understandable. He is now in a strange and hostile forest. All that he cherishes has been left behind. In a sense even his youth as his flight of independence has transformed him from an eaglet into a mature eagle.

Still Jason has ventured into a new realm full of danger in harm's way. The many sounds of nature throughout the woodland appear frightening to the young eagle. In an attempt to console himself, he reminisces about the security he had enjoyed in a warm nest amidst loving parents. Eric and his queen following the death of Jason's real parents have raised him as their own. Also according to the will of the Great White Eagle (Creator) they have educated him in the knowledge of life and the skill of flight. The lighthouse has been a good home typical of sound values. Thus the meaning of love and friendship will follow upon his wings forever. Even the fondness of the Old Man by the sea and his mate who had befriended him. In blessing Jason has been given an edge on life. Yet it remains for him to survive.

A light rain begins to fall as he like so many young eagles before him asks who am I? Only time can truly answer this inquisitive self inquiry. Although given his inner love and sensitivity, he is quite like Eric. Nevertheless apart from the grace that his mother has bestowed upon him during his years at the lighthouse, there are characteristics that attest to his own individuality.

With ambitious enthusiasm to continue his learning Jason devotes his attention to studying the events about him. He is acutely aware that knowledge can be pursued from a variety of unlimited sources. Even his immediate surroundings can provide wisdom essential for survival.

Perhaps because of the importance of rapid ascent he feels cause to gaze upward at the raindrops falling upon the forest. A north wind blows hard against the tree tops causing them to sway violently. With awe he wonders about the ravaging power of nature. How resourceful he ponders the wind that gives flight to his wings. Yet it also brings forth rain and sustains life within a forest. It further carries the seeds that sustain life upon the barren ground. Nonetheless it can equally be a destructive force as well. Perhaps the turbulence is neither a friend nor foe. But rather a necessary occurrence to be reckoned with. It appears evident that the importance lies in how I react to such a force upon my wings. Thus it will be my own initiative that will determine whether my flight is successful or fatal. If this is true about wind and wings, it would seem to parallel the whole of life as well. For the turbulences that blow upon each life are nearly the same.

While looking downward, Jason's keen eyes fix upon the forest floor. His thoughts become intrigued by the dense growth of plants and vines. The vegetation is not new to him. However considering his newly acquired independence a vast and different perspective on life is revealing itself. His youthful spirit is overflowing with curiosity.

A venturous flight has brought him to the wilderness. He is eager to soar through the skies. Life in his youth seems so simple and eternal. However survival is beginning to demand a more serious and deeper contemplation of an unfriendly environment. Also if he is to determine who he is in a hostile world, he must gain a thorough understanding of all aspects of life.

As Jason observes the raindrops falling from the leaves of the plants and the needles of the pine branches, he wonders about the other intricate parts. Water although vital quenches only one of life's sustaining needs. Certainly not all life is so simple in form. Yet he concludes it is the root system of the growth that essentially nourishes the plant.

Some he analyzes grow shallow while other roots develop more deeply into the soil. In complexity they not only nourish but sustain the growth against the winds of storm. Through this purposeful function Jason further concludes that the survival of all life depends upon promoting sound rooting. As the storms which form will try the worth of all.

By these thoughts Jason is beginning to acquaint himself in the wilderness. Although in perspective, he does not believe that the winds, rains, or roots of growth, come about by chance. For to conclude such would be to rule out interaction and orderly purpose. Thus through a greater understanding of life he is preparing himself to serve the Great White Eagle to the best of his ability.

As the rain ceases to fall, darkness gradually spreads across the wilderness. Jason rests. However his mind trails in thoughts and dreams of fantasies about what he might become in life. While much of his thinking continues to reflect realism it remains that he is still young. To this end some of the characteristics of an eaglet lingers within him.

It is with youth that foolishness is often associated. In contrast, wisdom is identified with maturity. Certainly wholeness depends upon both. But a time has been set aside for each. Thus the benefit of experience is measured through learning. Often in nature the exactness reflects the difference between being the hunter rather than the prey. Jason will learn soon enough that time, instinct, and knowledge, will promote flight. However accuracy and effectiveness of flight do not rest upon wings alone. For it is wisdom that makes knowledge effective.

As the hours of nightfall pass, the twilight forms. Slowly the rays of the sun begin to shine across the wilderness. A heavy dew sparkles in the brightness of the new day. Everything appears more radiant and the moisture enriches the beautiful colors of the flora.

The air is fresh when Jason awakes. However there is an unusual silence throughout the woodland. Nevertheless in the coolness he feels the pangs of hunger and gives thought to a hunt. Although as he spreads his wings to ascend, he surprisingly notices a fish lying beside him upon the tree branch. As he begins to eat, his eyes rapidly scan the area. In the distance his vision fixes upon a perched white dove.

For a brief time the two birds merely gaze upon one another. However Jason becomes intrigued by a white glow transcending from the dove's feathers. He also remains perplexed to understand the mystical silence and how the fish came to be placed at his side. To Jason's astonishment the dove abruptly begins to chirp. Eagle! "Your meal is a gift of love from me." "How is that possible? You are a small bird incapable of carrying such a large fish." "Oh Jason. Although you have been tutored well, you still have much to learn. It is not one's size in life that moves mountains. Rather it is one's faith."

Desiring Jason's full attention the dove does not wish to be distracted from his intended purpose. "As I renewed your foster father on a distant sandy shore, I am quite capable of providing for you. However, I did not make my presence known to provide what you can obtain by your cunning. Rather I have come at the beckoning of the Great White Eagle to further your learning. It is your destiny to serve His will." "Oh, Sacred One. I am extremely humbled. Also, I realize in spirit that you are Jesus."

My friend. "It is well that you possess love and respect. Both are essential qualities of a noble eagle. However on this day my profound interest is that you acknowledge the message that I have come to impart. Should my solemn resolve alarm you do not be afraid. Rather be of courage and take heed of the importance of my intended meaning. For it is destined that the severity of storms will cross upon your wings.

Furthermore upon your wings' rests an eternal standard of nobility. Thus it is intended that all of your flights represent a commitment to love and life's most esteemed values. I must further convey that due to your acute sensitivity to feel things in greater depth you will endure an unfair measure of suffering. You will also find that much of the world will ridicule your beliefs. Although with soundness of heart, it is important that you stay your direction of flight. For in the spirit and symbol of noble flight you are a representative of the life intended by the Great White Eagle.

In your flight through life seek the grace of Heaven for all things. However be wise in your expectations. Even this world does not satisfy the gullible and misdirected. Yet know that Heaven will not deny you the treasure and blessings deemed in your best interest. Also you have free choices in life. Do not squander worthwhile opportunities by merely fluttering your wings. Prepare wisely for the tomorrows will come soon enough. Remember further to keep an open mind lest you restrict your heart from all truths that will be revealed.

Never in dismay, turn from the storms of life. In noble cause they represent the responsibility that separates eagles from other birds. Also, as Eric has taught you, never panic. To do so will invite your destruction. While all creatures experience fear, be not afraid. Remember that I will follow upon your wings.

Jason. Always keep a true perspective on things. Life is a blending of both sunshine and turbulence. Although the Great White Eagle does not prevent the storms He will strengthen your persevering. Throughout nature all life is a struggle. It was willed that only the strong prevail. According to this eternal purpose, faith is served. Also the young are better endowed to endure the hardships that confront them. Still you should be moderate in your pursuits and seek a balance of harmony."

"Oh Master. If great demands are bestowed upon me, how can I achieve a balance in life?" Jason. "You are an eagle. More will be expected of you than other birds of a feather. However seldom in life are demands beyond your ability to persevere. Nevertheless some goals are of a sacrifice more worthy than ourselves. Thus there are certain essential values and priorities to uphold.

Jason. It is not the intended way of Heaven to put a premium on material things or esteemed titles. Rather, the emphasis is upon the rightful pursuit of love and the blossoming of good. Still you should aspire to be all that you can be. For there is a time for everything and a season for all things. Pursue knowledge and broaden your understanding. Should an eagle neglect his queen in the pursuit of perfecting flight and lose her, what has he gained? Especially, when her heart guides the wind beneath his wings.

You have a sensitive spirit. It is both a gift and an expression of your caring. However because you care so deeply, the betrayal or loss of one close will increase the pain of your sorrow. This will hold true of devoted friendships as well. Although the bond of love is not unique onto yourself, it is not common to the world. For there are many who will come to scorn the ideals and values that identify your noble calling. Although do not hate them, or be quick to anger. Rather with acquired understanding learn to forgive.

Those who take flight from the Great White Eagle will never know the treasure of flight. They betray themselves in the name of ignorance and greed. In the midst of true friends there are no betrayals. However remember that real friendship like faithful love is very rare. Both are nourished by devotion. Sadly not all hearts aspire to nobleness.

Jason. By nature you are a lone eagle. Social interaction is not particularly of your endowment. Still you are not alone in soaring through the skies. Relationships are the foundation of all life. Form friendships but always seek the truth through me.

"Master. Please do not think that I am being disrespectful. However concerning good and evil is the one who steals an egg not a greater benefactor than he who has lost it?" "Oh Jason. Like Eric in his youth, you are so naive. You should not cling so stubbornly to the false values of this world.

Look to your heart and seek flight above the chatter in the trees. Listen not to the temptations that obstruct your wings. Regardless of the rationale or the color attached, evil has only the reward of condemnation. Hearken unto my words. For he that does not walk with me is alone in the shadow of death. Apart from the law of nature this also holds true concerning your analogy about the stolen egg. The price of a stolen bird's egg is a loss of wings. In retrospect it is easier for the one who has lost the egg to replace it than for the thief to find another without coming into harm's way."

"Master. Your words are of pronounced wisdom. But I am curious why so many birds bent upon evil seem content." "Jason. Why do you persist to ask rhetorical questions of such insignificance? They are not of your heart or purpose to tempt me. Could it be that in your youth there is a slight lack of confidence without experience?" "Yes. However I cannot relinquish a feeling of envy that wealth often comes so easily to wrongdoers. Although I beg your forgiveness." "There is nothing to forgive. Still I must wonder why so much wisdom is wasted upon youth. Have I not already answered your question? Hearken unto my words. I am the Way. There is no other truth or lasting happiness. Besides what good can come from the suffering and misery of others? Surely even you must know that the vultures in life have already fallen into despair. Is their ugliness not befitting the greediness of their plight?" "Yes Master. It is so."

"Jason. I am aware that you have observed the roots of the flora. Some grow shallow in rock beds while others penetrate deep into fertile soil. Only the latter will survive the scorching sun and the turbulence of storm. The same holds true regarding the nature of all who walk the earth. With misguided purpose they pursue flight in vain directions. Ironically the roots beneath the ground represent an intrinsic need. Too often those above the surface become entangled in evil absent of noble serving. Concerning contentment do not be misled. Even swine are content to wallow in a mire of mud.

If you are pure in mind and heart, your wings will be true to you. As Heaven is sensitive to your needs, be charitable in your treatment of others. However be bold and ascend from the lowliness of the forest floor far above the highest mountains. Rise above the restrictions of your mind, in pursuit of a noble dream. Yet never forget that the glory of the Great White Eagle remains the guiding strength of your wings. Lest you falter and cease to serve what is good and righteous.

Now I must leave you. However my spirit will remain with you throughout the tomorrows. During the seasons of your life a few feathers may fall. Although in spite of storms, some happiness will trail upon your many flights. In your serving of the Great White Eagle may you contribute to the betterment of the world."

Before Jason can reply, his sacred friend lifts and ascends into the blue sky. Gradually the Dove of Love fades within a cumulus cloud. Yet in his wake Jason does not feel alone. Considering his size Jason could have held the small bird within a single claw. Although, it was not his intention to taint holiness. Also apart from stature it is he who remains humbled. Such is the pure power of love, wisdom, and good.

During the moments that follow Jason gives serious thought to the words divulged to him. He is aware that time will not erase them from his memory. Nor will he soon forget the gracious offering of a meal of fish. In value and gratitude they represent the greatest gifts of his life. Except for the honored presence of the Sacred One who came to him in the wilderness. Only in the Dove's vanishing do the sounds of nature return.

With determined vitality Jason begins to build a nest on high. During the next several weeks he crisscrosses the vast wilderness until he knows every tree and crevice. In his youth he is both exhilarated and happy. Many flights during this period often last from sunrise until sunset. Ascending aloft he fairs as well over the sea as above the land. It is during this season that he continues to perfect his skills as a worthy bird of prey. However because of his inner sensitivity, he finds it difficult to chase other birds away. Although as time passes, he becomes increasingly tired of a steady diet of fish. His instincts soon surface dictating survival and that he establish territorial rights. During an occasional encounter he sometimes loses a feather or two. Nevertheless it is a small price to pay to ensure an adequate supply of food.

New feathers will eventually replace those plucked. Perhaps, long before the loneliness for his loved ones at the lighthouse subsides. Nonetheless as a lone and bold eagle the transition from nest to the wilderness has enhanced his maturity in a significant manner. He is also acutely aware that his calling in life has been influenced by the Great White Eagle.

Many other young birds in spite of instinctive urging have found a similar transition to be much more difficult. Often regarding their reluctance to leave the nest a mother has instinctively forced their first flight. Amidst their screeching and unwillingness to face a hostile world even nature knows the importance of a time for all things.

Growing up even for an eagle is seldom an easy task. Some mothers who have prematurely pushed their young from the nest must take flight beneath them. As the young eaglet falters from the sky they find a haven upon her backside and a return flight to the nest. In contrast the lost security of the nest can seem like a harsh reality. However it is the intended way of life. Certainly the alternative would prove detrimental and cruel.

LIFE IS A STRUGGLE TO SURVIVE IN A VALLEY THAT
HARBORS BOTH
CALM AND TURBULENCE.
IN A WORLD OF GOOD AND EVIL THE DIRECTION OF FLIGHT
CAN BECOME
MISGUIDED BY ILL-FATED PRIORITIES.

CHAPTER II

Befriending A Boy In The Forest

One morning about midsummer Jason is gliding above the path of a rapid river. The mountains are beautiful and only a small patch of snow remains upon the highest peaks which tower above the dense pines. From the riverbed on his right the escarpment rises into the lower level of clouds. How esthetically the rays of sunlight reflect the multiple colors of the bare rock. Even the rushing water of the mountainous stream below sparkles against the deep blue sky.

Jason senses an awe about the majesty and serenity of the magnificent landscape. He is young and alive. Everything is new to him which excites his curiosity. With vibrant energy he extends his wings in search of his destiny.

The warm rays rising from the rock bed lift him higher and higher. Gliding upon the currents of air he follows the contour of the meandering river. Aligning his wings to glide around a bend in the stream his keen eyes become fixed upon a young boy sitting upon a large boulder. It is an area where the stream broadens into an adjacent wide pool of standing water.

Again aligning his wings Jason begins to descend. Normally he would avoid making contact with a human. However he has been alerted by the emotional stress and sobbing of the youngster. Also he does not feel threatened. The lad is only eleven years of age.

As he makes his approach a short distance away the boy seems uninterested in the large span of wings that have descended upon him. But with somewhat of a puzzled glare Jason feels empathy for the pain that the lad's tears convey. Also due to Jason's inner sensitivity a compelling desire to render assistance develops. With a modified screech he gains the lad's attention. Initially the boy bolts. However he does not panic nor flee from the huge boulder. Perhaps due to his inner feeling of a shattered world, fear has been shadowed in obscurity.

Ever so patiently Jason inches his way to the edge of the boulder. Then by taking cautious steps he approaches the boy's side. Still overwhelmed by grief the lad does not look upon him. Although as the moments pass, he slowly extends his left arm and gently draws Jason to him. It is an uncommon gesture in a search for consoling. Certainly a rare incident within the realm of nature. Still it represents the beginning of a true friendship. Perhaps for the innocent love is capable of crossing many untried boundaries.

As the hours pass, a friendship and a rudimentary communication develops between them. Kevin's tears cease to fall. Also Jason becomes the first eagle in the wilderness to receive a hug from a very affectionate boy. It is a unique embrace that radiates both innocence and a genuine need for companionship. A oneness with nature is not restricted to age. However trust is more easily conveyed by the young. Perhaps because of their limited experiences in a hostile world. In any event Jason slowly begins to comprehend the reason for Kevin's sadness. Within the wilderness not far from the river stand two cabins. The one nearest the stream is Kevin's home. The other is occupied by two middle aged brothers of questionable esteem.

Kevin has never known the love of a father. However his devoted mother lives only to provide for him. She is a good person and sacrifices much for him. How hard she has worked to provide for his fine stallion. But recently poverty required that the thoroughbred be sold to the two brothers.

In life there are countless youth who have been obliged to relinquish animals that they have come to love. Indirectly the loss often proves to be a valuable lesson about life. There is little permanence in this world of perpetual change. Even Kevin partially realized the need for his mother to sell the horse. Still awareness and acceptance are two entirely different entities. Also parting is a bitter sorrow when fondness clings to the heart. However, Kevin's sadness is due to the cruel beatings that he has observed the brothers inflict upon the animal.

Although quite young, the responsibilities of a man have fallen upon Kevin's shoulders. Nonetheless numerous chores and his mother's guidance has brought forth early maturing. Also he has been quick to learn the ways of the forest. Yet the cruelty inflicted upon his beloved horse devastates his heart. Taking a small stone into his hand he strikes it against the huge boulder several times in a displacement of anger. Perhaps equal in number to the whip he has seen lashed across the horse's back.

As the days pass, the bond of friendship between Jason and Kevin deepens. It is also while aloft that Jason comes to observe firsthand the mistreatment of the unfortunate horse. In agony of such cruelty he screeches across the heavens. It is also within a realm of caring that he and the young boy devise a plan of mercy.

The cabin of the brothers is unfamiliar to Kevin. He is forbidden to visit the horse. At the time of the purchase it was expressed that it would be in the best interest of the animal. In truth the brothers have no appreciation for the sleek black that bears a white marking on the forehead. Also the stallion is of superb champion stock. Kevin had been awarded the animal two years prior. A teacher in the lower valley unknowingly to Kevin had thoughtfully entered his name in a town drawing.

If the black beauty has any purpose to the brothers it is only to drag logs. They have long operated an illegal tree cutting business. Frequently in their disregard, foam flows forth from the overburdened stallion's mouth. A heavy rigged harness and chains further add to a grueling toil that exceeds his endowed purpose in life.

Sadly the stallion is worked from sunrise until sunset. On some occasions during moonlit nights the task is unending. Often instead of being given rest the animal finds the two brothers determined to sit his back. Even they in their cruel misgiving are aware that his spirit represents speed. However Dasher named by Kevin even in dwindling strength will allow only the boy who befriended him to ride upon his backside.

The periods of drunkenness are the worst. Whenever one of the brothers would attempt to mount the stallion would heel and buck him off. His brother in mocking laughter would bring forth rage by reason of embarrassment. The mark of the whip would soon follow without mercy biting into Dasher's hide. Only when the brothers pass out from an over indulgence of whiskey does the horse find rest. Fortunately Kevin never witnessed this inhumane treatment inflicted at the cabin. However the abuse he saw in the forest became branded upon his heart and the agony would not subside.

It is clear to Jason and Kevin that unless their plan is soon put into motion Dasher will not survive. In flight Jason has observed Dasher's ruthless treatment and the deterioration of his spirit. Also the brothers have begun to hobble the stallion. They have further tied him to prevent his lying upon the ground. Also they have placed large bags weighted with rocks over his back. Given their evil intent the brothers are determined to break the animal's spirit and ride him. If in the process the horse should die it is of little consequence to them.

On the following night beneath a star lit sky both Jason and Kevin make their way to the brothers' cabin. Thoughtfully Kevin has left a note upon his pillow not to arouse his mother should she check on him during the night. It is a simple message. "I have been unable to sleep. Therefore I have gone for a walk. Do not worry about me." Previously Kevin had informed his mother about his newly formed relationship with Jason. It is unlikely that she believed the story. However she did not question her young son's imagination. Although in concern, Kevin never told her about the cruelty inflicted upon his beloved horse or the plan to free the animal.

As they near the brother's cabin Jason ascends into flight and Kevin begins to climb the steep slope along the south boundary of the property. It is time consuming and a difficult task. However it is the only blind side leading to the structure to avoid being detected.

If Jason is reluctant to fly at night Kevin is near panic with terror that he might be apprehended by one or both of the brothers. Nevertheless both rescuers are encouraged in heart. To them the mission represents something greater than themselves. In consideration of their devoted friendship neither foolhardiness nor risk seem important to their youthful minds. Rather in their oneness with nature the freedom of a distressed horse fully dominates their quest.

Upon completing his climb to the summit Kevin waves to Jason. It is a signal for the befriended eagle to descend to the corral below. Jason circles in a wide pattern to avoid detection by the brothers. He lands several feet away from Dasher to avoid spooking him. Although hobbled it is fortunate that the stallion is not tied to a post or weighted by bags of rock.

After making his presence known, Jason cautiously closes the distance to the suffering horse. Initially Dasher becomes skittish and begins to paw the ground. However within minutes he seems to sense that the eagle is no threat. Perhaps he also has caught the faint scent of Kevin's presence. Notwithstanding as he settles down, Jason begins ripping with his beak and claws the rope that binds him.

Meanwhile Kevin crawls along a shallow ditch that runs parallel to the east side of the corral. Eventually he closes the distance to the gate. The latch securing it is rusted shut. However as good fortune would have it there is no padlock. As he silently lies in the shallow drainage the moments seem like hours. Across the way Jason continues to rip apart the tough rope. Sadly in the moonlight the whip wounds of Dasher shine as a testimony of his mistreatment.

As Jason is about to sever the binding rope a pack of wolves howls in the near distance. Abruptly the rear door of the cabin bolts open. The two brothers step out briefly to investigate the surroundings. An eerie feeling fills the air and near panic gnaws at the courage of the young rescuers. Jason hugs the shadows of the split rails of the corral. His instincts tell him to burst into flight as one of the brother's approaches. However he restrains his fear and remains motionless. To his relief the brother pauses momentarily after a few additional steps.

From his hiding place Kevin observes the large framed man gulp several swallows of whiskey before smashing the empty bottle upon some nearby rocks. Thereupon the brother with staggering movements reenters the cabin. Kevin feels hate for the cruel man who has abused his stallion. However this is not the true nature of the young boy's heart. Thus his animosity will eventually pass like a storm in the night.

The cabin door slams shut in the same dilapidated condition that depicts the degenerate state of the two brothers. The vibration causes a lone kerosene lamp to swing to and fro across a small window of the structure.

The reflection into the night reminds Jason of his former home at the lighthouse. However the source of the light silhouettes neither friendliness, nor passage of safe travel. In passing thought he resumes the task of severing the rope that binds Dasher.

While tearing at the rope, Jason glances upward at the magnificent horse. In esthetic perception and appreciation of nature's eloquence his loathing of evil becomes enhanced. In flight he had gazed at the sores upon Dasher's back. Yet his sensitivity had enabled him to see beyond in recognition of the thoroughbred's quality of spirit. Also in renewing he senses further that the sleek black stallion will again represent the epitome of swiftness.

The rope is all but severed as Jason lifts upon the top rail. Dasher sensing as much kicks hard with his right front leg. In an instant the graceful animal is freed from the binding. Slowly turning his head and extending his tongue the grateful horse licks Jason with such force that the young eagle topples to the ground. Thereupon with obvious determination Dasher rears up and gallops to the east side of the corral. He seems to sense that the direction will lead to his waiting friend. Actually Kevin has only traveled half the distance when Dasher jumps and clears the corral. In near disbelief Kevin becomes frozen in place.

However Dasher in his bid for freedom has been careful not to bring harm to the small boy. Also his love for him is stronger than his inner desire to seek refuge far into the mountainous wilderness. With fond devotion he gently rubs his large head back and forth upon him. Overcome with joy Kevin reciprocates the love being shown to him as a river of tears flows down his cheeks. However their ears soon hearken to the screech of Jason who has befriended both of them. It is a warning of the imminent danger that continues to lurk within the cabin. In harm's way Dasher kneels down allowing the young boy to grab his mane and mount. Kevin is careful to sit close to the horse's neck to avoid undue pressure upon the open wounds caused by the whip. Also his lightness of weight fades in comparison to the harsh beatings inflicted. Furthermore the joy of freedom far outweighs any discomfort. However much time will pass before Dasher's wounds heal and his strength returns.

In his prime, Dasher knows the way home. Thus there exists no need for Kevin to urge him to begin the journey. Still Kevin is troubled in thought. What will happen when he arrives? For he is acutely aware even at age eleven that he has become a horse thief. Also life is not always just. Nevertheless he feels that in view of the cruelty inflicted upon the stallion that the action taken was right.

However some confusion perplexes Kevin's young mind. Fear begins to grip his imagination. He visualizes himself being taken to jail and Dasher being returned to the wicked brothers. No! He exclaims. "I can never allow that to happen." In resolve he concludes that if necessary he will flee into the wilderness back country. Still his mind flashes in search of other alternatives to such a drastic measure. Furthermore he does not wish to abandon his mother.

Perhaps he contemplates "I can relate that some stranger set Dasher free. I could also say that the horse broke loose on his own accord. It would also be advantageous to add that due to his mistreatment that he should not be returned." However deep down Kevin knows that he cannot lie to his mother. He simply does not wish for further harm to come to the thoroughbred that he has come to love so fondly.

As Jason circles in a vigilant flight high over the brothers' cabin a bizarre occurrence develops. The calm air broken only by the arguing of the drunken brothers fills with the whispering of a strong breeze. It assails the trees and pine needles. Upon the ground the fallen debris begins to swirl violently. In the distance dark gray clouds have formed erupting both thunder and lightning. Oddly it is a wayward wind absent of a clear direction. Yet there is little doubt to Jason that the converging summer storm will soon unleash a deluge.

To avoid the turbulence Jason begins to descend towards a huge hollowed out oak stump located on the edge of the brothers' property. Upon landing his thoughts of concern remain for Kevin and Dasher. He has remained behind in defense of them and would in desperation have attacked the brothers. However as the air again stills, he ponders his friend's protection from the elements.

It is an eerie silence and phenomena that Jason has never before experienced. Not even the chirping of a cricket breaks the silent calm. Nor does a blade of grass wave against the blackening sky. Even the human sounds coming forth from the cabin have ceased to echo into the night.

In restlessness the hours pass by ever so slowly. However Jason believes that the delay of the deluge has given Kevin and Dasher time to reach safety. Suddenly the sky lightens from the pitch black veil to a gray white mixture of thunder clouds. The wind resumes with a furious roar. It is as though the world is coming to an end. Somewhat fearfully Jason ponders if he will ever experience flight again. Not to mention if death might deny his destiny and day in the sun.

From a crack in the stump Jason can clearly see the brothers' cabin and the surrounding area to the tree line. He can also gaze to the east where the land has been cleared. Even to the road that gradually slopes toward Kevin's home and the lower valley. However, it is above the dirt road leading west, that Jason's keen eyes fix upon one of nature's most awesome and destructive forces. The huge cone shaped tornado likens in comparison to nothing he has ever seen before.

Dipping from the sky the tornado sweeps along the ground before periodically rising. It soon destroys the road as it moves along an irregular path. Dirt and debris fill the sky in the wake of its destruction. The velocity and forceful suction of the wind pounds against the trees whipping the branches in frightening proportion.

Against the partially lit sky the cone shaped tornado moves ever consistently closer. Although in an instance, it suddenly traverses the mountainous road. It begins to move towards the upper crests directly in line with the brothers' cabin. The roar of the wind becomes deafening. It is greatly magnified by the cracking noise of the large pines being downed along the sides of the roadway. Yet nothing seems to compare to the exploding impact of the tornado striking the brothers' cabin. It is in comparison as if all the thunder in the heavens had come to bear upon one single spot.

The force of the tornado against the cabin causes it to blast into a fireball of thousands of splinters. The bellowing smoke at great velocity is drawn into the twister. It resembles swift dancing fog lifting rapidly from the surface of an ocean. Oddly as the tornado treks to the northwest the cone suddenly rises from the ground and dissipates.

In the aftermath a cold drizzle begins to fall. It whips through the trees extinguishing the burning debris that covers the region. Jason is bewildered as he gazes upon the former site of the brothers' cabin and corral. Not a single trace remains. Nature in flexing her hand has wiped away all the evil and the eyesore that had been.

For a brief period Jason ponders in thought about the two distinct cabins. They were but miles apart. Yet one seemed to represent good while the other exemplified bad. He inwardly searches for an explanation of why Kevin's cabin still stands? Is it a mere coincidence or stroke of luck? Perhaps it is a purposeful act of the Great White Eagle? Or an interaction of evil bringing destruction upon itself? After all it is well known that evil begets evil. Yet it is also possible that the destructive force of nature formed inadvertently when certain conditions developed. Still it is puzzling to know that grace may have directed the force once formed to serve a positive end.

Amidst these thoughts the rain ceases to fall. Shortly after, the rays of the sun begin to filter through the clouds. In humbleness Jason graciously thanks the Great White Eagle for protecting his friends and himself through the violent storm. However in feeling of awe full understanding remains elusive. Yet to him it is conclusive that certain happenings in life though not explainable are much more than mere circumstantial events. Often given the nature of these situations all that can be surmised is our heartfelt faith and trust. Respectively a just purpose that works to the good of the whole of the creation.

Emerging from the trunk of the fallen oak Jason stretches his wings in full extension. Thereupon in the light breeze he lifts into flight in the direction of Kevin's home. The road below has been greatly altered by the trek of the tornado. Except for the felled trees and the scattered uprooted growth the path has taken on the resemblance of the adjacent wilderness. Approaching the small barn near the cabin Jason comes to view the nearby river. The swollen rapids rush violently near the top of the banks. However as he descends upon the loft of the shelter a rainbow begins to grace the sky. It symbolizes not only the end of a turbulent storm but the dawning of a brighter day.

Gazing downward Jason looks upon Kevin's mother staring at her son and Dasher asleep on the freshly laid straw. No doubt she is wondering with concern how long the peaceful reunion will last. In appearance she is old for her years. Also given the love within her heart she does not wish for the same toil for Kevin. Also not being aware of the fate of the two brothers she believes that eventually the stallion will need to be returned. But for the moment everything is right. Leaning down she places a blanket upon Kevin and rubs healing salve into Dasher's wounds.

As Kevin, Dasher, and Jason rest the hours pass by. However about mid afternoon the regional magistrate makes an official visit. He conveys to Kevin's mother the fate of the two brothers. He further divulges the obliteration of their cabin in the disastrous storm. Reluctantly she informs him about Dashers mistreatment and that the horse is stabled in the barn. He advises that by law he is obliged to verify her story. Although in heart, he never doubts a single word that she has uttered. With some hesitation she invites him to enter the structure.

A short while later Kevin awakes to a warm hug and a cup of hot chocolate. "Sit down son. Your mother has something to tell you. What you did was wrong. God has willed that one should not steal. Apart from this I can only say that the two brothers and their cabin were lost in the storm." Kevin expresses neither sorrow nor pleasure upon hearing the news. Yet the hate within his heart had dissipated like the turbulence when Dasher reached safety.

"My son. You are too young to understand all the details involved. Nevertheless the magistrate has informed me that Dasher is yours to keep." Tears of happiness begin to fall upon Kevin's cheeks. However because of their poverty, he cannot refrain from asking: "Will we not need to sell him again to make ends meet?" His mother leans near and kisses him upon the cheek. Then with a choked voice she whispers softly, "Not in a million years!"

As the weeks pass, Dashers wounds heal. He also becomes renewed in spirit through Kevin's affectionate caring. It appears that not even poverty can deny happiness between a boy and a horse that seem born for each other. Whenever Kevin mounts the majestic stallion the horse is sensitive in guarding against throwing him from the saddle. However when they venture across the open meadow at a fast gallop, the stallion's black mane and tail toss in the wind.

Often in the joy of frolic play Jason descends upon them. In response Dasher always heels upon his hindquarters and snorts with great delight. Frequently Kevin observing at a distance rolls upon the ground after jumping with immense elation. He feels himself to be the richest eleven year old in the world. A few days hence he is moved in heart while his eyes fill with tears.

Because of the confinement and mistreatment of Dasher at the hands of the two brothers he leads the stallion to the edge of the meadow near the tree line. It is a difficult and sad gesture as he bids the horse good bye. With a mere slap on the hindquarter the stallion is given his freedom to roam wild in the wilderness. Only reluctantly does Dasher depart from his young friend. Occasionally he paws at the ground while looking back at the lad who has given him so much love. However with emotional determination Kevin simply urges farewell.

A short while after Dasher disappears into one of the mountainous ravines. Sadly Kevin returns home. His noble gesture is followed by another week at school and the completion of his daily chores. Although the passing of time does not erode the loneliness he continues to feel for the black stallion. Still he does not search for him. However eventually he and Jason decide to trek to the huge boulder by the river. Again the lad is embraced by the eagle who feels his grief over the loss of a beloved horse.

By late afternoon both he and Jason return home to the nearby meadow. But even the pleasure of play is not the same without Dasher. However with an unselfish heart Kevin is aware that freedom has a price. As the sky becomes overcast, Jason takes to flight and Kevin sets out towards his cabin. A few moments afterward thunder echoes in the distance across the heavens. As the bolts of lightning intensify, Kevin begins to wonder if he might reach home before the storm unleashes a deluge of rain.

The tall strands of grass dance wildly in the strong breeze. Aloft Jason's feathers flutter. Yet in keeping a vigilance over his friend he will not seek shelter swiftly. In the near darkness a flash of lightning arcs across the sky brightly lighting a portion of the meadow. However in lonely despair Kevin's thoughts are not focused upon the approaching storm. Nor is he aware of the slithering mountain lion stalking toward him.

However the carnivorous cougar has not escaped Jason's keen vision. Aligning his wings he begins to dive upon the beast that has greatly narrowed the distance to Kevin. However he does not pursue at a high velocity of flight. For unlike the young boy he has dinstinguished another source of thunder from Dasher's pounding hoofs against the ground.

As the galloping stallion closes the distance he whinnies loudly and rears high above the grass. With crashing blows his hoofs begin to find their marks upon the cougar. In harm's way the assailed wild cat cries out and attempts to escape. However there is no relenting of Dasher's fury. Soon the cougar slumps to the ground in deadly silence. In triumph Dasher rears and whinnies before trotting over to his dismayed but grateful companion. With jubilant expression he licks the lad with such force that the young boy falls upon the tender grass. Thereafter he nudges him with his large head rolling the youngster over several times in joyful play.

In a meaningful sense Dasher had never abandoned Kevin's side. Nor had the boy forsaken him. The bond of memory is so enduring within the heart. Although Dasher had tasted freedom in the wilderness and would many times again he yearned to remain foremost with Kevin. The gentle boy had shown him such unparalleled love and kindness. With immense excitement Kevin places his arms around Dasher's neck. The unrestricted embrace so represents the innocent fondness that only an eleven year old and his horse can feel so divinely.

WITH UNTOLD EXAGGERATION SAILORS HAVE RELATED
STORIES
FROM SHORE TO SHORE DEPICTING THE PEACEFUL
GUARDIANS
OF THE DEEP AS DESTROYERS OF HUMAN LIFE AND BOAT.

HOWEVER IT IS THE COURSE OF TIME THAT ESTABLISHES
THE TRUE INTRUDER. ALSO IT IS THE NEAR EXTINCTION
OF THE WHALES THAT ATTESTS TO THE FIRING OF THE
HARPOON.

CHAPTER III

They're Killing My Whales

Banking his wings Jason turns in flight to his nest in the wilderness. During the following weeks he becomes lonely and thinks often of Kevin and Dasher. The summer had been bountiful and the fond memories linger. However besides these friendly reminiscent thoughts there also is a growing desire for a mate.

Considering his youthful impatience he concludes that life is passing him by. Still he yearns to share all that he has learned and experienced in flight. However like the seasons his day in the sun cannot be rushed.

As the weeks pass, his many flights over the wilderness and the shorelines of the ocean bring little relenting to his restlessness. His inner spirit is a compelling drive to spread his wings. Perhaps not in the pursuit of prey but in proving himself in life. For he has not yet found the answer to, who am I?

In part Jason's quest for an answer is not long in coming. As he rests in the nest on a crisp autumn morning his attention becomes directed to a cluster of aspen amidst the pine trees. Intently he observes the golden leaves floating like soft feathers to the ground. Slowly he succumbs to a state of slumber in which a dream or vision ensues.

The vision reveals a mystified cloud of fog. Below the waves of the Pacific Ocean are tranquil save for a few small whitecaps that intermittently rise from the surface. The air is also still except for a faint eerie sound of slapping water against the sides of giant buoys. Strangely a red colored liquid flows from them into an unending sea.

Within the perimeter of the slightly bobbing buoys there is an open center. At this spot two smaller buoys lie anchored side by side from the rest. From the distant darkness a lone eagle takes to flight. A disheartened screech carries across the heavens. The sound defies the blatant cheering.

Upon awakening from the vision Jason is extremely startled. It is as though evil has touched his wings. However as he trembles, the voice of the Great White Eagle brings forth reassurance to him. "My feathered friend! The season is right for me to will purpose to your flight. I might add that the vision was not intended to frighten you. Rather it was meant to heighten your determination and courage for battle. First, as I have seen to your education explain the vision that I might know if you are a worthy choice."

For a moment or so Jason ponders in thought. Briefly he recollects the old adage, "Where fools rush in the wise fear to tread." Although his learning has enhanced much confidence he believes that the Great White Eagle will require preciseness. To him it is indisputable that the Creator of nature did not dwell in guesswork.

From a perch of humbleness Jason begins to reveal his interpretation of the vision. "Upon the surface of the ocean there exists both light and life. The waves of the sea in promoting life, roll in unison with the radiant light. In the absence of evil, life thrives and the air is pure. There is beauty and joy abounding in the peacefulness.

Unfortunately evil came through a dense fog of greed that tainted the air with the stench of death. It tainted the majestic balance intended. Also it destroyed the tranquility which sustains life for all generations." "Jason. How do you explain the whitecaps?"

"They represent the dying waters of the ocean regarding the life being excessively harvested from it. The red colored liquid is the blood spilled wastefully for there are no buoys. There are just great and magnificent whales. The two in the center were but calves dependent upon their mothers.

The hurrahs represented the seafarers cheering when the harpoons found their mark. Great White Eagle it was your resounding across the sea that drowned the hurrahs. It was an expression of your painful regard for the slaughter of the whales. In message you were asserting that the ravaging of the sea must end. Thus the lone eagle ascending into flight during the night has been beckoned to serve your will."

"Jason. It pleases me that you understand with clarity the meaning of the vision. You shall be that eagle in the night. I created the oceans as a garden of food. A blessing meant to sustain all life. But a wayward vessel is menacing my whales. They slaughter the young still with mother and it is an abominable act. The joy of killing has already brought many of my beloved to a point of extinction.

I shall guide your flight to the destination of the whaling ship. Even as we speak, that wretched crew thirsts for more blood. Still they shall not perish by the thunder of heaven. Rather their fate will come from the storm upon your wings. You shall have even the wind at your beckoning. However be prudent. Your flight will take you into harm's way and I wish to limit my intervention."

Shortly after dusk Jason lifts into flight. Upon reaching a desired altitude he begins to glide along a jet stream. The autumn air is cool but the night sky is unobstructed beneath a bright moon. Aloft Jason is humbled that the Great White Eagle has chosen him for such a noble task. Yet in solemn thought he is extremely perplexed about how to succeed in his mission.

After what seems like an endless journey the mist of the jet stream gradually dissipates. Below in the outer bay the wayward whaling boat lies anchored. Towards the bow the vessel lights magnify the hideous harpoon

gun. It was mounted for the sole purpose of killing whales and it does so with violent effectiveness.

The huge protruding harpoon bearing gruesome barbs rips deeply into the flesh of the whale at an enormous velocity. In dire pain the assailed whale seeks only to escape. However the barbs hold the harpoon secure denying any chance of the mammal escaping. A strong rope or cable attached to the harpoon prevents all attempts to survive. For most afflicted whales in spite of being mortally wounded death does not come quickly. Wrought with fatigue in a fruitless bid for freedom they eventually drown upon the open sea. Yet their wasteful suffering will bring forth a wind of atonement.

In the whole of nature only man kills for greed. Also rare is the creature that kills for sheer joy. Even Jason is baffled to understand the random destruction of the whales. In their beauty and grace many have befriended man. Only in the protection of their young and when threatened do they become aggressive. Most simply churn the water in a turbulent manner with their large tail fins in warning. Throughout time many whales have ventured along ships in curiosity. Some have even allowed themselves to be stroked in bidding of friendliness. However many in trust have been betrayed by a harpoon sailing through the air.

With untold exaggeration sailors have related stories from shore to shore depicting the peaceful guardians of the deep as destroyers of human life and boat. However it is the course of time that establishes the true intruder. Also it is the near extinction of the whales that attests to the firing of the harpoon. Notwithstanding it is equally verifiable that in the splendor of the oceanic migrations not a single whale has ever learned the meaning of greed.

In memory Jason recollects the whales that seasonally passed by his home at the lighthouse. He is mindful that learning had taught him the value of all life. With similar thought he recalls that all life has a right to freedom. A whale can communicate sound for hundreds of kilometers beneath the sea. Yet he cannot communicate an end to his own slaughter.

Jason is slow to judge all humans for the wickedness of a few. However below in the calm waters lies an evil scourge upon the sea. In serving the will of the Great White Eagle it is not for him to question but to be obedient.

During the remaining hours of darkness Jason rests along the inland shore. Still his mind continues to race in search of a plan to achieve his goal. In collective thought each idea becomes evasive in soundness of the undertaking. His frustration mounts. In near panic he begins to fear failure. Although, in regaining his composure he asserts, "where there is a will there is a way." He recalls the words of the Great White Eagle. There will be a storm upon your wings. You shall have even the wind at your beckoning.

With immense satisfaction Jason concludes his plan from the wisdom of the message.

During the next four days the whaling boat remains anchored while taking on provisions. The lapse of time proves to be a blessing for the sake of the whales and for Jason to implement his plan. Due to their extraordinary intelligence Jason befriends a young dolphin by the name of Tobal.

Although Tobal's flight is within the sea he strives for the same nobility as Jason does in the sky. They both seek their destiny in life as well as a day in the sun. Also both have been graced by the Great White Eagle. While their friendship is somewhat uncommon the higher plane they seek in life is never aspired by mediocrity of thought.

Expressing trust Jason reveals his enterprising plan to Tobal. At first the dolphin is reluctant to participate in such a destructive venture. However, Jason is able to persuade him, by quickly pointing out that the victims are his relatives. Tobal responds by expressing, "I will be your voice and wings beneath the sea."

On the fifth day the whaling boat pulls anchor and embarks upon a northwest route to the open sea. The vessel then circumnavigates the southern tip of mid island. Approximately fifty miles out the course becomes due north. Meanwhile pursuant with Jason's plan Tobal arranges for several whales to gather twenty-five miles north by northwest of the island. The whales are to serve as bait.

The boat of medium class size steadily sails up the coast of Mid Island. Although, the island is uninhabited due to its remote location and heavy rainfall, the tall trees come into view along the starboard side of the vessel. At this location in the hunt for whales the ship's lookouts climb to their stations.

Meanwhile Jason has descended upon the island to rest. A short time after, he again ascends aloft. The whaling vessel is now due west of him. Banking his wings he slowly glides to a position behind the boat. His path of flight follows the wake left by the large propeller. Somewhat ingeniously he pursues at a distance to blend in with a flock of trailing sea gulls.

According to Jason's plan the whales are soon sighted to the northwest by the vessel lookouts. The old familiar alert soon resounds from high above. "There she blows!" In earnest the blasting devices are affixed to the harpoon gun. A seaman further pulls the pins allowing the weapon to swivel upon the pivotal mount. The burden upon Jason's wings weighs heavily. He begins to wonder about the success of his plan. With troubled concern he is acutely aware that failure will result in doom for eighteen whales in addition to a dolphin and himself.

Jason's plan has been wisely implemented by Tobal in positioning the whales at the proper distance from the mouth of the narrow strait. It is tantamount to draw the ship within this area that connects the ocean with the neighboring sea. Still it is a feat that will not be easily accomplished. The straits are bordered on both sides by high mountains known to be active volcanoes. Many vessels in the past have met their fate in these waters. However as there has been few survivors most of the sinkings have remained a mystery. The exceptions being explained by the shelling of warships attempting to escape the strait during past wars.

Jason has no worldly knowledge. Yet he seems to sense that the vessel will be reluctant to enter the strait. Perhaps his instincts convey that the waters of all straits are dangerous and formidable. But even in the wild he has observed a prey lured into a trap. However this is nature's way of balancing numbers in harmony with available food supplies. In this instance greed will be the enticement of temptation. Thus Jason is turning evil upon itself.

Gradually the vessel begins to close the distance to the whales. Tobal begins to chatter nervously. He can only estimate the range of the harpoon gun. Alerting the whales he begins to lead them through a path of the strait which he has previously determined to be safe. Not a single whale dives which would minimize the luring of the boat.

Initially the vessel pursues. However near the entrance to the narrow strait the captain orders the craft to a full stop. Then to Jason's dismay it begins to turn about. Feelings of failure begin to cause doubt. However with revitalized determination he gives thought to a battle not being over until it actually ends.

Given his youth Jason lacks patience. He further tends to judge himself too harshly. Certainly his plan is sound. Furthermore life has taught him that regardless of the undertaking it is wise to have an alternate course of action. Accordingly Jason calls for a second group of whales to be positioned further to the West.

This second group of whales consists of seven. Although mature they are somewhat younger and faster swimmers than the other eighteen. For this reason they have been selected due to the greater distance to the mouth of the strait. It is not long before the lookouts aboard the vessel also sight them. "There she blows!" As the boat comes about, the ship begins to steam towards them. But the seven whales abruptly turn and begin swimming towards the primary group. Meanwhile aboard the vessel the harpoon gun is loaded. A dashing pursuit to close the distance commences.

The ship cuts through the water faster and faster. Acting like a huge knife the bow spews water high upon the hull. In a shrewd maneuver the well-experienced captain attempts to bypass the whales and position the vessel at the entrance. However the seven whales swim pass the opening before this can be accomplished. Again the captain orders the ship to a full stop. Gradually the vessel slows and becomes still in the water except for the rocking motion caused by the waves. However the anchor is not lowered.

Meanwhile Jason is beginning to tire as he continues to hover above and somewhat behind the stern of the ship. Even the hours and distance of flight leading up to this moment have sorely tested his endurance. Nevertheless the task requires perseverance and he has not ventured this far to give up now.

Aboard the vessel a chaotic disturbance ensues. The tone of the argument on the decks indicates that the crew vehemently wants to enter the narrow strait. Even the tone of their voices expresses greed. Surely they are tempted by the number of whales beyond the bow that has increased to twenty-five.

For the whalers it represents the potential catch of a lifetime. An opportunity too lucrative to abandon. Also in their eyes there is little risk involved. In the air of this immense delusion the ship's powerful engines are restarted. Slowly but cautiously the vessel moves through the gateway into the strait.

To escape harm the whales begin to swim through the strait towards a neighboring sea of warm water. Watching over them Tobal attempts to maintain a distance beyond the range of the harpoon gun. However as the whales reach the eastern side placing the ship at midpoint a gunner takes aim upon a straggler. The sighting device on the harpoon gun bears true to the target. Although before the charge can be fired, the seafarer becomes an object of prey himself.

In a desperate move to save the whale Jason soars downward upon the crew member. His sharp eagle claws sink deep into the man's shoulder. The assailed seaman reels in pain inadvertently setting off the firing mechanism of the gun. Fortunately the harpoon and spiraling cable arching through the sky embeds deeply into the nearby wall of volcanic rock. Efforts by the crew to free the device prove fruitless. Thus the craft remains bound to the cliff that gradually slopes towards the surface.

Believing that the crew members have other weapons Jason immediately ascends in flight. His attack had both the elements of surprise and confusion. However as he swiftly climbs in altitude, shots ring out from the deck of the ship. Yet only a single bullet enters the path of his ascension. With a twitch of pain, two of his tail feathers are ripped away.

At several hundred feet aloft Jason rocks his wings to signal Tobal to begin leading the whales back towards the open ocean. Due to the narrowness of the strait and the need to pass close to the vessel the escape begins on the surface of the water. However the whales soon submerge and absent detection they are able to reach freedom.

Beyond the strait the graceful mammals of the deep resurface and breath in the fresh salty air. Soon after, the whales blow through their air holes spewing mist and thunder above the rolling tide. Observing the wondrous spectacle Jason understands more fully the Great White Eagle's anger over their random destruction.

To the men aboard the ship the magnificent beauty of the whales brings only an outburst of wrath. For them it is a missed opportunity and loss of fortune. As the great whales fade in the distance the crew of the ill-fated vessel vilify both the giant mammals and the Sacred One who created them. In desperation they attempt to sever the harpoon line that anchors them to the cliff. It is still their hope to break free and to resume the hunt.

In their thirst for a big kill the crew's gluttonous appetite remains unsaturated even in peril. They are in the culmination of evil parallel to the frenzy feeding of sharks. Even when speared, certain species of sharks will not break from their wild quest to feed. The inner force that compels the shark to feed is greater in a frenzy than the weapon which has penetrated its cartilage. They will even feed upon their own kind in such a lethal state. Although their own afflicted wound is no less mortal in outcome.

A story well documented describes "a thirty ton whale which was brought alongside a whaling vessel to be hoisted aboard. Before it could be hoisted, the mammal's spewing blood attracted approximately two-hundred great white sharks. In a frenzy of feeding the sharks devoured nearly half of the whale before it could be hoisted above the surface. It was an agonizing death for the whale, that had come into harm's way."

Jason vows that the evil whaling vessel still dead in the sea will meet with a similar fate. It does not seem to matter to him that the cable anchoring them to the lava rock has severed. As the ship begins to drift the captain orders the engines restarted.

Tobal had revealed to Jason the frequent volcanic eruptions that plague the narrow strait. Similar to the wind beneath his wings' nature now begins to flex a more turbulent force. From the depths of the strait boiling hot bubbles begin to rise to the surface. The pressure being released from massive craters soon causes the molten lava to spew with exploding velocity. As numerous fireballs spiral through the cool water violent waves erupt.

The explosions from the floor of the strait rapidly intensify. Rock and tons of water assail the sky like gigantic geysers. With cyclone force the waves crash against the lava rock formations that have risen above the surface over centuries. They stand like huge jagged figurines against the landscape. A testimony of former storms that have laid havoc to the region.

Torrents of water spew over the sides of the vessel onto the decks. However due to the large size of the ship in spite of losing some control it remains afloat. Also the engines continue to respond. Although as the waves reach colossal size the stern of the ship occasionally rises above the surface. The exposed propeller dangerously vibrates the connecting shaft. This causes an eerie and fearful resounding that echoes throughout the hull of the craft. It is a voyage of catastrophic proportion that the seasoned crew has never before experienced.

The storm's unleashing continues to batter against the vessel's hull. Yet surprisingly the structure holds together. In strength the infamous flotation bears the pride of skilled construction. Thus it appears to have survived nature's pounding elements.

Still upon a field of battle the tide often turns. With nature a final blow is always lurking. For the wanton whaling vessel that has spilled blood from one end of the ocean to the other fate awaits. In a last surge of violent force a powerful wave strikes against the stern on the starboard side. The ship lists sharply. However it does not break apart. Within moments the storm begins to subside.

The helmsman having been knocked down by the impact resumes his place at the helm. Spinning the steering mechanism for the first time since the storm erupted he again feels the power of control. Subsequently he brings the ship about on a course out of the strait. In disillusionment regarding their survival the crew bursts forth with loud cheering. However their boasting only exemplifies their wretched pursuit of taking life needlessly.

Although control of the vessel has returned to those aboard, they are disillusioned in believing that fate lies within their hands. While the helmsman continues to bring the boat about, a loud echoing sound erupts from the hull. The crew becomes alarmed as the noise intensifies and traverses the length of the hull. Initially they conclude the damage as minor. However the ripping and twisting of steel has sealed their fate. Within moments, water rushes in through the enormous gouged openings.

In a desperate move some of the crew members begin to lower lifeboats. However their efforts are in vain. Upon the choppy waves the small inflatables quickly capsize. Also as water floods the lower compartments the ship begins to list hard to the port side. Steam rises from within the vessel and the hot metal of the engines emits a loud groaning. Gradually the ship begins to breakup. Terrifying screams of men trapped throughout the vessel emerge. Others in a vain attempt to survive seek elusive safety on the rising bow.

Perched upon a shoreline tree Jason observes the tilted bow of the vessel slide beneath the surface. In the wake of the vessel hissing steam and sea water rises several feet into the sky. Symbolically it seems to represent a protest of the fate befallen the doomed ship. However it is the last.

Gradually the waves calm and serenity replaces the turbulence that had risen from the fathoms. On the ocean floor the evil whaling vessel rests upon a watery grave. Greed has sent the ship to the bottom. Although ironically, death has resulted from collision with the upper structure of a World War II sunken ship. The storm had altered her position when the plates on the ocean floor shifted. During the upheaval the vessel had risen sufficiently to bring disaster to another.

The records of man will give an accounting that the whaling vessel was lost at sea. There are no survivors and the cause of the sinking remains unknown. However throughout the realm of nature the screech of a lone eagle is a testimony that the will of the Great White Eagle has been served. Jason regrets the tragedy suffered upon the crew. Yet upon the wings of noble flight only a righteous breeze can prevail.

The wanton killing of the magnificent whales had wrought death to a ship and crew. It seems a cruel act to cause their demise. However on senseless hunts the flotation had harpooned and ripped apart countless mammals that had been ruthlessly stalked. Notwithstanding those whales on the high sea that had escaped detection by the lookouts can now swim somewhat freer and safer out of harm's way.

Certainly the sinking of the whaling vessel could be construed as the result of natural causes. Perhaps, the catastrophic sequence of both timely and unfortunate events. Reason might even dictate the sinking as a mere coincidence or matter of poor judgment. But to an eagle named Jason and a dolphin named Tobal, the sinking in memory will remain a flight of profound serving. Their flight has been guided by a sacred force known as the Great White Eagle. For He alone directs the wind and accomplishes the impossible in life.

As the rays of sunlight spread over the region Jason ascends into flight towards Mid Island. Upon arriving he is cheerfully greeted by Tobal's chattering along the shore. Until the end of autumn they share in the play and joy of the lighter side of life. The sinking tragedy had strengthened their appreciation and respect for the value of life. Now in carefree flights' one upon the surface of the sea and the other in the heavens, they race across the open waters. In their soaring the experience further promotes the true value of friendship as well.

With the passing of the season and the approaching of colder weather Tobal departs for places unknown. But warm memories' shadow and the formed bond of friendship will endure for a lifetime. Jason remains on the island throughout the months of winter before returning to the wilderness in the spring.

Since leaving the lighthouse and his beloved parents, Jason has rapidly matured. He no longer seems to mind the solitude of his lone existence. It inadvertently affords him the time to contemplate the events that have so recently influenced his life. He has found a worthy purpose and a destiny in the sun. However though sanctified, the glory that has come upon his wings has resulted from the clawing of one human and the death of others. Within his spirit a storm of conflict seeks resolution. Peace comes to him a few days hence when the first snow begins to fall. The pureness of the white flakes upon the land and across the sea appears to be a cleansing of the blood that had been spilled.

THEY ARE EAGLES TURNING INTO THE WIND. HOWEVER
THEIR UNISON OF MOVEMENT IS FAR GREATER THAN
EXTENDED WINGS ALONE.

HE IS THE EPITOME OF HER LIFE. ALSO SHE REPRESENTS
ALL THAT HE DESIRES.
IN THE WHOLENESS OF THEIR FLIGHT THEY SHARE ALL
THAT IS NOBLE IN THE JOURNEY OF EAGLES.

CHAPTER IV

Spring And Love Find Flight

The warmth of spring brings forth thawing. Also the buds form upon the branches of the trees. Amidst nature's renewing Jason has come to think of the wilderness as home. Also in the freshness of the season a desire is rekindled to find a suitable mate.

A few days hence in the early morning sunlight Jason ascends into flight. He has not forgotten young Kevin nor a stallion named Dasher. Again at a lofty altitude he glides along the meandering river towards the cabin. However after about half the distance, he hears the screeching of two eagles on high. The smaller of the two is a female. She is being pursued by a larger male. Without being threatened Jason concludes it wise not to interfere into a courtship of nature. Nevertheless he ascends on high.

While rising in elevation, his attention focuses upon the beauty of the forest. It appears more beautiful than ever before. Some snow still lingers on the mountain peaks which loom above the scattered clouds. How esthetically the white flakes sparkle in the warming rays of sunlight. Below the crests new foliage covers the slopes between the towering pines. Even some of the early wild flowers have begun to bloom.

There is a tranquility in the air. However the harmonious sounds of nature are suddenly broken by the stress in the female eagle's screeching. Gazing in her direction Jason becomes aware that she is not interested in the dominant male's advances. Also the aggressive eagle has put her in harm's way.

Ever cautiously Jason maneuvers his wings to position himself above and behind the larger marauding bird. Although he hesitates to attack. "Who appointed me protector of the skies?" Yet when he sees her viciously attacked he inwardly feels compelled to drive the intruder off. The large male eagle distracted by the flight of the petite and graceful female is caught unawares. Diving with his claws extended Jason strikes hard upon his back. It is not Jason's intention to injure the male eagle. Thus he does not sink his claws. However the startled bird is swift to seek safety at a far away refuge.

In boldness Jason screeches across the region proclaiming his territorial right. He further rocks his wings in gesture of the female eagle's well-being. Thereupon he resumes his flight towards Kevin's cabin. However in journey he is no longer a lone eagle soaring through the sky. Through his noble caring he has gained an admirer. Also in the heart of the young female eagle is the fondness that he will never be alone again.

The two of them perch in the warm afternoon sun upon the huge boulder where Jason had befriended Kevin. In the magnificence of eagles she is special. It is also her gentle nature that attracts Jason. Perhaps due to their compatible nature a oneness of heart soon embraces their spirit. Thus joyfully they find favor in each other.

During the weeks that follow the love between Jason and Nicole deepens. There is a time for all things and a season for all. Their many flights through the wilderness and over the ocean seem to reflect this caring fulfillment. For with natural expression intuition rather than an uttered screech provides devotion to every need. Never to part they build their nest on high. Also the beginning of summer encourages further frolic flights amidst the clouds.

Through blessing the two mating eagles find both abundance and happiness. Life is good and within the fanciful realm of their youth it will last eternally. It is as though the sky was created for them alone. When love is right, the treasure of the heart begins to flow. It is equally true that when the sun shines it radiates ever so brightly.

The tips of their wings touch across the heavens. Also upon the white sand of the ocean shore a oneness of silhouette graces both their love and flight. Aloft they ascend into the clouds. In the pleasure of each other they embrace the happiness of their season. On occasion while circling and zooming in flight, Jason drops a small pine cone. Often it comes to land softly upon Nicole. How much she cherishes his attention.

Jason and Nicole are eagles turning into the wind. However their unison is of a greater depth than extended wings alone. He is the embodiment of her life. Also she represents all that he desires. Within the realm of this wholeness they share all that is esteemed in the journey of eagles. Rare is their elegance that eludes so many over a lifetime. It is as Grace has meant it to be. Thus should a storm darken the horizon the radiance of their love will obscure its shadowing.

The days of summer pass by like a gentle breeze through the trees. However time alone cannot accurately measure the gift of their love. Nobleness guides their every flight. In the expression of fondness it is an inspiration for all who follow to appreciate.

Summer draws to an end. However the wonderful memories of their sharing will endure far beyond. Autumn brings a slight chill to the region. Although in the afternoon sun both Jason and Nicole continue to glide upon the warm currents of rising air. While nesting they gaze upon the golden and crimson colored leaves fluttering on the branches of the trees. The tones of nature appear greatly enlivened during this particular season. Perhaps it is the richness of their love and happiness that makes it so.

Jason is anxious for Nicole to meet Kevin and Dasher. She enthusiastically desires to meet his friends. The conveyed story about their experience together has warmed her heart. Therefore shortly after sunrise they ascend into flight towards Kevin's cabin.

Nicole is especially high-spirited during the flight. She playfully teases Jason as they follow the path of the meandering river. Yet in a more solemn mood she affectionately brings the tip of her wing to touch his. Although she knows of his fondness for her, it is most reassuring when he expresses his love in a likeness as never before.

Life was meant to be enjoyed. In flight Jason and Nicole are enjoying it to the fullest. Their love is innocent and pure like the freshness of a morning breeze. There is not a single feather of discord upon their wings. The storms of life have taught them that the moments are both precious and numbered.

While many birds of a feather prefer independence and time apart, their hearts desire only togetherness. For in their season there is only a longing to share. Also within the treasure of love their spirits have joined in the oneness of flight. Thus as Jason and Nicole gaze upon the river below where it moves the slowest there is but a single silhouette of a lone eagle towering above.

As they approach a bend in the river Jason's keen vision fixes upon a camouflaged man lying amongst a cluster of aspen trees. Instinctively he senses danger. Experience has taught him not to trust humans. However only good had come from befriending Kevin. Still he ponders about the presence of this intruder into the forest.

In spite of his instinctive alertness Jason is reluctant to panic Nicole. Still he recalls the danger which Eric had taught him about mans' weapons. He also recollects his more recent encounter when fired upon by the crew of the whaling vessel. It further remains that this human is in hiding. Upon alerting Nicole he banks his wings and descends to investigate.

As the distance closes Jason does not observe a weapon. Although repeatedly, he sees the man put a small tube to his mouth. As he blows through the mouthpiece the strange instrument emits an incoherent sound. Jason is perplexed to understand the repetitious pitch. However he gradually detects a pattern to the strange noise. It seems similar in relationship to the commands given by the captain aboard the evil whaling vessel. But if this is true, what possible purpose could these commands have in the wilderness?

With great concern he turns in view of Nicole. He screeches a loud warning. However she is too distant to hear. Swiftly flapping his wings he ascends towards her. Unfortunately his efforts are in vain. With strickened terror he observes a larger than average trained hawk pounce down upon her. In carefree thought about Jason she never saw the danger swooping through the sky.

Female eagles are usually larger than their counterparts. Yet her petite body bolts as the hawk skillfully breaks her neck. Perhaps she was mistaken for a duck or an owl due to her small size. Nevertheless as the life leaves her, her wings go limp. As she falls to the ground Jason's heart trails as well.

As a noble eagle it is expected of Jason to perform all flights with dignity. Even those through the storms of sorrow and tragedy. In purpose the meaning of the flight is always greater than the eagle. To this end Jason controls his grief and does not descend to his beloved below. Rather he ascends into the heavens placing the advantage of the sun to his back.

With fortitude, courage, and the wind beneath his wings, Jason dives unrelenting towards the hawk. Soaring with aroused fury he screeches defiantly that the trained bird will know in advance his own fate. Alerted the hawk fearful of a larger eagle banks his wings to escape. However as swiftly Jason with ravaged intent pounces upon his back. His extended claws sink deep into the hawk's flesh. Feathers assail the air and blood spews as Jason snaps his neck with a single thrust. The dead hawk falls into the rapids below and is soon carried downstream. Perhaps he had once been a proud bird. However regarding his training evil had come upon his spirit and wings.

Infuriated with anger Jason aligns his wings and begins to descend towards the vicinity of the poacher. He seems to sense that the greater burden of responsibility rests with him. Nicole had died for want of her feathers or to become a trophy. The hunter trekking to claim her has no scruples. Nor does he believe himself to be in danger. Rarely has an eagle ever attacked a human being.

However soaring with fury in his eyes Jason keenly scans for the poacher's movement. He soon spots him nearing the edge of the clearing. As the hunter moves towards the rocks adjacent the river Jason further observes the limp body of Nicole. The pain of his loss causes him to thirst for revenge. It does not matter to him that the poacher has a side arm. If fate brings death he will find peace with his beloved.

About midway into the clearing the indiscriminate hunter happens to glance upward. His eyes fill with terror as he observes Jason diving down upon him. In panic he begins firing his side arm while racing along the river's edge. One of the bullets nicks Jason's left wing. It stings slightly and a few drops of blood assail the air. However the wound is not serious nor does it impede his dive.

In vehement pursuit Jason extends his claws and attacks the poacher. The impact is so devastating that the man's blood spews profusely upon the rocks. Using his sharp beak Jason further inflicts injury upon the beleaguered human. As Jason lifts from the attack the poacher staggers into the rapids and drowns. His body like that of the trained hawk is swiftly carried downstream.

Upon regaining his normal composure Jason cleanses himself in the river. Grief tears at his spirit. He has lost Nicole. Yet he is also plagued by remorse for having killed a relative bird and human being. In the morning air he has tasted the sweetness of revenge. However the spoil is bitter. The pain within his heart will not end soon. Perhaps because he has loved so deeply and is so sensitive to the fulfillment of its embrace. But also in consequence he is acutely aware that he has displeased the Great White Eagle.

In the early hours on a morning so bright Nicole had accompanied him in flight. Now only agony shadows his side. In torturous thought he ponders if only their ascending had been of another day. She would still be alive! How sorrowful the "what ifs" and the tragedies that occur at the crossroads of life. They are inevitably bound to the reality of "what is." Also the pain of acceptance bears the fury of an inner storm.

While perched next to Nicole, he frequently nudges her. Perhaps by doing so he feels that some of his own life will flow into her. It does not. How precious are the moments of love and sharing that are so often taken for granted. Yet in their season they wasted not a single one. In the growing darkness Jason instinctively knows that he must consider his own survival. Reluctantly he slowly ascends into flight.

The remaining weeks of autumn represent a time for healing. Although considering his hurt, the wilderness no longer holds the same meaning. He longs to venture elsewhere. Eric had told him about the remote island where he had found the footprints in the sand and a renewing of spirit. In the desire to be alone at a special place where Nicole could rest peaceably he concludes his destination.

A light rain begins to fall as the sky becomes overcast. With gentleness he unearths Nicole and lifts into flight. Occasionally he looks down upon her. Given his caring even in death he is concerned about her well-being. As the raindrops cleanse her, he is further saddened. For in appearance he sees the beauty that has always enlivened his heart.

The flight is long and difficult bearing both grief and the weight of his lost love. Still he endeavors to honor the one who has given to him so much in their season. Gradually the gray clouds dissipate and the drizzle ends. Darkness soon shadows beneath a partial moon. Below the silvery water of the ocean glitters in the moonlight. Aloft a calm breeze beckons the tragedy of the day. However his inner hurt conveys that neither dreams nor wishful thinking can deny the consequences of yesteryear storms.

Against the rhythmic sound of his flapping wings that seems eternal in motion the remote island finally appears in the distance. How serenely the endless waves flow upon the sandy shore. Gradually descending Jason is most impressed by the sprawling beauty. "Truly it is a befitting place to lie to rest my beloved." A fair distance inland stands a young tree surrounded by driftwood. It is at the base of this perennial that he buries his Nicole deep within the sandy loam. Thoroughly exhausted he thereafter perches upon one of the pieces of elevated driftwood.

Believing to hear his name being resounded he awakens in the early twilight. Initially not being fully alert he believes the voice to be Nicole's. But soon the loneliness of her passing returns as he gazes upon the shore. He is further disappointed that there are no footprints in the sand. The agony of his heart compels him to take flight. However as he extends his wings he hearkens to the calling of his name.

"I am here." Somewhat startled by the nearness of the voice Jason bolts. His eyes soon fix on a large gray eagle perched upon one of the upper branches of the young tree. "Who are you?" "I am Alexander. Your father Eric once befriended me. Although in spirit, I have been sent by the Great White Eagle. Also while I am not worthy of the Sacred One who makes footprints in the sand I bear His love."

"Is it possible for you to breathe life back into Nicole?" "No, my son! The grace that you speak of is not upon my wings. Also as you have learned the Great White Eagle does not prevent the storms of life. Rather He helps those who seek him to weather them." "I understand. However did the Sacred One not restore life to a human long ago?" "If you are referring to Lazarus, yes. But not wholly for the sake of he that died. He did so more for the glory of the Creator. Thus revealing that the power of love and good is greater than evil and death.

Console your pain by accepting the love of the Great White Eagle. Know through acceptance that all life of this world is mortal. I sense that your understanding Jason has already conveyed this wisdom. For you are acutely aware of the true meaning and importance of why the moments are precious. Nevertheless Nicole is alive. She is spiritually of a splendor that transcends all suffering on this earth. Someday you will join her in the ecstasy of all flight. Believe in my words as my own spirit and wings have experienced the same and long to return."

"Should I accept the truth of eternal bliss would it not be better to escape this imperfect world and crash myself onto the rocks? For without Nicole, life upon the earth no longer has meaning to me." "No Jason! The wisdom of the Great White Eagle is greater than our own. You must trust in Him. There is a reason for all things. Just as in parallel, you have learned about a season for all things.

It is not your time. Life is a blessing. A relationship of profound value linked to all living things. Think of it as an interacting chain. Nature nourishes. Yet she also extracts to provide for those strong enough to survive. It is a measure of balancing to maintain life through the ages. May I remind you that upon your wings rests an eternal standard. Your serving represents an aspiration for all eaglets to follow. As a noble eagle you have an obligation of responsibility to benefit all life.

Certainly life is difficult. I cannot make your pain go away. Perhaps all that anyone can do is to attempt to console. Even the gesture of expressing that I am here if you need me can be comforting. The loss of love causes great pain. However the presence of it can bring healing.

In spite of your grief the winds of time will abate your hurt. Be patient and resume flight. Self pity and isolation will only add misery and prolong the healing process. Nor should you allow yourself to become bitter. Remember that negative experiences arising from the past can jeopardize the happiness of days to come. Certainly there is a time for mourning. However keep abreast of a true perspective as other seasons await you. As Nicole enriched your life, cherish the sharing. Let those precious moments in memory sustain you in continued flight. For her loving spirit remains alive within your heart.

The Great White Eagle is pleased with your serving. Also all things are forgiven. Still I caution against bitterness as you quickened to anger. Although in your sorrow, I will say little more. Except I wish to convey that a gift from the Great White Eagle awaits you." "Alexander! You have exceeded my message." "I beg your forgiveness Creator." Somewhat bewildered Jason next observes Alexander gradually fade from his perch in the tree.

Jason feels somewhat consoled through the love of the Great White Eagle. He has also found caring from Alexander. With profound understanding he further appreciates the endearment of friendship between Alexander and Eric. In this thoughtfulness the hurt of his loss is not curtailed. However the sorrow has become bearable.

In the freshness of the morning air Jason lifts from his perch on the driftwood. He comes to rest by Nicole's side. A moment after a small pine cone falls from a nearby conifer. Taking it into his beak he drops it gently over her as he had so many times before in playful flight. Thereupon with immense inner pain he looks upward and screeches across the heavens that all might know of his agony. In the silent wake Jason expresses his love and bids Nicole farewell. He then plucks a white feather and plants it next to the pine cone in feeling of endearment. It further expresses a territorial message that she is guarded in rest.

Ascending in flight Jason is distracted in thought by some chattering near the shoreline. It is Tobal. "Do not leave my friend. I have traveled a long way to provide you with a meal of fish." Jason is grateful for Tobal's presence. He also concludes his companion in a time of need to be the gift referred to by Alexander.

The loss of Nicole has tempered Jason's appetite. However due to Tobal's insistence he reluctantly consumes the fish laid upon the sand. "How did you find me?" "Jason! Do you not believe that I have informative relatives throughout the sea? Why do you doubt me? Oh all right. It seems that we have a mutual friend in the form of a large gray eagle.

Come my friend. Although I hold empathy for your loss it is time for us to leave this island." A part of Jason wishes to remain forever. However he senses the importance of healing in Tobal's words. Ascending in flight Jason glances back upon Nicole's resting place. He is pleasantly surprised. A gleaming White Dove is perched upon a nearby twig. He is grateful that his beloved lies within the wings of a sacred fold.

Larry Slauson

MY FORTUNE LIES WITHIN YOUR FRIENDSHIP. I
CHERISH YOUR ALLEGIANCE AND SUPPORT THROUGH
THE STORMS OF LIFE. I ALSO HOLD SACRED OUR
TIME TOGETHER BENEATH THE SUN.

CHAPTER V

The Stalking Of An Eagle

As Tobal swims upon the surface of the sea Jason follows in his wake overhead. The caring dolphin senses that his eagle friend will not be at peace anytime soon. Therefore to prevent his vulnerability in the wilderness he directs their journey to Mid Island.

Gradually the crisp autumn air begins to warm. Below, the blue of the ocean reflects a deeper shade. The rays of sunlight seem to bring forth all the colors of the season with heightened vividness. Is this actually so? Jason ponders. Perhaps it is only my inner relief of being alive. Still it does not seem fair that I have been spared while Nicole perished. There is so little justice in this world. Reality can be so cruel. I can but wonder if might makes right. Certainly my own action in attacking the poacher and causing his demise is of questionable concern.

I control my wings but not the wind beneath them. The span is great and my claws are powerful. Still the choice of using them for good or for evil is mine. The feeling of hate and revenge is so detrimental. Surely I must find strength through healing as the seeds of bitterness have taken root within my spirit. I feel such loneliness. How could Nicole abandon me? No. It was not her fault. It is wrong for me to think negative thoughts.

If pity has rained upon my heart I must align my wings and ascend above the clouds of sorrow. However it is not wrong to feel grief. A time for mourning has been set aside. Yet I must be mindful that the needs of the living are greater than those who have passed on. Also in purpose the flight remains greater than the eagle."

Within a turbulence of agony Jason has become lost from the world about him. However, he is attempting to persevere and his maturity will grow in the process. It is an endeavoring to survive. While neither thoughts nor screeches of pain can bring an abrupt end to a storm of hurt he is learning the composure of a noble eagle. Also he is warmed in memory by the fondness shared with Nicole.

In these thoughts the distance to Mid Island passes quickly. Below the bright colors of the foliage cover the region and the white sand sparkles along the shore. Although the area is not home it represents a familiar nesting place. As the sun sets low on the horizon the two companions descend upon the island. Tobal procures food and thereafter they seek much needed rest. However Jason stirs frequently through the night. Perhaps yet another storm is brewing to give test to his wings.

213

Becoming more alert on the following day it occurs to Jason that Tobal is acting somewhat strange. But when questioned the prudent dolphin simply denies that anything is awry. However he is privately aware that danger awaits Jason in the wilderness. Knowing that Jason is still grieving he intends to delay his friends return to that area. Thus at least for a day the two of them engage in frolic play beneath an unusual warm autumn sun.

Both are committed to each other and the continued serving of noble flight.

Nevertheless Tobal is obliged to divulge to Jason that again he has come into harm's way. Reluctantly he expresses that some of the local townsmen have branded him an outlaw eagle. The township in the lower wilderness valley upon retrieving the poacher's body determined that his death had been caused by the claws of a large bird. In haste and with vengeful intent the unlawful action of the poacher has been overlooked. Ultimately drunkenness has exacted a drastic measure to rid the forest area of all eagles. Hence a hunting excursion has combed much of the wilderness each day.

"Tobal. It is a terrible thing that other eagles will suffer because of me. There must be a way to avoid such a catastrophe. I must think." For a long while, Jason perches silently staring out to sea. Nearby Tobal patiently awaits for a plan that will put the odds upon his friend's wings.

Breaking the calm Jason reveals his proposed strategy. "My friend the risks will be grave. Also because of my wrongful deed in attacking the hunter it is unlikely that any assistance can be expected from the Great White Eagle. Certainly there is remorse within my heart. Although if Nicole was alive I cannot say that I would not do the same again."

"Jason. Through you I have found the true meaning of friendship. I know no eagle more noble than yourself. Your notable difference has inspired many birds of a feather. Even the whales that we saw today have continued life because of you. Do we not have the instinctive right to protect ourselves and our love ones?"

"Tobal. My fortune lies within your friendship. I cherish your allegiance and support through the storms of life. Also I hold our time together sacred beneath the sun. But my dear friend I sense your bitterness towards man growing in the tide of my threatened flight. Still considering your concern for me, I remain humbled. Let us both remember that the message of love is for all life. Nevertheless we cannot avoid this confrontation. Therefore we shall not attempt to escape into the night. Rather we will turn into the wind and give battle."

Early the next morning as the sun peaks over the horizon Jason and Tobal venture towards the wilderness. The waves of the sea are choppy. Also a strong breeze blows aloft. Jason attempts to maintain a normal composure. However he is wrought with anger. Still he flaps his wings in the direction of harm's way.

According to his plan Jason screeches to Tobal before ascending to a higher plane. Thereupon he turns in flight towards the vicinity of the nest that he and Nicole shared. He is aware that the hunters will congregate upon this elevation known as the Domain of Eagles. At this locale he spreads his wings and begins to glide in a circular pattern on the rising currents of warm air.

The other eagles have abandoned their nests. Perhaps they were frighten off by gunshots. Scanning the area with his keen vision Jason detects no trace of any birds upon the ground. He is relieved. However, there is no way to determine if a wounded eagle has flown over the edge of the escarpment and perished at sea. Although quite unexpectedly, he sees a young eaglet far below in the distance flying towards one of the nests. Apparently it wants to return to the security of a once tranquil abode. Jason does not wish to be cruel. However for the eaglets' safety he screeches a loud warning of territorial right. The alerted eaglet not wishing to contest with a mature eagle swiftly abandons the mountainous area. Eventually he will return.

The hours pass uneventfully. But early into the afternoon Jason sights a man stalking up the side of the mountainous slope. Almost instantly the familiar sounds of the forest cease to an eerie stillness. Jason senses that the hunter is not alone. Aligning his wings he descends in altitude to scan the dense underbrush and standing trees. Leveling in flight he spots eleven additional hunters. Slowly but cautiously using the camouflage of the terrain they are advancing towards the crest.

To entice his pursuers Jason glides lower. However he remains well out of range of their weapons. Thereupon he aligns his wings initiating a circular pattern of flight. Closer and closer he moves in direction towards the edge of the escarpment and the ocean waters. The hunters aware of his presence continue to parallel his every movement.

As the hours pass, the ordeal becomes a battle of nerves for both hunters and prey alike. The terrain is extremely rugged and the thick underbrush impedes the pursuers. Aloft while rising upon the warm currents and keeping a vigilance on all twelve stalkers, Jason becomes plagued by fatigue.

In a surprise move Jason observes three of the hunters begin to retreat from the mountain. He is perplexed to understand why? Nevertheless he is not disillusioned in believing that their slow departure has ended the threat of danger. Nor is he blind to the flanking movement of two other hunters that are attempting to reach the edge of the cliff.

It appears obvious that the maneuver is a trap to catch him in a crossfire. To counter his pursuers flanking movement Jason descends even lower. He breaks from the circular pattern of flight and begins to zigzag. It is a calculated risk. He now is a more potential target along a broad line.

Late in the afternoon the edge of the escarpment comes into view. The two flanking hunters are well approaching their selected point of advantage. At this critical moment Jason bolsters his strength to attempt an escape flight over the sea. There is no time for him to ascend in altitude. Also he must rely upon swiftness to elude the seven pursuers approaching from the opposite direction.

With his life in the balance Jason rapidly begins to flap his wings. In seconds he will be within range of the two hunters lying concealed in ambush. They are perpendicular to his escape path to the sea. His wing muscles begin to ache as if they were being torn from his body. Still he endeavors to reach a speed of flight that few eagles dare. His heart pounds for that second burst of energy. He is in harm's way about to fly through a gauntlet maze of OO magnum buckshot.

Blood rushes through his veins like the rapids of a river to replenish the oxygen being consumed by the momentum of his flight. The pain is excruciating and at optimum flapping his wings can deliver no additional velocity. Yet with dire determination he zooms into the field of gunfire. In an instance he hearkens to the thunderous resounding coming forth from the muzzles.

A barrage of buckshot whizzes upward at a terrifying speed. However in the shadow of death he traverses unharmed past the edge of the cliff over the ocean. The two concealed hunters rapidly race across the escarpment firing additional shells. Believing that he has reached a safe haven Jason gradually reduces the speed of his flight. It is a consequential mistake. As the final shots echo against the walls of the cliff his left wing stings and grows limp.

Soon the irregular flapping of his wings causes him to spiral slowly downward towards the surface of the sea. Upon the escarpment the two hunters cheer. In defiance and drunkenness they celebrate their achieved vengeance. However it is a deplorable injustice absent of compassion. Meanwhile Jason in dire pain has come to float upon the calm waters. To the stalkers it is a befitting fate. Although only wounded, the lone eagle will soon drown or be consumed by a scavenging shark.

A few moments hence the sun begins to dip beneath the horizon. A short while after the twilight forms spreading darkness over the region. It signals the near end of another day. Yet in the lingering rays of sunlight upon the scattered clouds the hunters depart.

As the chilly waves spew over Jason exposure begins to take a toll. He tucks his head beneath his unimpaired wing to avoid drowning. It brings some comfort. However it does not alleviate the pain of his wound. Nor does it lessen his distress that soon a roaming shark will find him. Bobbing incessantly in the water his fanned tail feathers shine in the moonlight. Still they are not a beacon in the night that will guide Tobal to him.

In the frigid water he begins to numb. Attempts to lift into flight are in vain. He further fears for Tobal. In desperation he spreads his wings to bolster himself over the tide to reach shore. His efforts are futile and he is merely hurled haphazardly about.

In the near freezing temperature the warm colors of autumn have become hostile. Also his agonizing flight over the forest has exacted a tremendous amount of energy. Now the elements take an even greater toll. Unless rescue comes soon he will perish. Gradually he succumbs to sleep.

In dreams of happy flights with Nicole the Noble Eagle finds peace. The pain and violence of life's storms begin to fade. In a tragic sense he appears almost pleased that his journey has ended. Often in life the best laid plans do not always prevail.

A rhythmic pain in Jason's side causes him to regain consciousness. Poking his head out from beneath his wing he is greatly startled. Floating nearby is a water soaked tree. Apparently the choppy sea of the day before had caused it to uproot along the edge of the shore. Stabilized in the water by the branches Jason extends his claws and retrieves himself onto a dry limb.

Also to Jason's surprise the tide has changed and he is much closer to shore. With revived hope he shakes the excess moisture from his feathers. Steadily the warmth of his body heat begins to return. Yet in spite of his good fortune he is still too absorbed with moisture to ascend in flight.

Directly to his front is the sheer cliff. The only sandy area lies several yards away. Still he has survived the night and is out of immediate danger. Furthermore the wound to his wing has stopped bleeding. Hopefully the morning sun will bring additional warming and a drying of his feathers. With concern his thoughts again turn to Tobal. However in the darkness of the night there is no trace of him.

Totally exhausted Jason falls into a deep sleep. Although he occasionally stirs, a peacefulness prevails in the absence of dreams. However in the early twilight an odd sensation of movement comes over him. In duration it seems to last a long while. Upon awakening he is extremely astonished to see that the tide has carried him near the shore.

However all is not well. In the shallow water not far away is Tobal. Jason's heart pounds with joy. Although his elation is short-lived. Tobal lies motionless in the water with only his head protruding slightly above the surface. Worse there is a deep cut in the upper part of his dorsal fin. Notwithstanding, his entire body bears numerous gashes. It is obvious that he has been mauled by a shark.

As Tobal lies unconscious, Jason gathers a variety of moss inland from the shore. He places it into the openings of Tobal's most serious wounds. He also puts a clump into his own injured wing. Still it is questionable whether Tobal can survive the temperature of the frigid water. In any event Jason is helpless to render further aid. It is well that the dolphin had beached himself to prevent drowning. But now only the benefit of the warm rays of sunlight shining over the horizon can aid the strickened mammal. Although as the hours pass, Tobal shows no visible signs of improvement.

However by late afternoon his eyes begin to show life. His head moves slightly and his body twitches near the wound. Apparently the moss is eradicating the infection along with the rising mist of salt water. Jason sighs with relief. Still it is near sundown before he awakens to his friend's chattering.

Jason. "Please forgive me. Regrettably I was not there when you needed me." "There is nothing to forgive my friend. Not all paths in life are as timely as we would like them to be. Besides it was not your fault that you were pursued by a shark." "Perhaps not. Still I want you to know that I did my best to outdistance him. He was so unrelenting. Nevertheless I struck him several times with my blunt nose. In the end he contorted and died before my eyes. Unfortunately not before he assailed me."

"Tobal! We have both experienced dire encounters before. I did not question your courage then. Nor do I do so now. You are an entrusted friend and a dear companion."

For several additional days Jason and Tobal remain on the island. Slowly but gradually their wounds heal. However Tobal will bear forever a scar from his near fatal battle in the deep. Yet in the struggle for food within the depths a vast number bear the marks of near tragic ordeals. This is also true of life as a whole. Yet within this storm both eagle and dolphin have emerged victorious. However as one turbulence subsides, another often forms, and rainbows are ever so fleeting.

With renewed energy Jason and Tobal bid each other farewell. In the wake of their trail, winter is rapidly approaching. Tobal has set a course for parts unknown. But Jason whose heart has been unwavering continues to long for the young boy and his horse that befriended him in seasons' past. He is also concerned that Kevin might be worried about his fate in the aftermath of being stalked by the hunters. Ascending into flight he turns into the wind in the direction of the cabin.

As he treks across the open sky he does not follow the meandering river. His heart still clings to the painful loss of Nicole. Nor has he forgotten with increased alertness the misfortune of being fired upon. Still the time has come to continue on in life. As his wing muscles relax, he observes the beauty of the wilderness below. His ears further hearken to the harmonious sounds of nature.

As he approaches the cabin his keen eyes fix upon Kevin riding Dasher in the distant meadow. With his wings fully extended he glides toward them. Then at the right moment he screeches his presence. Immensely excited Kevin waves his arm wildly. Dasher whinnies and heels with joy. However young Kevin not expecting the thoroughbred's sudden bolt nearly topples to the ground.

Jason circles the meadow before descending. Perhaps his near fatal experiences in harm's way has taught him to be more alert of possible obscured danger. However Kevin is not so cautious. Upon dismounting, he races towards Jason and embraces the eagle whom he loves. Dasher in a less gentle manner initiates a tongue licking spree that topples Jason head over claw. In protest Jason screeches and flaps his wings. However Dasher continues to ruffle and dampen the bird's feathers with his saliva until Kevin intervenes.

Until dusk the three uncommon friends frolic in the meadow. With great delight they bask in the fondness of sharing that had brought such bonding in the past. However for Jason the reunion holds an additional benefit. In the joy of the day his heart is mending. Apart from this Kevin is taller and Dasher no longer abused by the deceased brothers is much more spirited.

As the three companions stroll towards the small barn, the first snow of the season begins to fall. Upon entering the structure Kevin lays fresh straw for Dasher in the stall. He also prepares a special place in the loft for Jason. In his caring and articulate manner the young lad seems to sense that Jason will remain until spring.

The snow intensifies throughout the night blanketing the region. High winds howl between the cracks of the barn planking. Beyond the structure the snow drifts higher and higher. However both Jason and Dasher remain warm nestled in the straw. Perhaps their greatest warmth comes by way of an innocent boy's caring.

Several days hence Jason becomes bewildered. It seems odd to him that Kevin and his mother after cutting down a tree are dragging it into the cabin. Observing from his nest through an opening in the opposite wall he becomes even more intrigued. Through the darkness he gazes upon the candles and other strange ornaments fixed upon the branches. How much the candle light dances and shines through the window upon the outside snow. However his attention becomes focused upon the replica of a white dove placed on top of the tree. Although the meaning of Christmas exceeds his understanding a special love sparkles in his heart.

When not attending school or doing chores, Kevin devotes much time to Jason and Dasher. Apart from his mother they represent the world that he loves most as a young boy. Also during periods when school was dismissed due to heavy snow Kevin would frequently sit next to Jason in the loft. He seemed to find both pleasure and security by gently placing his arm around the eagle. In speech to each other the sounds are always incomprehensible. However their fondness always expresses great clarity.

On one such occasion Kevin's small fingers happen to touch the feather hidden scar in Jason's wing. He seemed to understand that a bullet had made the wound long ago. Yet in feeling a tear of empathy rolls gently down his cheek. Sometimes in life there are unique times when curiosity should be respectfully refrained. Even when communication is possible adverse results may occur. Trust is most fundamental in preserving innocent love and warding off past hurt laid to rest.

It is through trust that Kevin's heart denies the allegations against eagles. The local hunters were willfully wrong in their actions to inflict such harm upon noble birds. In anger he wonders if it was one of them who had caused Jason's suffering. It is quite probable. However, Kevin can only speculate and he has no knowledge about the evil whaling vessel. Nevertheless it is possible that his youth blinds him to the truth. Still through his trust he knows that Jason would never attack a human unless extremely provoked.

In the valley of the wilderness the weeks of winter pass slowly by. However both happiness and meaningful sharing abound at the cabin. Thus in their youth during a season of friendship the moments are precious. Neither the snow flurries nor the chill of air can still the whispering message that life goes on.

Absent of storm Kevin delights in building snowmen in the meadow. The head of each becomes a suitable perch for Jason. However Dasher, believing them to be intruders in nodding gesture always encourages their departure. But in their melting and motionless stance he simply gallops about the meadow in assertion of territorial right. His gait being restricted only by the depth of the snow. Perhaps his frolic is merely intended to bring a smile to a young boy's face.

A month hence the warming of the sun intensifies. The thawing snow upon the branches of the pines begins to fall in clumps. Icicles drip along the overhangs of the cabin and barn. A few days hence the grass turns green. Also life becomes renewed throughout the forest. The river swells with clear running water as the snow disappears from the lower elevations of the mountains. With esthetic splendor a new spring is dawning. It is further enlivened by the sounds of the newborn.

Excited in spirit Dasher yearns to roam beyond the meadow. He seems to yearn again to be with a herd of wild horses which run free. Although not confined by a fence, he had chosen Kevin over the herd in the past.

However on this occasion his going to the far edge of the meadow and shaking his head seems somewhat peculiar. Kevin is confused about whether the thoroughbred wants him to follow. Certainly he is far too skittish to mount. Aloft Jason screeches for Kevin to retreat to a safe distance.

Meanwhile Dasher at a slow gait goes several yards beyond the meadow into some lush grass. Then he halts and whinnies. Within moments a well-bred mare appears from a nearby ravine. At her side is a foal. As she approaches, Dasher rubs her head fondly. Thereupon turning his head and long neck downward he proudly sniffs the scent of his newborn son.

High in the sky Jason screeches with elation while performing a rollover. On the ground a jubilantly surprised Kevin jumps and shouts enthusiastically. He then begins to run energetically to fetch his mother. Upon returning her joy for Kevin is both tearful and emotional. Taking his hand the two of them dance about in a circle.

Only the foal is indifferent to the excitement. He prefers instead to indulge in his mother's warm milk. In the calm that follows all but Jason come to lie beneath the radiant rays of sunlight. He prefers to perch upon a branch of a nearby tree. The wilderness has gained a family that will long be cherished in the fanciful heart of a young boy.

Amidst the bloom of a rainbow of flowers, the mare and her foal accept their new home. Although they are free to roam, seldom do they leave the meadow and the security of the barn. The dilapidated cabin still bears the struggle of poverty. Yet it is a season enriched with happiness.

Contentment has satisfied Dasher's longing. However Jason's sense of yearning has not found such peace. Although he will miss his friends an inner restlessness urges a return to the lighthouse. It is an uncommon feeling as eagles do not normally return to their parental nest. Maybe he is driven by the tremendous love that he had known there? Also in spite of storms subsiding the turbulence often lingers within far longer. Perhaps he is merely searching for inner peace while anticipating that his flight will again cross the path of yet another storm in harm's way.

Sensing Jason's restlessness Kevin begins to favor him with his love. Then one morning he ventures towards the large boulder adjacent the river. He urges Jason to follow. However the cautious eagle is reluctant. Nevertheless Kevin's coaxing by waving his arm is too influential. Jason descends by his side. Reminiscent of seasons past Kevin gently begins to run his hand over his feathers. As the morning passes, Jason accepts the absence of danger.

A fair breeze fills the air with the fresh fragrance of the wilderness. The river runs clear save for the calm of the pond. Occasionally a leaf falls upon the still water. In their parting from the branches of the trees they seem to convey the passing of a season. As Jason ponders the beauty of the landscape and the value of life, he comes to observe teardrops upon the boulder. Looking upward into Kevin's moisture laden eyes he sees the sadness of his leaving. Plucking one of his white tail feathers with a slight groan he presents it to his young friend. The gift brings forth additional tears. However in time Jason knows that a smile will dawn again.

In the presence of love there is always good. Furthermore the kindness of Kevin's spirit whispers of destiny. His fanciful heart will eventually yield to the valuable lessons of poverty and the ruggedness of the wilderness. Struggle is also building the strength of his character. It almost seems predictable that in years to come that Kevin will devote his energies to the preservation of the forest. However far and wide his journey evidently the region has already laid claim to his heart.

Kevin cherishes the feather presented to him. Perhaps in part due to the pain Jason endured to pluck it. In gratitude he leans over and to Jason's unexpected surprise he kisses him upon the head. With a puzzled look Jason screeches loudly. However Kevin only responds amusingly while removing himself from the boulder. It is time to return to the cabin and Kevin knows that Jason's wing span exceeds his height.

At sunrise on the following morning Kevin gives Jason a final meal and a warm embrace. Thereupon not wishing to prolong the agony of his friend's tender heart by a long farewell Jason lifts into flight. Aloft he rocks his wings over the meadow in bidding respect to Dasher.

As Jason soars through the sky he is troubled in flight. He does not wish to leave the boy whom he has grown to love. He is also aware that he may never see him again. Still it remains in life that each of us must take journey to the horizon that beckons our spirit. In journey there are the inevitable farewells.

WHERE HAVE ALL THE EAGLES GONE. THEY HAVE
GONE WITH THE WIND. AND THOUGH IT WILL LONG
ENDURE THAT IN PREVAILING THERE WILL REMAIN
A GATHERING OF EAGLES, THEIR NUMBERS WILL LIKELY
CONTINUE TO DWINDLE. PERHAPS EVEN TO EXTINCTION.

CHAPTER VI

The Homecoming

Upon reaching a desired level of altitude Jason aligns his wings in the direction of the lighthouse. However after only a short distance in flight, he changes course towards Mid Island. It is a beautiful day and in the season of spring there is a chance that Tobal will be in the surrounding waters.

While gliding over the pines of the wilderness, Jason observes a rabbit in one of the small clearings. As a bird of prey he swiftly begins to dive upon the delicacy. However as he approaches ground level he abruptly zooms upward to his former position aloft. In gesture of charity it is a day of sparing mercy.

With the wind beneath his wings Jason continues in flight over the meandering river. The beauty of the landscape is spectacular. Still he is morose as he flies over the area where Nicole was felled. In a respectful farewell he rocks his wings. Life must go on! Yet it must be a joyous journey not one of mere existence. The grace of Nicole's flight in sharing had bestowed a treasure unto his heart. Although in waning sorrow, he must accept a renewing of spirit and turn in flight to the shores beyond.

By late afternoon Mid Island comes into view. Beneath the setting sun a light breeze sways the branches of the trees. The fluttering leaves portray a serenity that he had known in the past. Before descending he circles far and wide over the ocean in search of Tobal. Although his efforts are unsuccessful. As darkness spreads over the region he heads for the shore. He is extremely disappointed in not finding his friend. However perhaps tomorrow the result will be different.

There are many disappointments in life. Still there are also many joyous surprises. As Jason nears the shoreline he begins to hear the familiar chattering of his dolphin friend. His heart fills with excitement and relief. Tobal has survived the rigors of his environment during his absence.

As the sun dips sharply on the horizon the two companions feast on a meal of fish. Soon after, the sound of their voices carries into the night resounding over the surface of the tide. Only when the moon reaches high into the heavens does the silent calm of the uninhabited island return.

Tobal persuades Jason to remain on the island longer than he had intended. Yet it took little coaxing considering the meaningful bond of their friendship. Although the realm of their domain remains uniquely different they continue to indulge in carefree flights. They further share in purpose their devotion in serving the Great White Eagle.

On their last day together Tobal rises early and takes leave of the island. However he soon returns with his mate Amy and a newborn daughter. "Jason! This is Beth." "I hesitated to tell you before due to your recent loss of Nicole." "I am quite honored." "Tobal, there is a season for all things. I wish the three of you much happiness. Cherish each other and remember to make precious the moments."

In thoughtfulness Jason bids Tobal and Amy a few private moments. Thereupon he indulges in frolic play with Beth. Swooping from the sky he causes the little one to make several unexpected dives into the depths. It is in keeping with the ways of nature. For often what appears to be idle play, is actually a valuable lesson of survival. The two companions screech and chatter endlessly in delight. It is a joyous but rare occasion when the sea and the sky are bridged. Although nobleness knows no boundaries.

After a couple of hours Beth's endurance begins to wane. She and her guardian in the heavens head for the shore. When Tobal and Amy return, they bring yet another meal of fish. In the distance the lingering pastel rays of sunlight shine through the clouds. The end of another day draws near. In their remaining time together the adventurous times of the past are not reflected. However often in the peaceful calm the quiet moments become the most valued and remembered.

Darkness gradually spreads across the island. The sounds of the night begin to fill the air. In the moonlight the crested waves roll upon the shore. Amidst the splendor, sleep drifts upon the island's only eagle and dolphin family.

The silence of the morning sunrise is broken by a screeching and chattering of farewell. Then hovering just beyond the shore Jason drops a ball of fruit close to Beth. With immense delight she begins to push it about the water in youthful play. How meaningful the little things in life can be to a receptive heart.

Tobal and Jason through purposeful flight in serving the Great White Eagle found blessing of friendship. Their path of noble ascent enhanced a journey of gloried good. Their deeds became a culmination of aspiration worthy of others to follow. Also in their calling to harm's way they exemplified courage. Still they remained humbled.

In their sharing they had experienced the daring of adventurous flight. Through boldness they survived the storms to claim their destinies. When afflicted they bound up each other's wounds. Together they have matured in the ways of the world. Thus in parting they will remain together forever in memorable friendship.

Aloft Jason aligns his wings toward the lighthouse. It is a beautiful day with cumulus clouds dotting a velvety blue sky. A fair breeze over the sea forms a few white caps upon the waves. How much he has come to appreciate the magnificence of the surroundings.

Like the flapping of his wings the hours of flight seem endless. Perhaps it is only his excitement in returning home. Yet with only a few miles remaining in his journey he hears the frantic cries of a young orphaned whale. She is beached upon a sandbar located to the Northwest.

In response to her cries of distress Jason screeches and turns to the area known as a sanctuary for small migrating birds. However he does so reluctantly. "Why should I not ignore the mammal and continue my journey home? Is there no limit to noble goodwill? After all, is it my fault that she beached herself? Perhaps the fate of the whale is the will of the Great White Eagle. If this is true I should not interfere. Besides what possible assistance can I render? Certainly miracles do not extend from the tips of my wings.

If only, I could renounce my inner sense of responsibility." However Jason cannot elude from his valued and virtuous ways. Even the devotion of his faith compels rendering to the needs of others. Thus, he is mindful of his appointed role in life.

Upon descending Jason approaches the stranded whale. Fortunately she has not been beached long. She still retains much of her vital strength. Nevertheless the chances of saving her are slim. A plan must be formulated. Also in Tobal's absence a rudimentary simple message is essential.

Under the watchful eyes of the suspicious whale Jason lifts a leg and extends his claw out to sea. Thereupon with a discernible screech he utters loudly: "Very soon it will be high tide. As many sharks as I have tail feathers will gather to glut you." Initially the young whale fails to respond. In frustration Jason attempts other means of communication. However nothing seems to stir the stressed mammal from her predicament. Then in a bolstered stance Jason snaps his beak several times. Terror suddenly shines in her eyes as she gazes back towards the depths.

A moment after the whale vainly bolts to free herself from the sandy bottom. Jason, to escape being harmed, ascends towards a cluster of trees on higher ground. In seclusion he patiently waits for nightfall and the changing tide.

Gradually the sun comes to set on the horizon. Twilight forms and slowly the water begins to rise. The splashing waves bring soothing moisture to the dry skin of the whale. However as if guided by some mysterious death wish she does not attempt further to free herself. Yet oddly she occasionally glances out to sea in anticipation of the sharks. She seems to sense their ability to close the distance in the rising shallow water. Her groans also appear to accept Jason's abandonment. However he is perched with vigilant eyes nearby.

As the hours pass, the tide rushes in with a fury submerging the sand bar. Although due to the large size of the mammal and the dissipating waves upon the shore, she remains greatly exposed. Still she has become increasingly more alert and equally more fearful. Yet in spite of additional attempts to free herself the sand will not release her.

The water continues to rise higher and higher. It brings the hope of a bid for freedom. However when almost at the desired level, the tide peaks. As the water begins to recede, the beached whale exerts no further effort to survive. Perhaps because of her youth she has not learned the value of an extra surge of determination which so often when applied renders success. But in contrast Jason is a matured eagle and experience has taught him the ways of life.

Spreading his wings Jason swoops down towards the whale that has succumbed to rest. It is a silent flight as if he were pursuing game. Soaring through the sky the distance closes rapidly. Then with an aggressive loud screech he extends his claws and sinks them into the whale's head. In startled fear more than pain the female whale lurches back violently. Sand assails into the heavens similar to the retracting funnel of a tornado. It is all that Jason can do to escape the pelting granules.

With wild twisting of her body and frantic resounding the whale finally slithers herself about to the security of deeper water. In her rapid trek to the depths the gathering sharks become distant in the wake. Jason feels gratified by his deed. He further knows that the salt water will bring healing to the minor wounds caused by his claws. In time a sense of calm will return to the strickened whale. However she may never conclude a noble eagle as being less than belligerent.

Jason took no pleasure in resorting to an extreme measure to free the stranded whale. Often the mean does not justify the end. Although in this situation, fear became a positive solution. On occasion in life it is necessary to stimulate latent strengths to achieve designated and worthy goals.

Jason remains at the sanctuary throughout the hours of darkness. It has been a rewarding day. Still with a slight murmuring he ponders if the freed whale will eventually forgive him for his daring tactic. Perhaps it does not really matter considering that noble caring often exceeds understanding.

Beneath an overcast sky Jason again ascends into flight towards the lighthouse. In spite of the threatening storm only an occasional drop of rain falls. Yet even these droplets evaporate in their downward descent. How different he concludes his journey home from his solo flight into the wilderness. Growing up is not easy in a hostile world. Still with fortitude and the right kind of preparation the odds of surviving are enormously enhanced.

In youth Jason had found his place in the sun. Also destiny eventually came upon his wings. He had not ascended in flight in search of youthful glory. However the price became sorrow and the spilling of blood. Certainly those who have searched and striven to achieve the more noble and worthy treasures of life, have often experienced the greater turbulence of storms. Yet in reward they have known a more radiant shining and a greater sense of accomplishment.

As the rays of sunlight begin to spread over the region Jason can see clearly the home of his youth. Eager to see his parents he descends a few feet over the surface of the sea. He quickens the flapping of his wings. So fresh is the mist rising from the cresting waves. It is good to be alive.

In the distance the black roofed lighthouse towers high into the sky. To Jason it is as breathtaking as the sea. Nearby the magnificent waves crash against the huge boulders along the shore. Torrents of water spew upward with a force resounding of thunder. Although beyond where the verdant grass grows and the rows of trees stand as monuments there is only a calm breeze. It has been said that "one can never go home again." For in the days since, one's youth has been lost. Nevertheless Jason has returned at least in flight.

It does not surprise him that other eagles have neglected to ascend in assertion of territorial right. In spite of few birds migrating along this path all are welcomed. Especially amongst the grove of trees and the pool of sacred water that honor endeared friends. The most revered being a Pure White Dove.

Respectfully Jason circles the lighthouse before descending by the nearby garden. He screeches to give notice of his presence and friendly intentions. There are several feathers that have been shed upon the ground. Jason concludes that Eric has been instructing several students. Although on this day, only one young and attractive female is perched in attendance. Notwithstanding he is soon greeted by his elated parents.

His caring mother soon embraces him within the fold of her wings. Eric being more reserved merely extends a wing in a welcome home gesture. However Jason longing for his father's affection breaks from formal tradition and hugs his father. Although Eric does not admit it he is gratified by his son's love for him.

Jason is puzzled that the young female eagle has chosen not to acknowledge his presence. Perhaps she is merely shy? Besides it is of no great importance. If Jason had contemplated his loneliness no thought had been given to ever mating again. Yet there is an attraction about her that exceeds his understanding.

"Son! We have been expecting you. Also there is someone we wish for you to meet." For a moment or so Jason does not respond. It seems strange to him that his flight could have been anticipated. "Well, come along son. There is no need for you to be bashful." "Father. You always said that I took things too literally." "True! I have also expressed that all things will be revealed when the time is right."

"Jason. Your coming home is a rare quirk of nature. Still it pleases me immensely. I am a fortunate mother. Few others ever see their sons after they leave the nest. I suppose that the reason is just. Still I find blessing in this exception." "Mother! It pleases me when you express your heart so fondly." "Well Jason! Let us not dally away the day."

Slowly they walk towards the perched female eagle. She is eager to meet Jason but patiently awaits the respectful greeting of his parents. Initially Jason is slightly nervous. He seems to sense that the fondness radiating from her is for him. There is a loveliness about her. Also the look in her eyes reveals much devotion. Soon he becomes lost in her charm that eludes his understanding.

Jason's mother approves of the interest her son shows for the fair bird. With a soft murmur she expresses "this is Jody!" "I am honored to make your acquaintance. May I add that your name is most befitting for one so gifted with noble etiquette and beauty." "How very gracious of you to say."

A moment or two hence both Eric and his queen depart leaving the newly acquainted in the privacy of their attraction. It is a rightful match. A coming together of two eagles that adoringly possess to the fullest the natural qualities of irresistible harmony. As the hours pass, a sense of belonging grows and blossoms into the meaningful fold of love. It almost seems as though they had shared in closeness another time and place.

In the beginning of their season Jody expresses that she has come to him as a treasured gift. Jason is moved in heart. Yet he asks "by whom?" "A very spirited and faithful messenger on a mission by the Great White Eagle. He bestowed upon me a worthy purpose in life. A devotion that I have long yearned for in oneness of flight. Jason. You are my direction of journey and the messenger who sent me is known as Alexander."

Jason does not respond immediately. Rather in humbleness he perches silently in thought. Then with jubilant gratitude he screeches upward into the heavens. How much Jody soothes his loneliness. Yet it was never intended that she replace the memories of Nicole. Rather it is the natural evolving of love amidst a caring breeze sent forth by the Great White Eagle. He does not prevent the storms but in the aftermath are the mending rainbows of His grace.

As Jason and Jody ascend in flight over the ocean the ecstasy of their fondness trails. They are meant for each other and the silhouette of their oneness shadows upon the sea. As they spread their wings towards the sun their spirits shine of happiness. Upon descending in a gliding pattern over the currents the tips of their wings touch in splendor. The wind beneath their wings has found blessing.

As the weeks pass, their love matures in the sharing of both bliss and storm. In likeness the season of spring ebbs into summer. Shortly after dawn on a bright sunny morning Jason and Jody are aloft in a frolic game of chase over the sea. While flying forth from a cumulus cloud, a group of whales far below rounds the tip of the peninsula.

They are a magnificent sight. As they blow through their air holes a thunderous echo resounds high into the sky. There are eighteen of them comprising the entourage. Three are young and smaller. While approaching the lighthouse, Jason and Jody bank their wings to view closer the mammals of the deep. How gracefully they cut through the water in near perfect stride.

As the distance closes to the whales a strange occurrence takes place. The larger of the three smaller whales breaks from the others in the direction of the two gliding eagles. He abruptly dives. However upon surfacing she vigorously slaps her large tail fins against the surface. She thereupon blows through her air hole and comes to lie still in the water. It appears to be a strange mode of behavior.

Cautiously Jason and Jody come to hover in front of the majestic mammal. Almost instantly the huge dark eyes of the whale train upon them. Jody becomes nervous and screeches to Jason a desire to depart. However Jason is reluctant. He senses a look of trust in the discerning eyes below. Still he bolts slightly as the ruler of the ocean bellows a high pitched sound that vibrates the air beneath his wings. A heavy mist follows as the young female again blows through her air hole.

Jody further urges that they take flight from harm's way. Yet Jason in response merely conveys that all is well. He has come to recognize that the female whale is no other than the one beached upon the sand bar.

In a bold maneuver that terrifies Jody he slows the flapping of his wings and descends upon the mammal's head. The whale twitches slightly remembering Jason's embedding claws during her ordeal. However, she soon relaxes as he gently clings to her tough hide. Against the backdrop of the splashing waves a rendezvous of friendly regard is gestured.

Still somewhat frantic Jody again screeches for Jason to lift into flight. In acknowledgment of her beckoning he ascends aloft. However he rocks his wings in a bid of farewell before joining in flight with his mate. The female whale responds by slapping her tail fins hard against the surface of the sea. The water heaves in gigantic waves. Then the orphaned whale dives before surfacing with the other mammals who have welcomed her as one of their own.

As Jason and Jody approach the lighthouse, the Old Man and his mate are working in the garden. Jason assures Jody about their friendliness. She has observed their gentleness in the past. However given her faith in Jason's judgment she further accepts their good intentions. The two warm hearted humans are elated by Jason's return. In their presence he finds a certain peace. Yet instinctively his memory lingers to the tragic encounter with a poacher and subsequent hunter.

Time has aged the Old Man. Still he seems energetic. In his familiar manner he waves to Jason and Jody to follow. "Behold" he exclaims as they near the lighthouse. "I have built you a home. It is similar to the splendid nest that I fashioned for Eric and his queen." Jody screeches with immense happiness. However Jason though pleased is slightly reserved. Nevertheless he extends his wings in gratitude.

While Jody comes to occupy the nest Jason departs to the area of the pool and grove of trees. He so loves the peace and tranquility there. As he perches in contemplation he senses an inner urging. The meaning of such is unclear to him. However in trailing thought his mind turns to the sea.

How much the ocean reminds him of the whole of life. A constant realm of interchanging calm and turbulence amidst a vastness of beauty. It is like a caring mother's love for the life within her. Each species having a time and place within the depths to seek the essential needs that sustain life. Many pursue the light that shines beneath the surface. Others seek their abode within the darkness of the depths. Like the trees that shed their leaves upon the land, the mistress claims her dead. Yet as the buds of spring that form anew, she rejoices of her new born. In the past their numbers were endless like the perpetual waves flowing upon the sandy shores.

Jason is realizing the importance of pondering life. For its intrinsic value and in relationship to not rushing the seasons. While the moments are precious they are so only because of their timely and unique unveiling.

In the newness of a season Jason has found bliss. Still he chose not to divulge to Jody the sorrowful encounters of his past. However Alexander informed her that she might better understand. She in turn shared this knowledge with his parents. In purpose they are aware that the Great White Eagle will again call upon him. Coincidental to his serving Jason gazes upon the pool of still water. He sees the reflection of a White Dove ascending across the sky. It has a glow of sacredness transcending from every feather.

Upon concluding his thoughts Jason longs to return to Jody's side. However as he partially spreads his wings his attention focuses on a new seedling in the grove. He is moved in heart. The Old Man by Eric's encouraging has given honor to Nicole.

The next day, a summer storm unleashes its fury over the region. Beneath an overcast sky the incessant rains driven by a strong wind pelt the landscape. The heavy droplets crash upon the boulders and surface of the sea rebounding at great height. How clearly the gigantic beacon shines a path through the maze of torrential downpour.

As the rain subsides, a new dawn brings forth a rainbow's gleaming. In the wake of the fury the beauty of a calm summer's day returns. Amidst the freshness of a morning heavy with dew Eric, his queen, Jason, and Jody lift into flight. Aloft they bank their wings in an easterly direction towards the mountainous forest. Although the spring spawning of the salmon is over, several of the tasty fish remain in the lower basin of the river.

As they glide over the tree tops the river that divides the forest comes into view. Sadly the warm rays of sunlight shine upon the devastation of human greed. East of the river is the barren landscape resulting from over cutting and careless burning. However to their relief the western side remains unscathed in all of its natural beauty.

With their wings extended the four eagles descend upon the basin. The water runs clear and cold. But of greater importance the sprawling streams are full of dying adult salmon. By spawning they have served their purpose in life. As the eagles feast the stones in the rock bed glimmer beneath the silvery waters that drain into the sea. However as the sun comes to rest upon the horizon the noble birds again ascend into flight. Banking their wings they glide over the ocean towards the lighthouse that they call home. In their wake other eagles will gather to feast. For it is a time of abundance.

As the twilight spreads across the heavens the four eagles approach the lighthouse. They soon hearken to the familiar clicking sound of the gears that rotate the huge beacon. Although to them, it shines not as a warning to vessels at sea. Rather it is a second moon towering over their domain. Secure from harm's way they soon settle into their respective nests. However the gray clouds lingering on the horizon are an omen of storms to come.

Following a brief hunt the next morning both Jason and Jody visit the grove of trees by the garden. Nearby Eric is instructing an eaglet who had come upon the pool in the early twilight. The young bird is full of enthusiasm. He also appears to be an orphan. Eric seems to take great pleasure from the eaglet's quickness to learn and manner of response. It seems imminent that the Great White Eagle has given the youngster direction in life. Perhaps it is a preparation to lift the burden from Jason's wings? Just as he was destined to fill the wake of Eric's serving.

As Jason and Jody look upon the newcomer his eyes become trained upon Jason. Yet they soon shift to the chirping and the fluttering of wings on top of a nearby tree branch. As the familiar Pure White Dove lifts into flight a small twig breaks and falls before the distracted young eaglet. Both his eyes and attention revert immediately to Eric. In message he understands that his learning preparation cannot tolerate the typical distractions in life that so often promote failure.

With greater attentiveness Jason and Jody also continue to listen to Eric's revealing wisdom. Then abruptly but in a respectful manner the young eaglet exclaims: "Master! Master! Where have all the eagles gone?" "Son! Many remain bringing nobleness to flight. However that which gives question to your heart brings sadness even to myself. There was a time when eagles filled the sky like drops of rain. They graced the heavens and traversed the horizons.

Where have all the eagles gone? Son! Like the virgin forests they have fallen to be no more. The winds of time have blown them from their duly appointed course. However do not lose heart. An eternal standard of nobility continues to rest upon the wings of the devoted. Hopefully in time these same aspiring values will yield your rightful destiny.

So many eagles have been felled by humans. In man's quest to conquer the land and the sea the tide of their destruction has never ebbed. However several eagles have caused their own decline. They have become as vultures in their abandonment of noble pursuit. Essential sacrifice to achieve worthy goals are too often compromised. Few are willing to make dire sacrifices in a world that tempts of immediate gratification. Thus there are more birds upon the forest floor than those in number soaring on high.

The cause of nobility is supported by Grace. However this particular sphere is one of sacrifice and struggles in an upward climb of flight. Though the rewards are worthwhile most birds choose the gliding path of descent. It is less strain upon the wings. Even when the warm currents make easier the rise aloft, many in ignorance and laziness refuse the true wind.

Unfortunately the values of seasons' past are no longer deemed important by many. During the months of summer the flight of pleasure often takes precedence. Too little regard is given for the coming of winter. Laxity of preparing for the future will fail to sustain during times of scarcity and cold of storm.

Time has brought change. Yet not all who share the world are responsible caretakers. The attributes of noble character must be preserved to promote the value of all life. Thus in spite of feathers shedding the proven qualities that enhance the betterment of life must be perpetual.

Frequently those who speak of change are selfish in heart. Often they are unwise to the ways of nature. Certainly there is imperfection in the world and some change has merit. However, the winds of life blow in many directions. Not all are favorable of positive ends. Also there are those who value the feathers of eagles more than the bird.

My young student. So many eagles have vanished with the wind. Although several flocks remain in prevailing to gather about the continents vast numbers will dwindle further. Amidst the encroachment of man the eagle is no longer secure. As the links of the chain that complement various types of life are broken the shadow of extinction will exact an increasing toll.

When a forest is ruthlessly felled it is not just the trees that are lost. The animal life, beauty, and sounds of communication are destroyed as well. The wilderness is a domain for numerous wildlife. In the name of progress, development is spreading like a prairie fire. To argue that man is greater than nature is a futility. Is the ocean greater than the land? In the beginning of time the world was given to all life. It is a place under the sun for all things."

"Master! The situation that you describe appears so wasteful and bleak. Why should I prepare for a flight through life that depicts such despair?" "My young friend. The spirit of our journey gives hope to all life. Without noble flight there is no quality to inspire or preserve.

It is important that you equate your purpose with the values espoused by the Great White Eagle. In your asking about where have all the eagles gone remember not to hover long in the wind. The idle fluttering of your feathers will not provide journey to the treasure of life. The flight is greater than the eagle. As knowledge brings forth wisdom you will cease to ask where have all the eagles gone? Rather you will inquire about the loss of meaningful values that have enriched life throughout the ages.

It is well that you ask questions. A curious mind will search out knowledge. Now take journey to the pool of water and gaze upon your reflection. Ask yourself, Who am I? The answer will be long in coming. However, it is important that you learn who you are. This knowledge will reveal your strength and direction of serving. Thereafter when the sun is directly above, ascend in playful flight. I do not wish for you to become too serious and neglect recognizing the need to balance all aspects of life."

"Master! Before departing I would like to know if the devotion of an eagle beckons moderation?" Lad. "The measure of commitment is determined by the measure of our responsibilities. However be mindful that the Great White Eagle advised to be moderate in all things. Always let wisdom be your guide. Certainly you cannot defend yourself moderately. Nor should love be constrained. However let your wings rather than your emotions guide you through a storm.

Apply sound reasoning in every situation to maintain control. Never relinquish a successful flight by allowing the whims of others to influence you in a negative manner. Notwithstanding be moderate in those things that warrant forbearance and spread your wings fully when sound judgment demands greater application. In time your remaining confusion will yield to a confident stride. I believe this to be true as you have a spirited and humble heart."

A few moments after Eric, his beloved, Jason, and Jody take flight towards the lighthouse. However upon approaching the magnificent tower Jason aligns his wings and comes to perch alone upon a large boulder along the shoreline. As he gazes across the open waters he cannot escape the persistent longing within his spirit. It is not his wish to bring unhappiness to Jody who has grown fond of their home at the lighthouse. Yet the wilderness has claimed his own heart. With each passing day the urge to return grows stronger.

As the waves splash upon the sandy shore the Old Man ventures to Jason. In his lifetime he too has experienced a few longings. Now he senses Jason's. "When I was quite young my feathered friend I yearned for the sea and this lighthouse. However when I informed my friends and relatives, they quickly pointed out several misgivings.

In my attempt to satisfy their wishes I remained on the mainland for seven additional years. They meant well. However not a single one fully understood my love for the ocean. Eventually they pursued their dreams and I lost my feeling of happiness. Throughout most of my childhood and early adult life my parents wisely knew what was best for me. But in spite of good intentions many relatives and well-meaning folks do not even know what is best for themselves. Several do not even follow their own advice. The so called experts are the worst of the lot.

I do not wish to sound critical. Yet I offer no apology either. My dream was sound. Had I not been so eager to please everyone else I would have found happiness by the sea much sooner. Also concerning all the things that they said I would miss, there is not a single one that comes to mind. Perhaps to feel the loss of something one must acquire an attachment. Still I have compromised and there have been regrets.

In the nobleness of your wings always consider others. However as you have attested there are certain values in life that cannot be compromised. I am further emphasizing that certain ambitions and longings cannot be denied either. Consider the things that I have spoken carefully as we all have a heartfelt dream. Often it is the hope of realizing such that gives meaning and worth to our lives.

We all make mistakes. However it is wiser to pursue a dream and fail then to regret a lack of effort. A miscalculation aloft can cost your life. The same is true regarding a critical error on the ground. Therefore do not rush your lifelong ambition. Also weigh the value and consequence as everything in life has a price. Thus the seeds sown today can enrich or deny the happiness of tomorrow."

As the Old Man comes to his feet and departs, he utters, "Good fortune in hunting my feathered friend." Although Jason does not fully understand the words expressed he does feel the sincerity of love. He further knows in reference that the meaning intended will compromise Jody's contentment at the lighthouse.

A few moments later Jody also senses that all is not well with Jason. With concern she goes to him. While perched upon the boulder Jason reluctantly divulges to her his longing to return to the wilderness. She is obviously disappointed. Why she asks with a bewildered look, "do you wish to leave this beauty that we have come to share?" Jason does not reply. However in a low murmur she begins to express several advantages of remaining at the lighthouse. However inwardly she is aware of his long developed appreciation for their domain. After all he has spent more seasons than she in the region. Nevertheless he remains unmoved in his yearning to ascend beyond the shore.

With aroused anger she spreads her wings and lifts into flight. Amidst the ruffling of his feathers Jason almost topples into the water. However upon regaining his composure he too ascends aloft. As he pursues her path of flight he loudly screeches his displeasure with her somewhat brash behavior. Although as he is about to overtake her in flight he abruptly aligns his wings and returns to the huge boulder.

In devotion to his mate Jason would willingly sacrifice himself for her. Yet there will be other days and seasons in which he will cater to her wishes. Yet on this occasion he believes that the flourishing of their future happiness must come forth from the wilderness.

Jody soon returns and while hovering over him she again screeches her disapproval. However as her anger subsides, she descends by his side. He affectionately embraces her within the fold of his wings. "Sometimes my love your spirit is exorbitant. Still your asserted independent manner often delights me. It is also possible that I have spoiled you? Might this be true?" "No, my beloved. However I am wise enough to know the benefit of following my mate. Not because it is the way of eagles or simply what is the norm. Rather it is the expression of my love and earned respect for you. Still we shall not depart before summer's end."

Jason screeches in frolic protest. However with understanding he agrees to her expressed desire. In gesture he again embraces her with all the love of his grateful heart. Then with noble regard he accompanies her to their home high in the tower of the lighthouse.

During the flight of life all relationships are subject to conflict. It is only through compromise that the bond endures. The measure of devotion determines the degree of understanding. In humbleness both mates must be willing to make great sacrifice for the benefit of the other. Perhaps not at the same moment but within the season of precious moments as the breeze requires.

The weeks of summer pass by joyfully for Jason and Jody. They find tranquility in their many flights over the sea and the land. Through meaningful sharing they come to experience the desired happiness of many. It is a treasure of lasting bliss which only a few in life come to realize.

Their numerous flights with Eric and his queen provide fond memories. During the heat of the summer Jody deepens her friendship with the Old Man by the sea and his warm hearted mate. To the delight of all Nathaniel and Larisa come to visit. Soon after, the familiar chattering of Jubal swimming around the tip of the peninsula adds to the excitement. The dolphin friend's unexpected and timely visit further gratifies Eric.

It is also during mid summer when the young eaglet under Eric's instruction spreads his wings aloft. In preparation for potential storms and battles he learns the cunning of eagle flight. With admired grace the orphaned eaglet soars through the heavens with great prowess and quickness of reaction. However with youthful exorbitance his pride swells making him vulnerable in harm's way. With daring confidence he flaps his wings bearing hard upon Jason. However the impatient youngster has yet to learn that there is much more to noble flight than swiftness.

Alerted to the eaglet's frolic mischief Jason aligns his own wings. With skillful intent he maneuvers the youthful bird along a path of entrapment. As the distance to Jason narrows, Jody dives down from the glaring sun. With her sharp beak she plucks one of the orphan's tail feathers as she passes by. The humbled eaglet screeches in the pain of his error. However as he slowly descends to the ground in understanding he humbly accepts the value of an important lesson.

The young eaglet will learn other valuable lessons or perish. Although it would seem that destiny is written upon his wings. Still it is well known amongst the flight of eagles that to procrastinate will result in freezing in the winter. One must prepare for a worthwhile goal earnestly to realize a harvest. Often the neglect of preparing for the tomorrows will result in jeopardizing a season. Too many wasted seasons can also lead to the loss of a dream or life. Thus all moments are precious. Yet some are more important in purpose than others.

Similar to all things that have a beginning and an end summer wanes. Autumn dawns again in all of its splendor. How magnificent in beauty are the golden and crimson colored leaves upon the trees. As a crisp breeze blows across the ocean both Jason and Jody ascend into flight towards the wilderness.

High aloft they rock their wings in farewell. Although their journey will take them to new horizons the fond memories shared at the lighthouse will long endure within their hearts. For they have been graced by the real glory of life that is love.

While gliding upon the warm air currents they circle the grove of trees. It is a bidding gesture of honor. In tribute respect is the shining radiance that lends nobleness to love. Below there is a stillness upon the water of the pond. Yet amidst the lingering lilies is the image of a Sacred White Dove. Also beyond is the Silhouette of their Oneness with Him.

The End

About The Author

Larry Slauson resides near the coastal waters of North Carolina. He is a veteran and a former teacher of history and philosophy. He received his Bachelor of Arts degree from the University of Upper Iowa and his Master of Arts degree from the University of South Dakota.

Larry is a bachelor whose romantic interest focuses on the American Civil War era. He is presently finalizing four other novels about this great tragedy. One of the stories reflects his personal interest in boating and the sea.